THE PROVINCIAL COUNCIL OF MANILA OF 1771

(ITS TEXT FOLLOWED BY A COMMENTARY ON *ACTIO II, DE EPISCOPIS*)

THE CATHOLIC UNIVERSITY OF AMERICA
CANON LAW STUDIES
No. 376

The Provincial Council of Manila of 1771

(ITS TEXT FOLLOWED BY A COMMENTARY ON *ACTIO II, DE EPISCOPIS*)

A DISSERTATION
SUBMITTED TO THE FACULTY OF THE SCHOOL OF CANON LAW
OF THE CATHOLIC UNIVERSITY OF AMERICA IN PARTIAL
FULFILLMENT OF THE REQUIREMENTS FOR THE
DEGREE OF DOCTOR OF CANON LAW

BY THE
REV. PEDRO N. BANTIGUE, J.C.L.
PRIEST OF THE ARCHDIOCESE OF MANILA, PHILIPPINES

THE CATHOLIC UNIVERSITY OF AMERICA PRESS
WASHINGTON, D.C.
1957

NIHIL OBSTAT:
EDUARDUS ROELKER, S.T.D., J.C.D.
Censor Deputatus

Washingtonii, D.C., die 22 julii, 1957

IMPRIMATUR:
RUFINUS J. SANTOS, D.D.
Archiepiscopus Manilensis

Manilae, 28 junii, 1957

Printed by The Abbey Press, St. Meinrad, Indiana, U.S.A.

RESPECTFULLY DEDICATED
TO
HIS EXCELLENCY
THE MOST REVEREND RUFINO J. SANTOS, D.D.
ARCHBISHOP OF MANILA, PHILIPPINE ISLANDS
AND TO THE MEMORY OF THE LATE ARCHBISHOPS
MICHAEL J. O'DOHERTY AND GABRIEL M. REYES

FOREWORD

Holy Mother Church has always used provincial councils as a fitting and salutary means for increasing the faith of her subjects, for preserving the unity of the faithful, and for the safeguarding of ecclesiastical discipline.

In the far Orient there is an archipelago consisting of more than seven thousands islands and islets, known to the world as the Philippine Islands (also known as the Pearl of the Orient Seas). These islands, for about four centuries, were under Spain, a Catholic nation. By the providence and mercy of God the Spanish missionaries uprooted from the Filipinos their abysmal paganism and successfully evangelized them, deeply implanting in them the doctrine of Christ, an achievement indeed without parallel and a most wonderful page in the history of the Far East.

In the capital of this archipelago, bearing the charming description *Insigne y siempre leal ciudad* (distinguished and ever loyal city), given to it by the Spanish Crown, in that city, commonly known by the name of Manila, an ecclesiastical provincial council was held in 1771. It was convoked by Basilio Sancho de Santa Justa y Rufina, Archbishop of Manila, upon the order of the Spanish King, Charles III (1759-1788).

The convocation of such a council was necessary, for almost two centuries had passed without the holding of any provincial council since Manila was established as a Metropolitan See in 1595. There was no doubt that Manila was in serious need of conciliar legislation pertaining to the particular needs of this ecclesiastical province.

The council was held, but its legislation received neither the approbation of the King nor the recognition of the Holy See. It was consequently void and had no force from the legal or juridical point of view. But it had a great value and importance from the historical point of view, for its texts shed light on the Church, the state and society of the Philippine Islands, especially at the latter part of the eighteenth century. This period was highly characterized by bitter struggles between the authorities of the Church and those of the state, and even among the various Religious Orders themselves.

It is about the text and legislation of the council that the writer treats in this work. But the requisite large number of pages to be produced in a rather short period of time, along with the fact that the recently located exceedingly damaged voluminous documents that pertain to the council are not yet available, made the writer limit his work to the history of the council with a presentation of the entire text followed by a commentary on its *Actio II*, entitled *De Episcopis.*

In this work the writer has considered it better to present in its first chapter some necessary background of the Manila Council. Since Manila was a part of the universal Church, the celebration of its provincial council had of necessity to attend to the Tridentine Legislation on provincial councils. But inasmuch as the Philippine Islands were evangelized as a Spanish colony under the regime of the *Patronato Real de las Indias,* in virtue whereof laws regarding the Indies provincial councils were enacted, the Manila Council was bound by these as well. For this reason the writer recounts briefly the Tridentine Law and the Laws of the Indies legislation on provincial councils as necessary background of the council. The Spanish monarchs' aim of colonization is also mentioned, namely, the promoting of evangelization among their subjects, and likewise the policy of sending missionaries who, after years of evangelical labor, prepared the establishment of dioceses and ecclesiastical provinces in the Indies, one of which was Manila.

In virtue of the *Patronato Real de las Indias,* the Spanish kings wielded a preponderant and decisive influence on the administration of the Church in their colonies especially during the reign of Charles III. His well-known absolutist tendencies served firmly to maintain regalism within the Church. The writer, consequently, presents also as necessary background Charles III's regalistic administration in

Spain, manifested principally in his conflicts with several Roman Pontiffs and in the suppression of the Society of Jesus. The same type of administration was wielded in the colonies by the local administrators, who looked upon the Spanish crown as a competent authority even in ecclesiastical affairs. An appendix to Chapter I contains the document on provincial councils in the Indies. This document will clearly show the point of departure from the common law of the Church regarding provincial councils as it existed in the legislation of the Laws of the Indies.

The second chapter is devoted to the history of the Manila Council (1771) itself. Its history had an abrupt ending. All that is known for certain is that the *Acta et Decreta* of the council were personally sent to Charles III through an appointed procurator, but the king refused to accept his credentials and ordered him to his convent, forbidding him to return to the Philippine Islands. Whether the king forwarded the *Acta et Decreta* to the Supreme Council of the Indies for revision before sending them to the Holy See is not known. What appears certain is that the *Acta et Decreta* do not exist in the Vatican Archives. Presumably, the Supreme Council of the Indies did not forward them to the Holy See as it did those of the VI Provincial Council of Lima (1772). In this second chapter, a short exposition of the famous *Real Cedula* (Tomo Regio) which Charles III issued on August 21, 1769, serves as a prelude to the presentation of the history of the council. It was in this *Real Cedula* that the order of the king to the archbishops of the Indies and of the Philippine Islands regarding the convocation of the provincial council was contained. In it were twenty points, enjoined by the king, to be proposed, considered and settled during the council. A copy of the abovementioned *Real Cedula* is appended to Chapter II.

The complete text of the decrees of the *Concilium Manilanum Provinciale Celebratum Anno MDCCLXXI* is presented in the third chapter of this work. The text itself is prefaced with a short history and physical description of the text. Since this is the first time the text will be published, and in view of the time and effort spent by the writer in the presentation of this text, the kind indulgence of the reader is presumed though the text does not appear as an appendix to this work.

The last chapter is a commentary on *Actio II* of the Manila Council (1771). Although it had been the original plan to offer a commentary on the whole text, nevertheless the shortness of the time available and the difficulty of exploring the sources of information rendered it impossible to accomplish that task in this work. In commenting on many parts of the *Actio II,* the writer had to depart often from the field of canon law and correspondingly had to revert to history. It is for this reason that historical commentary has prevailed in this work. Some provisions, however, are simple and need no commentary whatsoever. As a basis for the commentary, the writer has referred principally to the provisions of the Council of Trent in its Sessions on Reform, since the Provincial Council of Manila was itself convoked for the purpose of ecclesiastical reform in the Philippine Islands; to the provisions of the famous councils of Milan, held at the time of St. Charles Borromeo, which councils the Fathers of the Manila Council used as sources for many of the council's decrees; to the provisions of the Laws of the Indies, which were used as a basis of colonial government, and which showed the intimate relation between the Church and the State in the Spanish colonies; and finally, to the provisions of the III Provincial Council of Mexico (1589), by which Manila was bound until the time of the Manila Council (1771). The writer has referred also to the contemporary provincial councils, the IV of Mexico (1771) and the VI of Lima (1772), which shared the same fate as the Manila Council, since they, too, did not receive the approbation of the King or the recognition of the Holy See. Needless to say, the history of the Philippines as written by various authors has been very useful for this work.

The writer wishes to express his sincere appreciation to all those who helped him in the preparation of this work. He wishes to express in a special way his grateful thanks to

Dr. Schafer Williams (a one-time Hispanic Specialist of the Manuscripts Division, Library of Congress) for his kindness in placing his transcript of the text of the Acts of the Manila Council at the disposal of the writer; to Rev. Pedro Achutegi, S.J., for his effort and patience in locating the original manuscript of the Council of Manila, as requested by the writer through the Archbishop of Manila; to Rev. Josè Billiet, C.I.C.M., Rector of the Archdiocesan Major Seminary of Manila, for his untiring and patient assistance in collating the copy of the manuscript of the Library of Congress with the original manuscript and with the other contemporary manuscript, and thus a faithful copy of the authentic original manuscript of the Manila Council could be used in this dissertation; to Mr. Sigismund Pniower for his solicitude in sending the writer whatever documents he found in connection with the council; to Dr. Stĕphen Kuttner for his wise, solicitous, and patient direction; and to the faculty of the School of Canon Law of the Catholic University of America for their benevolent concession to shorten the subject matter of this work. Most of all, the writer wishes to express in a very special way his sincerest and most grateful thanks to his Archbishop, Most Reverend Rufino J. Santos, D.D., of Manila, for the opportunity to pursue graduate studies in Canon Law at the Catholic University of America.

TABLE OF CONTENTS

CHAPTER I

INTRODUCTION

ARTICLE 1. LEGISLATION ON PROVINCIAL COUNCILS FROM THE COUNCIL OF TRENT

So great and constant is the solicitude of Holy Mother Church for the well-being of her subjects that she insists again and again on the fulfillment of her laws, which often are not complied with. She tries to find out what may be the cause of the nonfulfillment or of the lax observance, and then, if necessary, and with due care and prudent provision, introduces some modifications or reforms conducive to the exact observance of the laws. Such were her laws or enactments regarding provincial councils. Since provincial councils are for the good of the people, the Church has always been insistent on holding them. But in spite of the frequent renewal of the canonical enactments regarding the holding of provincial councils, their celebration in some places was delayed, and in some places completely neglected. In this connection the Council of Trent (1545-1563) decreed the following:

> Provincial councils, wherever they have been omitted, shall be restored for the regulation of morals, the correction of abuses, the settlement of controversies, and for other purposes permitted by the sacred canons. Wherefore, the Metropolitans in person, or if they are legitimately hindered, the oldest suffragan bishop, shall not neglect to convoke, each in his own province, a council within a year at least from the termination of the present council, and after that at least every third year, after the octave of the Resurrection of Our Lord Jesus Christ or at some other more convenient time, according to the custom of the province, and at which all bishops and others who by right or by custom are under obligation to be present shall be absolutely bound to attend, those being excepted who at imminent danger would have to cross the

> sea. The bishops of the province shall not in the future be compelled under pretext of any custom whatsoever to go against their will to the Metropolitan Church. Those bishops likewise who are not subject to any Archbishop shall once for all choose some neighboring Metropolitan, at whose provincial council they shall be obliged to be present with the other bishops, and whatever has been decided therein they shall observe and cause to be observed. In all other respects, their exemption and privileges shall remain intact and entire.[1]

The Metropolitan, according to the Council of Trent, had the right and duty of convoking provincial councils.[2] It was a personal obligation.[3] He could not carry out this obliga-

[1] Sess. XXIV, *de ref.*, c. 2: translation by H. J. Schroeder, *Canons and Decrees of the Council of Trent* (St. Louis, Mo., & London, W. C.: Herder Book Company, 1941), pp. 192-193.

[2] "... quare Metropolitani ... non praetermittant synodum in provincia sua cogere ..."—Sess. XXIV, *de ref.*, c. 2; Cf. Stephanus Quaranta, *Summa Bullarii earumve Summorum Pontificum Constitutionum* (Venetiis, 1672), p. 210, n. 2; Vincentius Petra, *Commentaria ad Constitutiones Apostolicas seu Bullas Singulas Summorum Pontificum in Bullario Romano contentas secundum Collectionem Cherubim* (5 vols. 1, Romae, 1705-1726) I, 472, n. 39. This obligation of convoking provincial councils as imposed upon Metropolitans by the Council of Trent was a restatement of the twentieth canon of the Council of Antioch (341)—Bruns, *Canones Apostolorum et Conciliorum Saeculorum IV-VII* (2 vols., Berolini, 1839) I, 85 (hereafter cited as Bruns); c. 25, X, *de accusationibus, inquisitionibus et denunciationibus*, V, I, which incorporated the sixth canon of the IV Lateran Ecumenical Council under Pope Innocent III held in the year 1215—Mansi, *Sacrorum Conciliorum Nova et Amplissima Collectio* (53 vols. in 60, Parisiis, Arnhem, Lipsiae, 1901-1927), XXII, 991 (hereafter cited as Mansi); the provision of the Constitution of Leo X, *Regimini universalis* (1515) which states: "... cum conveniat nos circa ea ... desiderantes canones ipsos firmiter observari, eisdem ... archiepiscopis districte iniungimus ... concilia hujusmodi mandantes fieri, quocumque privilegio non obstante, inviolabiliter observent ..." —*Bullarum Diplomatum et Privilegiorum Sanctorum Romanorum Pontificum Taurinensis Editio* (24 vols. in 25, 1857-1872), V, 617-621 (hereafter cited as *Bull. Rom.*)

[3] "Quare Metropolitani ... per se ipsos ... non praetermittant synodum in sua provincia cogere ..." *Conc. Trident.*, Sess. XXIV, *de ref.*,

tion through his Vicar General, even with the issuing of a special mandate; if he convoked the council otherwise than personally, he convoked the council invalidly.[4] But if the Metropolitan was legitimately impeded,[5] the senior bishop *(antiquior coepiscopus)* according to the Council of Trent,[6] acted in place of the Metropolitan. In this connection the problem arose as to whether the words *"antiquior coepiscopus"* of the Council of Trent were to be understood as referring to the oldest bishop among the suffragans alone, or among all the bishops of the council, including also the exempt bishops. (It must be noted that the Council of Trent decreed also that exempt bishops, i.e., those who are not subject to any Metropolitan, should once and for all choose some neighboring Metropolitan at whose provincial council they were to be present, and that whatever was decided therein they should observe and cause to be observed—Sess. XXIV, *de ref.*, c. 2). The problem was resolved by the Congregation of Cardinal Interpreters, who declared that, if the Metropolitan was impeded, the senior suffragan, and not a non-suffragan bishop, though the latter was exempt and immediately subject to the Holy See, was to convoke the provincial council and act in his stead.[7]

c. 2; J. L. Selvagio, *Institutionum Canonicorum* Libri Tres (3 vols., Neapoli, 1839), I, p. 95.

[4] "Non potest per Vicarium Generalem concilium provinciale fieri sed per seipsum . . ." Petra, *op. cit.*, I, p. 469, n. 18; Bouix, *De Concilio Provinciali* (3. ed., Parisiis, 1862), p. 101.

[5] Vacancy of the see was considered a legitimate impediment—S.C.C. *Tarraconen.*, 2 dec. 1623; 10 febr. 1624. "Sacra, etc. partibus auditis, censuit ius provinciale indicendi concilium ac celebrandi sede vacante . . . ad antiquiorem Episcopum pertinere."—*Codicis Iuris Canonici Fontes*, cura Emi Petri Cardinalis Gasparri editi (9 vols., Romae, Typis Polyglottis Vaticanis, 1923-1939), n. 2444; n. 2448 (hereafter cited as *Fontes*); Petra, *op. cit.*, I, 469, n. 18. It was obvious that sickness or old age, or any such grave reason which would hinder the Metropolitan from performing his duties, was considered a legitimate obstacle for the Metropolitan in the matter of convoking the provincial councils.

[6] Sess. XXIV, *de ref.*, c. 2.

[7] *Conc. Trident.*, sess. XXIV, *de ref.*, c. 2, decl. 2. Cf Bouix, *op. cit.*,

In the case of *sede vacante* due to the death of a Metropolitan before the convocation of the council, the obligation was likewise transferred to the senior suffragan and not to the Metropolitan Chapter.[8]

The frequency of holding the provincial councils was decreed by the Council of Trent as once every three years. It specified that within a year after the closing of the Council of Trent a provincial council was to be held in every ecclesiastical province; and after that, a council was to be held at least once every three years. The time, sometime after the octave of the Resurrection of Our Lord, was to be decided according to the usage or custom of the province.[9]

pp. 67-68 *passim;* Juan R. Tejada, *Colleccion de Canones y de todos los Concilios de la Iglesia Española* (5 tomos, Madrid, 1849-1855), IV, 335; "Jus vocandi concilium provinciale, Metropolita impedito ... ad episcopum suffraganeum seniorem devolvitur"—Selvagio, *op. cit.*, I, 96.

[8] . . . sed quid dicendum si archiepiscopus ante convocationem obierit ad quem spectet convocatio, et an fieri valeat; et dicendum spectare etiam ad antiquiorem suffraganeum Episcopum et non ad capitulum Metropolitanae, ex verbis claris ejusdem concilii, quidquid antea fuerit; nam antiquitus Capitulum convocabat, si Sedes Archiepiscopalis fuisset vacans.——Petra, *op. cit.*, I, p. 469, n. 23; S.C.C. *Tarraconen.*, 2 dec. 1623; "Sacra, etc. partibus auditis, censuit ius provinciale concilium indicendi ac celebrandi sede vacante non ad capitulum Metropolitanum sed ad antiquiorem Provinciae Episcopum pertinere." —*Fontes*, n. 2444; sed also S.C.C. *Tarraconen.*, 10 febr. 1644—*Fontes*, n. 2448; "Cessat hodie potestas capituli Metropolitani Sede vacante celebrandi concilium provinciale ac suffraganeos convocandi."—Barbosa, *Collectanea Doctorum in varia Concilii Tridentini Decreta et Canones* (Lugduni 1672), p. 285, n. 4 (hereafter cited as Barbosa); Quaranta, p. 211, n. 2 in additione post quaestionem 3.

[9] Sess. XXIV, *de ref.*, c. 2. This enactment of the Council of Trent with regard to the holding of provincial councils at least every three years was just a reiteration of former enactments, v.gr., of the statute of the Council of Constance (1414-1418) calling for provincial councils only every third year. This statute was approved by Pope Martin V in 1425. Cf. Franciscus Xav. Wernz, *Ius Decretalium* (6 vols. 2. ed., vols. I-IV, 1905-1912, Romae; vols. V-VI, 1914 & 1913 resp., Prati), II, *Ius Constitutiones Ecclesiae Catholicae*, p. 1960, n. 843; See also the statute of the Council of Basle (1433), which ordained that a provincial council should be held at least every third

Despite the very explicit canonical sanction concerning the holding of provincial councils every third year,[10] in large parts of the Church these councils were for centuries of rarest occurrence.[11] Of course in some places there was a remarkable series of provincial councils, notably the ones celebrated in Milan under Saint Charles Borromeo (1538-1584).[12] In the United States of America provincial coun-

year—Mansi, XXIX, 77, and the provision of the Constitution of Pope Leo X in his *Regimini universalis* on May 4, 1515, at the V Lateran Council (session X), prescribing the holding of provincial councils every three years. Cf. *Fontes*, n. 66; *Bull. Rom.*, V, 617-621.

10 "... Quod si in his tam Metropolitani quam episcopi et alii supra scripti negligentes, poenas sacris canonibus sancitas incurrant."—Conc. Trident., sess. XXIV, *de ref.*, c. 2. The sanction contained in c. 7, D.XVIII, simply stated: "Si quis Metropolitanus hoc neglexerit agere absque necessitate vel in sua aliqua rationabili occasione, canonicis poenis subiaceat." The sanction, "*canonicis poenis subiaceat,*" was not specific. But provision with a specific penal sanction was made in the Decretals of Gregory IX: "Quisque autem hoc salutare statutum neglexerit adimplere a sui executione officii suspendatur (donec per superioris arbitrium eius relaxetur),"—C. 25, X, *de accusationibus, inquisitionibus et denunciationibus*, V, 1. This sanction was of a *ferendae* and not a *latae sententiae* character. "... non est ergo poena latae sententiae, quod bene expedit, nam et si omnes negligentes suspendantur, pauci possint exequi quod incumbit."—Hostiensis, *Commentaria in Quinque Decretalium Libros* (6 vols. in 4, Venetiis, 1581), Lib. V, tit. 1, cap 25, n. 9. Then Pope Leo X in his constitution *Regimini universalis* of May 4, 1515, had the same interpretation, a "*ferendae sententiae*" sanction: "Circa hoc autem negligentes, poenas in eisdem canonibus contentas se noverint incursuros." Cf. *Bull. Rom.*, V, 617-621; *Fontes*, n. 66. The Council of Trent retained this "*ferendae sententiae*" penalty.

11 S.C.C. Senen., 28 nov. 1699: "... cum in Provincia Senensi per integrum fere spatium unius saeculi celebratum non fuisset provinciale concilium."—*Fontes*, n. 2973.

12 Inter Synodos Provinciales post Tridentinum habitas eminent quoque Mediolanenses a Sancto Carrolo Borromeo celebratae ..."—Selvagio, *op. cit.*, I, 97; "His adnotasse sufficit, complura concilia etiam defuncto S. Carrolo, in Italia fuisse celebrata v. gr. VII concilium Mediolanense; concilia Firman. (1590), Aquilejense, Salern. et S. Severinae (1596); Amalph. (1597, concilia Beneventana (1599, 1656, 1693, 1698); Conc. Capuan. 1603, Neapolis (1699) ..."—*Acta et Decreta Sacrorum Conciliorum Recentiorum, Collectio Lacensis*

cils were numerous, especially in the 19th century. Though bigotry was quite generally in evidence, the U. S. Government itself showed neither opposition nor hindrance to the holding of these councils.[13] It must be noted that the chief obstacles to the holding of the provincial councils in many places, particularly in Europe, were the special circumstances of the place, the turbulent political conditions then current, or the interference of the temporal rulers.[14]

The proper aim of the provincial councils was the consolidating of ecclesiastical discipline through the regulating of morals, the correcting of abuses, the settling of controversies, and the achieving of such other purposes as were expressly delineated in the sacred canons.[15]

Provincial councils were not competent to deal with matters of the faith, either by defining or by condemning any belief, since they lacked the prerogative of infallibility, yet they could treat of such matters from a disciplinary point of view, by promoting religious teaching, by pointing out the

(7 vols., auctoribus G. Schneeman (Vols. I-VI) et T. Granderath (Vol. VII, Friburgi Brisgoviae, 1870-92), I, footnote 2 (hereafter cited as *Coll. Lac.*)

[13] D. Craisson, *Manuale totius Iuris Canonici* (5. ed., 4 vols. Pictavii, 1877), I, p. 47, n. 81; Baltimorense I (1829), Baltimorense II (1833), Baltimorense III (1837), Baltimorense IV (1840), Baltimorense V (1843), Baltimorense VI (1846), Oregonense (1848), Baltimorense VII (1849), Neo-Eboracense I (1854), Baltimorense VIII (1855), Cincinnatense I (1855), Sancti Ludovici I (1855), Neo-Aurelianense I (1856), Baltimorense IX (1858), Cincinnatense II (1858), Sancti Ludovici II (1858), Neo-Eboracense II (1860), Neo-Aurelianense II (1860), Cincinnatense III (1861), Neo-Eboracense III (1861), Baltimorense X (1869). Cf. *Coll. Lac.*, III, 1, 8-322 and 575-600.

[14] *Coll. Lac.*, I, 19a: Tejada, *op. cit.*, IV, 366, footnote a; Selvagio, *op. cit.* I, 98; Bouix, *op. cit.*, pp. 39-53 *passim.* The non-observance of the Tridentine law of holding provincial councils every three years was rather a corruption of the law"—Benedictus XIV, *De Synodo Dioecesana* (2. ed., 2 vols., Parmae, 1764), Lib. I, c. VI, n. 5.

[15] Conc. Trident., sess. XXIV, *de ref.*, c. 2; see also cc. 2-7, 9-14, D.XVIII; c. 25, X, *de accusationibus, inquisitionibus et denunciationibus*, V, 1 (c. 6 of IV Lateran Ecumenical Council)—Mansi, XXII, 991.

errors of the day, and by defending the truth.[16]

Regarding the membership, the Council of Trent decreed that all the bishops of a province, and others who by right or custom were under obligation to be present, were absolutely bound to attend the provincial councils.[17]

As to the place, the Council of Trent provided that provincial councils were to be held in each ecclesiastical province.[18]

They were, however, to be held in a place that suited the convenience of the members of the council. Accordingly, they could permissibly be held in any of the suffragan dioceses, but ordinarily they were to be held in the Metropolitan Church. The place was to be selected by the Metropolitan.[19]

In provincial councils the order of precedence, not only in the seating accommodation, but also for the casting of the vote or the subscribing of the decrees, was based upon the element of priority of episcopal consecration.[20]

A majority vote was necessary for the settling or deciding of the relevant matters in the provincial council.[21]

The ceremonies incidental to the celebration of provincial councils were regulated by the *Liber Pontificalis* and by the *Caeremoniale Episcoporum*.[22]

16 Wernz, *op. cit.*, I, 263 ff., n. 181; "In rebus dubiis et de jure controversis non facile definitiones fiant, praesertim ubi grave aliquod praejudicium parari potest velut in materia sacramentorum . . ."—Prosper Faganus, *Commentaria in Quinque Decretalium Libros* (5 vols. in 4, Venetiis, 1709), Lib. V, *de accusationibus*, c. *Sicut olim*, n. 82 (hereafter cited as Faganus).

17 Sess. XXIV, *de ref.*, c. 2.

18 Sess. XXIV, *de ref.*, c. 2.

19 "In loco intra provinciam magis apto commoditati convocandum. Potest etiam fieri in Dioecesi suffraganei, quae etiam dicitur in Provincia, tamen regulariter fieri debet in Metropolitana Ecclesia, ut censuit pluries S. Congregatio, et electio fieri debet a Metropolitano." —Petra, *op. cit.*, I, p. 469, n. 17; Tejada, *op. cit.*, IV, 335.

20 CC. 7 & 10, D.XVIII; Faganus, lib. V, *de accusationibus* c. *Sicut olim*, n. 30; Barbosa, p. 285, n. 14.

21 Petra, *op. cit.*, I, p. 476, n. 69.

22 Bouix, *op. cit.*, pp. 545 ff.; pp. 570 ff.

After the Holy See had examined and revised the *Acta* of a provincial council, these acts had to be promulgated to the community. Such promulgation could be effected in various ways, v. gr., through sermons, through the press, and through the posting of edicts at the doors of the churches.[23] Any other means serving to bring to the people a knowledge of these decrees could also be used, so that no occasion or pretence of ignorance would remain.

In passing, one may mention the following important post-Tridentine pronouncements of the Holy See regarding the provincial councils; and likewise the praises accorded by several Roman Pontiffs:

(1) In 1588, by virtue of the Constitution *Immensa aeterni* of Pope Sixtus V, the *Acta* of provincial councils were to be submitted to the Sacred Congregation of the Council for examination and revision.[24]

(2) On December 7, 1610, Pope Paul V in responding to the petition of the Spanish King granted permission for the holding of provincial councils every twelve years in the Indies.[25]

(3) Pope Benedict XIII at the Council of Rome (1725) reaffirmed the requisite convocation of provincial councils every three years.[26]

(4) Pope Pius IX in his encyclical letter *Cum nuper* on

[23] "Ne quis in hac provincia ignorantiae excusationem praetendere possit, quominus ea praestet, quae in provinciali Synodo decreta sunt, edicimus, ut, postquam haec ab Apostolica Sede probata fuerint, edantur et in valvis propanantur primum Metropolitanae, deinde omnium Cathedralium et collegiatarum provinciae . . ."—Decreta Concilii Provinciae Ravennatis, (1885) cap. X, II,—cf. *Coll. Lac.*, VI, 211d.

[24] ". . . et quoniam eodem concilio Tridentino decretum est synodos provinciales tertio quoque anno . . . celebrari debere . . . id in executionis usum ob iis quorum interest induci eadem congregatio providebit. Provincialium vero, ubivis terrarum illae celebrentur, decreta ad se, Sacra Congregatio Concilii mitti praecipiet, eaque singula expendet et recognoscet."—*Bull. Rom.*, VIII, pars 2, p. 991.

[25] *Bull. Rom.*, IX, p. 659, par. 3.

[26] *Coll. Lac.*, I, 46.

January 22, 1858, stressed the notion that provincial councils could provide opportune remedies and serve as sources of prosperity for the dioceses.[27]

(5) On August 28, 1893, in an encyclical letter of the Sacred Congregation for the Propagation of the Faith to the Bishops of the Indies, it was emphasized that peace and unity among the pastors of the Church were to be obtained and confirmed through the diligent and accurate maintaining of disciplinary norms enacted in the provincial councils.[28]

(6) In 1896 it was pronounced by the Sacred Congregation of the Holy Office that provincial councils enjoyed a true legislative power, superior indeed to that of any individual bishop or Metropolitan who was a member of the council.[29]

(7) In 1897 Pope Leo XIII authorized the Latin American ecclesiastical provinces to hold councils every twelve years.[30]

(8) In 1897 Pope Leo XIII, in his Apostolic Letter to the Church in the Philippines, declared that councils were useful for the fostering of charity and for the maintaining of a vigorous discipline, and that through them (the councils) unity in thought and action could easily be obtained.[31]

(9) On June 29, 1908, by virtue of the Constitution *Sapienti consilio* of St. Pius X, the duty of examining and re-

[27] "... Summopere optamus ut Provincilia concilia ex Sacrorum canonum praescripto concelebranda curetis. Etiam probe intelligitis, hoc sane pacto, Vos, et collatis inter Vos conciliis, et rebus omnibus perpensis, posse facilius et consultius opportuna adhibere remedia et vestrarum Dioecesium prosperitati providere ..."—*Fontes*, n. 523.

[28] *Collectanea S.C. de Propaganda Fide*, II, p. 297, n. 1848.

[29] S.C.S. Off., 10 sept. 1896, ad 1 & 2—*Collectanea S.C. de Propaganda Fide*, II, n. 1952; *Fontes*, n. 1184.

[30] "Leo XIII pro tota America Latina concessit ut concilii provincialis celebratio ad duodecim annos differri possit ..."—*Acta et Decreta Concilii Plenarii Americae Latinae in Urbe celebrata 1899* (Romae, Typis Vaticanis, 1901), c. XIII, p. 131, n. 283.

[31] Wynne, *The Great Encyclicals of Leo XIII* (3. ed., New York, Cincinnati, Chicago: Benziger Brothers, 1903), p. 549.

vising the *Acta* of the provincial councils became the duty of the Sacred Congregation of the Council even as it had been since the time of Pope Sixtus V.[32]

Canon 283 of the present Code provides that provincial councils must be held every twenty years.

ARTICLE 2. HISTORICAL ANTECEDENTS

It is a notable fact that Spain retained her vast colonial empire in the Indies for three centuries or more. Historians generally concede that there were grave defects in the Spanish system of administration; nevertheless, modern research is constantly revealing the fact that, considered from many viewpoints, Spanish colonial government was no less adequate and in fact was much more carefully planned than that of its contemporaries. The fact that before Spain embarked on a career of colonization, it had developed laws and institutions at home which were suited to the solution of colonial problems, and that it had no more to do than to inaugurate them in its colonies, certainly enabled Spain to put into operation within a short time a more finished and successful scheme of government than did any colonizing nation in any other part of the world.[33]

So closely related were Catholicism and Spanish rule in Spain's colonial empire in the Indies that the history of the one seems also the history of the other. Certainly, Catholicism had enabled Spain to achieve its greatest glories as a colonizing power in the Indies. The propagation of the faith (conversion of the infidels) was without doubt the cardinal aim of Spanish colonization, as was manifestly borne out by the Catholic spirit of Queen Isabella's last will, the Laws of the Indies and the policy of Spanish kings.

The last will and testament of Isabella the Catholic (1451-

[32] *Acta Apostolicae Sedis, Commentarium Officiale*, Romae, I (1909), 11 4, 3); *Fontes*, n. 682.

[33] Charles Henry Cunningham, "The Institutional Background of Spanish American History" *The Hispanic American Historical Review*, I (1918), 24-25.

1504) expressed the keynote of Spanish colonial policy as follows:

> Our principal aim has always been that of converting the Indies and the Tierra Firme to our Holy Faith, sending them prelates, missionaries and other learned persons to instruct them and teach them good manners.[34]

The Laws of the Indies[35] expressly provided that the spread of Catholicism was to be the main aim of Spanish colonization, and that the colonies were to be administered not for any political grandeur of the monarch or for the economic enrichment of the colonizers, but for the spiritual and cultural welfare of the natives. For instance, Law I, Title I, Book IV of the said Laws states:

[34] Nada mejor que el testamento de Isabel la Catolica para definir el spiritu religioso que siguio a los espanoles al Nuevo Mundo. Tres dias antes de su muerte el 23 de Noviembre de 1504 un codicilo al testamento del Octubre de 1504, decia la Reina: yten cuanto al tiempo que nos fueron concedidas por la Santa Sede Apostolica las Islas y Tierra Firme del Mar Oceano descubiertas e por descubrir, nuestra principal intencion fue al tiempo que lo suplicamos al Papa Alejandro sesto de buena memoria que nos hizo la dicha concesion de procurar de ynducir e traer los pueblos dellas e los convertir a nuestra santa fe chatolica, y embiar a las dichas yslas e tierra firme prelados y religiosos e clerigos e otras personas, doctas e temerosas de Dios para instruir los vecinos e moradores dellas en la fe chatolica e los ensenar a dotar de buenas costumbres."—Roberto Levillier, *Organizacion de la Iglesia y Ordenes Religiosas en el Vireinato del Peru en el siglo XVI* (2 vols. in 1, Madrid, 1919), II, 37 (hereafter cited as Levillier)

[35] In the Laws of the Indies, the intimate relation which existed between the Church and the State in the Spanish colonies can be seen. The Laws of the Indies were actually used as a basis of colonial government. While not always effectively enforced, they were by no means a dead letter until Spain actually lost its colonies. It is interesting to note that the first attempt to codify the laws regarding the Indies was made in Mexico in 1545, and approved by the King in 1548. It was not until 1681 that the work was published in Madrid in four volumes. Subsequent editions were printed in 1754, 1774, 1791, and 1841—Cf. Jose Maria Anteguera, *Historia de la Legislation Española desde los Tiempos Mas Remotos hasta Nuestros Dias* (Madrid, 1884), pp. 480 ff. and *passim.*

> Inasmuch as the principal end which inspires us to make new conquests is the preaching and extension of the Holy Catholic Faith and the instruction of the Indians to live in peace and civilization, we order and command that, before the conceding of new discoveries and settlements, orders be given that what has been discovered be pacified and made obedient to our Holy Mother, the Catholic Church.[36]

Book VI, Title X, Law I of the Laws of the Indies restated the contents of Queen Isabella's last will and testament regarding the Christianization and education of the inhabitants in the new lands discovered and conquered by Spain.[37]

Book I, Title I, Law 5, and Book VI, Title X, Law 3 of the Codified Laws of the Indies gave the missionaries all facilities to Christianize and educate the natives of the colonies.[38]

Book VI, Title IX, Law 1 of said Laws expressly enjoined all colonial officials to safeguard the temporal and spiritual welfare of the natives and to promote their conversion in the doctrines and precepts of our Holy Catholic Faith.[39]

Subsequent kings of Spain followed the colonial policy of Isabella, the Catholic. In proof of this, the laws of the Indies attest the following:

> . . . and we [the kings of Spain], imitating the Catholic and pious zeal of Isabella, do order and command the viceroys, presidents, *audiencias*, governors, and judges, and charge archbishops, bishops, domestic prelates to keep in mind the last will of Isabella and to safeguard the laws regarding the conversion of the natives.[40]

It was the policy of the Spanish kings (Queen Isabella and the subsequent kings from the 15th to the 18th century)

[36] *Recopilacion de Leyes de los Reinos de las Indias* (5. ed., 4 vols. in 2, Madrid, 1841), Tomo II, p. 93 (hereafter cited as *Recopilacion*).

[37] Cf. *Recopilacion*, Tomo II, Lib. VI, Tit. X, Ley I, p. 269.

[38] Cf. *Recopilacion*, Tomo I, p. 2, & Tomo II, p. 269.

[39] Cf. *Recopilacion*, Tomo II, p. 263.

[40] Cf. *Recopilacion*, Tomo II, Lib. VI, Tit. X, Ley I, p. 269.

to send missionaries with all the Spanish colonizing expeditions. Magellan's expedition which reached the Philippines in 1521 was accompanied by seven missionaries. Legaspi's expedition (1564-1565) was accompanied by nine Augustinian Friars.[41]

The missionaries were given the charge of conquering the natives of the Indies for the Cross of Christ.

After many years of arduous missionary labor it seemed suitable at last to create dioceses for the better local centralization of the ecclesiastical activities and for the facilitation of administration. Consequently, such dioceses were created in the Spainsh colonies of the Indies. Some of the early dioceses created in the Indies were Caracas (1503), St. Domingo (1504), Portorico (1511), Yucatan (1519), Panama (1520), Santiago de Cuba (1522), Puebla de los Angeles (1525), Mexico (1530), Nicaragua (1531), Cartagena (1534), Antequera (1535), Cuzco (1536), Michoacan (1536), Trujillo (1538), Chiapas (1539), Lima (1543), and Quito (1545).[42]

All these dioceses were suffragans to the Metropolitan See of Seville, Spain. But due to the increasing number of dioceses and their great distance from Seville, three archdioceses were created, St. Domingo, Mexico, and Lima in 1545. Consequently, the dioceses thus far created in the Indies ceased to be suffragans of the Seville Province.[43]

The creation of ecclesiastical provinces in the Indies necessitated the convoking of provincial councils, primarily for the strengthening of the ecclesiastical discipline, and for the observance of the common laws. It also served the

[41] Eladio Zamora, *Las Corporaciones Religiosas en Filipinas* (Vallodolid, 1901), p. 80; Gregorio Zaide, *Philippine Political and Cultural History* (2 vols. edition 1953, Manila: Philippine Education Company), I, 160-161 (hereafter cited as *Phil. Pol. Cult. Hist.*).

[42] P. Carolus Streit, *Atlas Hierarchichus* (Paderbonae in Guestfalia, 1913), 114-120.

[43] *Annuario Pontificio* (Citta del Vaticano: Tipografia Poliglotta Vaticana, 1956), p. 306; Cyriacus Morelli, *Fasti Novi Orbis et Ordinationum Apostolicarum* (Venetiis, 1776), Ordinatio LXXIII, p. 156.

purpose of legislating for the particular needs of the local provinces of the Indies.

Prior to the establishment of ecclesiastical provinces in the Indies, there were three important ecclesiastical meetings held in Mexico, in 1524-1525, 1539 and 1544 respectively. They were convoked by Fr. Martin de Valencia, acting Apostolic Delegate to Mexico. In these meetings the delegates treated baptism, confession, matrimony, the instruction to the natives and other needs of the Indies. Some writers called the first meeting a council or synod, but probably inaccurately, because in the meeting no archbishop nor any bishop was present. It was an apostolic meeting *(juncta apostolica)*. The second and third convocations, although called "provincial councils" by some, in the proper sense of the word were merely apostolic meetings like the first. There were some bishops present, to be sure, but there was no archbishop or metropolitan in attendance. The bishops were all suffragans of Seville, Spain. There was, as yet, no ecclesiastical province in the Indies. Though these were not provincial councils, they were, nonetheless, important and served as the beginning of the ecclesiastical legislative work in the Indies, and as a stepping stone for the provincial councils that were held later.[44]

Since the ecclesiastical provinces of the Indies were a part of the universal Church, they were consequently bound by the Church's universal laws. Hence the provincial councils, which legislated for the provinces, were also subject to the Church's common law. However, in virtue of the *"Real Patronato de las Indias"* enjoyed by the Catholic Spanish Monarchs, there were enacted by the Laws of the Indies some particular provisions with reference to the provincial councils in the Spanish dominions.

Real Patronato de las Indias was an extraordinary privilege granted by the Roman Pontiffs to the Spanish Mon-

[44] Morelli, *op. cit.*, p. 103; Fortino Hipolito Vera, *Apuntamientos Historicos de los Concilios Provinciales Mejicanos* (2 vols. in 1, Mejico, 1893), I, 1-8.

archs, in order to reward their zeal and to encourage them to establish and propagate the Church in the Indies. Such patronage implied a certain intervention in the government and administration of the Church, which could be granted only by way of a special privilege from the Pope.[45]

The royal patronage in the Indies was based on the bulls of Alexander VI, dated May 4, 1493, and November 16, 1501, and on that of Julius II, dated July 28, 1508. By the first two bulls the temporal and spiritual jurisdiction over the Indies was conceded to the Monarchs of Spain, and by the last one the universal *patronato* was given. Aside from the responsibilites of government, this concession involved the duty of Christianizing the natives and the right of collecting tithes from them. By virtue of these bulls, the Spanish rulers were granted the right of nominating prelates for the Indies, the right of the assignment of the benefices, the right of allocating the various provinces to the different orders, the right of confirmation for the minor ecclesiastical appointments, and in fact the right of a general supervision and control over the regular and secular clergy in the colonies.[46]

Beyond all these rights obtained by grant, the Royal Crown assumed several others. This was not surprising, especially during the reign of the Bourbons, who with their well-known absolutist tendencies firmly maintained the policy of regalism in their relationships with the Church, and challenged every possible ecclesiastical prerogative, particularly in the matter of patronage. The regalist doctrine taught that the king is master of the Church as well as of

[45] "El Regio Patronato Indiano es un Patronato extraordinario, concedido por el Papa a los Reyes de Castilla para premiar el celo de estos y alentar en orden al establicimiento y propagacion de la Iglesia en Indias . . . mas el patronato de aqui tratamos por lo mismo que indica cierta intervencion en el gobierno y administracion de la Iglesia, solo puede obtenerse por gracia especial del Romano Pontifice . . ." Matias Gomez Zamora, *Regio Patronato Espanol e Indiano* (Madrid, 1897), 287 ff.

[46] Charles Henry Cunningham, *The Audiencia in the Spanish Colonies* (Berkeley, 1919), pp. 36 ff.

the State.[47] Regalism may be defined as the inordinate exercise of royal power in Church matters and the concomitant subordination of the Church's interests to those of the State.[48]

It should be noted that Regalism reached its zenith during the reign of Charles III (1759-1788), as manifested in his conflict with the popes, in the subjecting of the Spanish clergy to himself, in his diminishing of the power of the Inquisition, in his reduction of the number of persons in religious Orders, and in his expulsion of the Jesuits.

The first conflict between Charles III and the Pope (Clement XIII) was occasioned by a papal brief, which condemned a book entitled *Exposicion de la Doctrina Cristiana* and written by the French theologian Mesengny. The king issued a decree prohibiting the publication of the condemnatory document which the Spanish office of the Inquisition was about to issue. He further decreed that no papal bull, brief, or other pontifical letter should be allowed to circulate or be obeyed unless it had been presented to the king, and in certain cases of lesser importance to the *Consejo*. This was the origin of the Spanish form *(pase regio)* of the claimed prerogative of Catholic Kings, called the *placet regi*. It was an assumed prerogative of the Spanish monarch to take previous cognizance of, with a view to confirming papal edicts or briefs, or such as were issued by other foreign ecclesiastics or by the superiors of religious Orders, before they could be valid in Spanish dominions.

As regards the Spanish clergy, Charles III and his ministers undertook many measures in order to subject them to the crown. In this connection, bishops were ordered to see

[47] Bannon-Dunne, *Latin America, An Historical Survey* (Milwaukee: The Bruce Publishing Company, 1950), p. 480.

[48] Mary Crescencia Thornton, *The Church and Freemasonry in Brazil 1872-1875*, The Catholic University of America Study in Regalism (Washington, D. C.: The Catholic University of America Press, 1948), p. 15; "Regalism is the illegitimate intervention of the civil authority with ecclesiastical affairs . . ." Marcelino Menendez y Pelayo, *Heterodoxos Españoles* (3 tomos, Madrid, 1880-1881), III, 32.

to it that priests should say nothing against the government or the members of the royal family, and even the *alcaldes* were given authority to assist in this regard in conserving the good name of the state and its rulers.

During his reign Charles III was responsible for the enactment of many other measures whose purpose was the subjection of the Spanish church to the Royal power. Some of these were the recourse of *fuerza*,[49] frequently employed in cases of the conflict of laws between the civil and ecclesiastical courts, with the jurisdiction of the former generally favored, the prohibition imposed upon bishops against appointing vicars without the prior consent of the king, and the subjection of the provincial councils and diocesan synods to the *Audiencias* with the authority to determine their convocation.

Concerning the Inquisition not much was done until the reign of Charles III. Prior to his accession to the throne of Spain, and while he was still the King of Naples, he had shown himself hostile to the Inquisition. One of his earliest acts as King of Spain was the banishment of the Inquisitor General, when the latter protested against the royal edict prohibiting the publication of the ecclesiastical document which condemned Mesengny's *Exposicion de la Doctrina Cristiana.* Charles III succeeded in limiting and regulating the Inquisition's sphere of action.

Charles III's reign was especially notable for the steps which he took to prevent an increase in the membership of the religious Orders, and to bring about a reduction in the list of benefices and chaplaincies.

Another prominent event during Charles III's sovereignty was the expulsion of the Jesuits from Spain—the land which gave birth to the soldier-saint of Loyola.

The Society of Jesus, influential both in Europe and

[49] "*Recurso de fuerza* is defined as the reclamation to a civil judge, made by a person believing himself aggrieved by an ecclesiastical judge, imploring the protection of the former in order that the *fuerza* or violence may be terminated or undone." Cunningham, *op. cit.*, p. 411, footnote 3.

abroad, was opposed by powerful enemies—the Jansenists, the Protestants and the free-thinkers—and was not always regarded in a kindly light by the religious and secular clergy alike. For a century and a half there had been conflicts between this or that Order and the Jesuits, sometimes on doctrinal issues, and sometimes on matters of ecclesiastical policy. The Spanish Universities, which had sadly decayed since their Golden Age, were envious of the efficiency and well-merited popularity of the Jesuit colleges. The fact that both Philip V (1700-1746) and Ferdinand VI (1746-1759) had Jesuits for their confessors furnished occasion to the society for unique political opportunities, which were increased as they gained virtual control of the still existant Inquisition. Frequent clashes, together with the rapid influx of ideas and sentiments often loosely described as Voltairean, led up to a crisis which was ended in 1767 by the expulsion of the Jesuits from Spain. In 1759, through the influence of the despotic Pombal (1699-1782) the Society of Jesus had been dissolved in Portugal. Three years later, despite episcopal opposition, the long struggle in France had ended in the Society's suppression by Louis XI (1715-1774). In France, the Jansenists, Gallicans, Regalists and Infidel Philosophers were united by a common hatred into a practical alliance for the war against the Society.

There were four events of political character that tended to increase the feeling of hostility toward the Jesuits. One of these occurred in the reign of Ferdinand when the Jesuits of Paraguay opposed the cession of that territory to Portugal in exchange for Sacramento. The Indians of Paraguay rose in rebellion against the transfer, and it was believed that the Jesuits were in some way concerned. The second of the events was the attempted assassination of the kings of Portugal and France, which was attributed to the Society of Jesus. Many were of the opinion that Charles III might be in danger of a like fate. In the third place, friction arose betwen Charles III and the Jesuits as a result of the former's advocacy of the canonization of Juan de Palafox de Mendoza (1600-1659), a seventeenth century bishop of

Pueblo de los Angeles in New Spain. The Jesuits opposed the king in this matter. The fourth matter was of far greater consequence—the riots of 1766, which broke out in Madrid. These were chiefly caused by certain changes which the minister ordered in the national costume, and were therefore known as the Revolution of the Capes and the Sombreros. The Jesuits were believed to be behind this revolution.

There were many charges made against the Jesuits. They were the following: the diffusion of maxims contrary to the royal and the canon law; a spirit of sedition; treasonable relations with the English in the Philippine Islands; monopolization of commerce and excess of power in the Americas; a too great pride leading them to support the doctrines of Rome against the king; advocacy by many Jesuit writers of tyrannicide; political intrigues against the king; aspiration for universal monarchy, and hatred towards the house of Bourbon. A further argument against them was found in the letter supposed to have been written by Father Lorenzo Ricci, the 18th General of the Society of Jesus (it was in reality the work of Choiseul), wherein the General was made to state that he possessed documents proving that Charles III was an illegitimate child, and, therefore, an unlawful occupant of the throne.[50]

In passing, one should here state that in the conflict between Church and State, but especially in the conflict be-

[50] Rafael Altamira y Crevea, *Historia de España y de la civilizacion Española* (4 tomos, 1909-1911), IV, 215 ff. and *passim;* Charles Chapman, *A History of Spain Founded in the Historia de España of de la Civilizacion Española by Rafael Altamira* (New York: The McMillan Company, 1941), 443 ff. and *passim;* Courson Barbara, *The Jesuits: Their Foundation and History* (2 vols., New York, Cincinnati, and St. Louis, 1879), II, 214 ff.; Edgar Allison Peers, *Spain, The Church and the Orders* (London: Burns Oates & Washbourne, Ltd., 1945), 54 ff. and *passim;* Martin Harney, *The Jesuits in History: The Society of Jesus Through Four Centuries* (New York: The America Press, 1941), 292 ff.; Thomas Campbell, *The Jesuits 1534-1921 A History of the Society of Jesus from Its Foundation to the Present Time* (2 vols., New York, 1921), II, 504 ff.

tween Charles III and the Popes, the Jesuits were involved of necessity more than of choice. During two centuries and under different aspects two diverse principles came into open opposition: the principle of the authority of the Church, which was the banner of the Society of Jesus, and the principle of rebellion against the past, proclaimed originally by Protestantism, adapted afterward into the encyclopedistic philosophy, and still later taking the form of the Liberalism of the nineteenth century.[51]

With Charles III's conviction that the Jesuits constituted an element prejudicial to public tranquility and to the monarchy, he issued the decrees of banishment of the Jesuits from Spain and the Indies on February 27, 1767, at El Pardo. This expulsion was viewed with either approbation or indifference by the Spanish clergy in general, in view of the widespread unpopularity of the Jesuits among other religious Orders and the clergy. In 1773 the triumph of the Society's opponents was completed through the Papal Bull *Dominus ac Redemptor Noster* which suppressed the society entirely.[52]

Such was the spirit of the insistent ambitious desire of the Spanish Monarch for control in ecclesiastical affairs. This idea of Regalism had been carried along in the Spanish colonial regime through the *Patronato Real* and grew apace during the eighteenth century.[53]

ARTICLE 3. LAWS OF THE INDIES ON PROVINCIAL COUNCILS

The convocation of provincial councils in the Indies required at the outset the order or permission of the king. With such an order or permission contained in a *Real Cedula* received from the king, the metropolitan, before convoking the council, had to make the necessary arrangement

[51] Emma Blair-James Robertson, *The Philippine Islands* (55 vols., Ohio, Cleveland, 1902-1909), 272-273.

[52] Rafael Altamira, *A History of Spain* translated into English by Muna Lee, Toronto, New York and London: D. Van Nostrand Company, Inc., 1949), p. 499.

[53] Bannon-Dunne, *op. cit.*, p. 480.

with the king's colonial officers, such as the Viceroy and the Captain General of the district, regarding the preliminaries of the council. After these arrangements had been made, the metropolitan had to inform the king that all was in readiness. This information was required in order that the king might offer further suitable suggestions. When the king had given his approval, the metropolitan could proceed to the convocation of the provincial council.[54]

The Archbishops could petition the king to issue a *Real Cedula* to convoke a provincial council if there was need for it. For instance, Archbishop Lanziego had a laudable desire of convoking a provincial council in Mexico, or at least a synod. So on August 16, 1720, he wrote to the king requesting him to issue a *Real Cedula* to convoke a provincial council. The reason he gave was that no council had been held within the last century. He explained to the king that his visitation of the province made it clear that it was necessary to restore and reform the ecclesiastical and Christian discipline in the region. This petition was granted by the king through the Council of the Indies.[55]

[54] "... y cuando se resolvieron a convocarlos sea dandonos primero cuenta, para que les advirtamos lo que fuere conveniente, y estando confirmado y ejecutado lo que por ultimo antecedente se hubiere determinado para la ejecucion y cumplimiento bastara que los prelados celebren sus sinodos particulares, y nos avisen de lo que determinaren."—*Recopilacion,* Tomo I, Lib. I, Tit. VIII, Ley I, p. 49; "Real Cedula de ruego y encargo al Arzobispo Metropolitano de la ciudad de los Reyes: que juntandose con el Virrey escriban a los obispos suffraganeos para que sin excusa alguna asistan al concilio provincial a que seran convocados. Badajos, 19 de septiembre, 1580."—Levillier, II, 150; "Muy Reverendo en Christo Padre Arzobispo de Iglesia Metropolitana de la ciudad de Manila ... propuse accordaros la obligacion que teneis por el concilio Tridentino a hacer concilio Provincial ... y asi os encargo, que juntandoos con el (e Don Alfonso Faxardo, mi Presidente y Gobernador) y con la audiencia si fuere necessario, o con algunos de ella, deis desde luego principio a esta obra Santa...."—Petro Frasso, *De Regio Patronatu Indiarum* (2 tomos, Matriti 1775), II, p. 325, n. 39.

[55] "En cumplimiento de mi pastoral oficio, debo poner en noticia de V. Majestad, que hace mas de cien anos que en esta Nueva España

Before the promulgation of the decrees of the Council of Trent (1545-1563) two provincial councils had been held in the Indies, namely, that of Lima (1552)[56] and that of Mexico (1555).[57] Other provincial councils in the Indies were held after the Council of Trent (1545-1563) and consequently were bound by its canons and decrees. The legislation of the Council of Trent was promulgated in Spain in 1564.[58] The Council of Trent provided for the holding of provincial councils in every ecclesiastical province every three years.[59] But on account of the great distance between the diocesan centers in the Indies and the great inconvenience encountered by the prelates, the provincial councils were not held every three years. A time interval of six or seven years between councils was granted to the Indies by Gregory XIII on April 15, 1583. Then, in the Bull of Pope

no se ha celebrado Concilio Provincial, y con la experiencia de las seis visitas a que he salido por casi todas las provincias de mi Arzobispado, estoy reconociendo la necesidad que hay de restablecer y reparar la disciplina cristiana y ecclesiastica, especialmente en un reino donde sus naturales gozan aun los privilegios de los neofitos: habiendo llegado a tanto muestra flaqueza que oigo decir no estar en uso ni observancia este muestro Concilio Mexicano, siendo para mi venerabilisimo. Suplico a V. Majestad se sirva interponer orden Real este efecto, a cuva sombra espero se logre este mi deseo, y en su consecuencia se sirva V. Majestad darme su consentimiento para pasar al Papa con esta mi determinacion y proponerle algunos dubios que en esta materia se me han ofrecido y se proceda con acierto. Nuestro Senor guarde la Real Persona de V. Majestad los muchos anos que cada dia le suplico, y todo esta su monarquia necesita . . . Del Consejo de Indias se le respondio que se atuviese al Concilio Tercero Mexicano. . . ."—Mariano Cuevas, *Historia de la Iglesia en Mexico* (4 tomos, Mexico, 1926), IV, 67.

[56] Ruben Vargas Ugarte, *Concilios Limenses*, 1551-1722 (3 vols., Lima: Tipografia Peruana, S. A., Ravago y Hijos, 1951-54), I, 3 (hereafter cited as *Concilios Limenses*)

[57] Francisco Lorenzana, *Concilios Provinciales, Primero y Segundo, 1555 & 1565* (Mexico, 1769) hereafter cited as I & II Mexico)

[58] Laureano Perez Mier, *Iglesia y Estado Nuevo, Los Concordatos ante el Moderno Derecho Publico* (Madrid: Ediciones Fax, 1940), p. 92.

[59] Sess. XXIV, *de ref.*, c. 2.

Paul V, on December 7, 1610, in response to a petition of the Spanish king, permission was granted for the holding of the provincial councils only every twelve years, unless some other disposition would be made by the Holy See, or unless the archbishops and bishops would subsequently consider a more frequent celebration of provincial councils as necessary.[60]

But in spite of the long interval between provincial councils which had been granted to the Indies, even this minimum observance was not achieved. Thus, the interval between the I Provincial Council of Lima (1551-52) and the II (1567-68) was sixteen years. Between the II and III (1582-83) there was an interval of fifteen years but the IV (1591) and V (1601) followed in relatively short succession. Between the V (1601) and the VI (1772), however, a long period of one hundred and seventy-one years elapsed.[61]

In Mexico, four provincial councils were held in 1555, 1565, and 1585 and 1771, respectively, reflecting intervals of 10 years, 20 years and 186 years, respectively, between the first and second, the second and third, and the third and fourth provincial councils.[62]

In the Philippine Islands a *Real Cedula,* dated February 9, 1621, at Madrid, was sent to Governor Alfonzo Faxardo de Tonza and to the Archbishop of Manila. In it King Philip III ordered that a provincial council be held; it was to be the first such council in the Islands.[63]

[60] Morelli, *op. cit.*, Ordinatio CLXIII, p. 285, & pp. 263-264; Petro Frasso, *op. cit.*, II, p. 325, n. 39. Matias Zamora Gomez, *op. cit.*, p. 401; Cf. *Recopilacion,* Tomo I, Lib. I, Tit. VIII, Ley I, p. 49. Levillier, II, 104-106; 109.

[61] Vargas Ugarte, *op. cit.*, I, 399 ff.; II, 7.

[62] *I & II Mexico; Concilium Provinciale Mexicanum III* (5 vols. in 1, Mexico, 1770) (hereafter cited as *III Mexicanum*); *Concilio Provincial Mexicano IV* (5 vols. in 1, Quertaro, 1898) (hereafter cited as *IV Mexicano*)

[63] "... y pues, veis cuan arda es esta materia y que en estas Islas se predica el santo Evangelio, no se ha hecho otro ningun concilio Provincial y esta es el primero, os encargo procureis asi en la sustancia como en las materias, y en su execucion se luzca vuestra prudencia y

This prepared provincial council, however, was not held. As a matter of fact, almost a century and a half later another *Real Cedula,* dated August 21 1769, at Madrid, was sent to the Archbishop of the Indies and the Philippines, and in it the king of Spain once again ordered the convocation of a first provincial council.[64]

So, from the issuance of the *Cedula Real* of February 9, 1621, to the year 1771, in which the I Provincial Council of Manila was really held, there was an interval of about one hundred and fifty years.[65]

Among the matters ordered to be treated in the provincial councils were the items decreed by the Council of Trent (Sess. XXIV, *de ref.* c. 2), such as the regulation of morals, the correction of abuses, and the settlement of controversies as the circumstances of time, persons and place demanded it.[66]

Just compensation of the priests, stipends for masses, and fees for assistance at marriages, funerals and the divine offices were items also dealt with in the provincial councils, as provided by the Laws of the Indies.[67]

The establishment of seminaries was one of the most im-

que mediante vuestra persona y cuidado se consigna un fin tan necesario para que Dios nuestro Senor sea servido. . . ."—De Madrid, a nueva de Febrero de mil seiscientos y viente uno."—Frasso, *op. cit.*, II, 326.

[64] "Cedula Real de 21 de agosto de 1769," cf. Vargas Ugarte, *op. cit.*, II, 207 ff.

[65] Jose Montero y Vidal, *Historia General de Filipinas* (2 vols., Madrid, 1887-1894), II, 245.

[66] Cedula Real, Feb. 9, 1621: ". . . se trate luego de convocar el dicho concilio Provincial . . . guardando en este lo que se dispone por el Tridentino, en las materias y cosas que alii se deben instituir, segun la intelligencia, tiempo, persona y necesidades de las ngocios presentes"—Frasso, *op. cit.*, II, 326.

[67] Cedula Real de Don Carlos y La Reina Governadora en Valladolid a 16 de Abril de 1528 y Cedula Real de Felipe II en Madrid a 27 de Febrero de 1575 y de Don Felipe. Cf. *Recopilacion,* Tomo I, Lib. I, Tit. VIII, Ley IX, p. 50.

portant matters proposed and approved in the II Provincial Council of Lima in 1567.[68]

The reformation of the clerics, the improvement of the condition of the Church, the imparting of instruction to the natives (Indios) and the administration of the sacraments to them were the matters treated in the III Provincial Councils of Lima (1583) and Mexico (1585).[69]

The Laws of the Indies provided that the viceroys, presidents or governors should assist at the provincial councils in the name of the King of Spain. These officers were empowered by the king to propose and discuss matters which they considered necessary in order that the council might prove successful. They were empowered to maintain peace and order in the council.[70]

In the II Provincial Council of Lima (1567), which was held fifteen years after the I, the "*Licenciado*" Lope Garcia de Castro, Governor of Peru, attended in the name of the king.[71]

Don Martino Henriquez, Viceroy of Peru, attended the III Provincial Council of Lima (1582-83) as a representative of the Spanish King.[72]

In the I Provincial Council of Mexico (1555), five laymen assisted as the king's representatives: three justices, a prosecuting attorney and a chief constable.[73]

In the III Provincial Council of Mexico (1585), the King's Legate was the Archbishop Pedro de Maya y Contreras, who at the same time was the Metropolitan and the president of the council, but there were other laymen repre-

[68] Levillier, II, 260.

[69] Cf. *Recopilacion,* Tomo I, Lib. I, Tit. VIII, Ley VII, p. 50; Levillier, II, 312-313.

[70] Cf. *Recopilacion,* Tomo I, Lib. I, Tit. VIII, Ley I, p. 49; Frasso, *op. cit.*, II, p. 322, Nos. 7-10.

[71] Levillier, II, 158-159.

[72] Vargas Ugarte, *op. cit.*, I, 261.

[73] "... concurrieron igualmente los Señores Herrera, Mexia, Montealegre, oidores de la real audiencia de Mexico, y el Licenciado Maldonado Y Gonzales Cerezo, fiscal y aguacil mayor de dicha audiencia ..."—Fortino Hipolito Vera, *op. cit.*, p. 10.

senting the king in that council, such as Pedro Farjan, Lope de Miranda, Valdez de Carcamo, and Cespedes de Cardenas.[74]

Resolutions and decisions of the provincial councils of the Indies could not become effective unless they were first submitted to the Supreme Council of the Indies[75] for correction, examination, revision or recognition, since the laws of the Indies demanded this.[76]

The *Cedula Real* of King Philip II (1556-1598) given in Toledo and dated August 31, 1560, provided that the acts of the provincial councils be submitted to the Supreme Council of the Indies before being published. This was incorporated into the laws of the Indies.[77]

Because of this law, the acts of the III Provincial Councils of Lima (1583) and Mexico (1585) were sent to the Supreme Council of the Indies for revision and examination. But in the meantime, Pope Sixtus V (1585-90) in his Constitution *Immensa aeterni* on January 22, 1588, enacted it as part of the universal law of the Church that before being promulgated all the acts of the provincial councils had to be submitted to the Sacred Congregation of the Council for examination and revision.[78]

So the acts of the said two provincial councils were submitted to the Sacred Congregation of the Council. The Congregation of the Council, after making some corrections in the acts of the Provincial Council of Lima (1583) decreed in 1588 its publication. It was Pope Sixtus V who gave his formal approbation for the acts of the Provincial Council of

[74] Vera, *op. cit.*, p. 14.

[75] "The Council of the Indies was a high court of appeal to which all cases from the colonial *audiencias* came for final adjudication. It was, however, not only a court of appeal in judicial matters but also a directive ministry for the supervision of the administrative acts of the colonial *audiencias* and executives." Cunningham, *The Audiencia in the Spanish Colonies*, pp. 15-16.

[76] Cf. *Recopilacion*, Tomo I, Lib. I, Tit. VIII, Ley VI, p. 50.

[77] Cf. *Recopilacion*, Tomo I, Lib. I, Tit. VIII, Ley VI, p. 50.

[78] *Bull. Rom.*, VIII, pars 2, p. 991; Coll. Lac. I, 17, d; 18, b.

Mexico (1585) in his Brief *Romanum Pontificem*, of October 28, 1589.[79]

King Philip II then issued the *Cedula Real Ejecutoria* for the said Provincial Council of Lima (1583), dated September 18, 1591, at San Lorenzo.[80]

For Mexico, however, King Philip III (1598-1621) issued the *Cedula Real* at Madrid on February 9, 1621. Both of these *Cedulas* were incorporated in the Laws of the Indies.[81]

The *Cedula Real* of Philip II, issued at Cordova on March 29, 1570, and that of Philip IV, given at Madrid on June 8, 1621, both of which were incorporated in the Codified Laws of the Indies, decreed that the archbishops and bishops in celebrating these councils were to avoid all excessive banquets, all idle expenses and all lavish demonstrations, which in the past had been the very factors that hindered the celebration of the councils.[82] Another *Cedula Real*, given by King Philip IV (1621-1665) at Madrid on August 8, 1621, which was also incorporated in the Codified Laws of the Indies, provided that the pastors, both secular and religious, had to possess a copy of the decrees and the resolutions of the provincial councils in order to learn their content and study their import.[83]

[79] *Bull. Rom.*, IX, 350-51.

[80] Real Cedula al Virrey y Audiencia del Peru y Gobernador y Correjedores de los distritos de ella, para que se guarde el Concilio de Lima approbado por su Santidad , en que se ordenaron diversos decretos tocantes a la reformacion del clero y estado eclesiastico, y administracion de los sacramentos en el Arzobispado de Limo y obispados sufraganeos... cf. Levillier, II, 312-313.

[81] Cf. *Recopilacion*, Tomo I, Lib. I, Tit. VIII, Ley VII, p. 50.

[82] Cf. *Recopilacion*, Tomo I, Lib. I, Tit. VIII, Ley IV, p. 49.

[83] Cf. *Recopilacion*, Tomo I, Lib. I, Tit. VIII, Ley VI, p. 50.

APPENDIX

LEYES DE LAS INDIAS

De los Concilios Provinciales y Sinodales

Libro I, Titulo VIII

Ley I

Don felipe II en Madrid a 21 de junio de 1570. En; :: a 30 de octubre de 1591. D. Felipe III en Madrid a 9 de febrero de 1621. Y Don Felipe IV en esta Recopilacion.

Que los concilios provinciales se celebren en las Indias, en conformidad del breve de su Santidad.

A instancia y suplicacion nuestra, y en atencion a la grande distancia que hay en las Indias de unos obispados a otros, y de las iglesias catedrales a sus metropolitanas, y costa que se seguiria a los obispos si se congregasen a celebrar concilios provinciales tan continuamente, y a que no estuviesen mucho tiempo fuera de sus iglesias, la Santidad de Paulo V por breve dado en Roma a siete de diciembre de el ano de mil y seis cientos y diez, concedio que se pudiesen diferir y celebrar de doce en doce años, si la santa Sede apostolica no ordenare y mandare otra cosa, o a los arzobispos y obispos no les pareciere que hay necesidad de celebrarlos dentro de mas breve termino, no obstante lo determinado hasta el dia de la data: rogamos y encargamos a los prelados que guardando lo que esta concedido y permitido por el dicho breve, no habiendo precisa necesidad de congregarse los concilios, sobresean en su convocacion el tiempo que les pareciere que lo pueden hacer; y cuando se resolvieron a convocarlos sea dandonos primero cuenta, para que les advirtamos los que fuere conveniente, y estando confirmado y ejecutado lo que por ultimo antecedente se hubiere determinado, para cuya ejecucion y cumplimento bastara que los prelados celebren sus sinodos particulares, y nos avisen de lo que determinaren.

LEY II

D. Felipe II en Barcelona a 13 de mayo de 1583. *Que los vireyes, presidentes, o gobernadores assistan en los concilios provinciales en nombre de el Rey.*

Mandamos a los vireyes, presidentes y gobernadores, que cada uno en su distrito asistan personalmente por Nos, y en nuestro nombre a los concilios provinciales, que para todo lo que ofreciere y les pareciere tratar de nuestra parte, a fin de conseguir el buen efecto que se espera de aquellas santas congregaciones, en las cuales han de tener el lugar que se acostumbra dar a los que representando nuestra persona han asistido en semejantes concilios les damos poder y facultad cuan bastante se requiere, y tengan mucho cuidado de procurar la paz y conformidad de los congregados, mirar por lo que toca a la conservacion de nuesto Patronazgo, y que nada se ejecute hasta que habiendonos avisado y visto por Nos, demos orden para ello.

LEY III

D. Felipe III en Madrid a 9 de Febrero de 1621. Don Felipe IV alli a 8 de Agosto de 1621. Y en esta Recopilacion.

Que en los arzobispados y obispados de las Indias, se celebren cado año concilios sinodales, y los vireyes, presidentes, audiencias y gobernadores procuren que tenga efecto.

Rogamos y encargamos a los obispos de nuestras Indias que cumpliendo con lo dispuesto por el santo Concilio de Trento, convoquen y junten en cada ano, concilios sinodales en sus iglesias disponiendo las materias de su obligacion de forma que se consiga el servicio de Dios nuestro senor y bien de sus subditos. Y mandamos a nuestros vireyes, presidentes, audiencias y gobernadores que escriban todos los años a los prelados de sus distritos, haciendoles particular memoria de lo referido para que por todas partes tenga efecto lo que tanto importa.

LEY IV

D. Felipe II en Cordoba a 29 de marzo de 1570. Don Felipe IV en Madrid a 8 de junio de 1621. *Que los concilios se celebren con la menos costa que se pueda.*

Para que el ejemplo comience de las cabezas, encargamos a los arzobispos y obispos de nuestras Indias que cuando celebraren concilios sinodales escusen convites, gastos y demostraciones suntuosas y populares, porque la ocasion que han impedido obra tan santa por lo pasado siempre se ha entendido que es el gasto escesivo, y esperamos que acordandose del descargo de sus conciencias y de la nuestra, cumpliran en todo con lo que son obligados.

Ley V

D. Felipe II en Aranjuez a 27 de mayo de 1568. *Que los prelados hagan buen tratamiento y dejen votar libremente a los clerigos y religiosos que fueren a los concilios.*

Rogamos y encargamos a los prelados de nuestras Indias que todas las veces que convocaren y celebraren concilios sinodales en sus provincias, hagan todo buen tratamiento a los clerigos y religiosos que se juntaren y asistieren en ellos y los dejen votar libremente y decir su parecer, sin les poner nungun impedimento.

Ley VI

D. Felipe II en Toledo a 31 de agosto de 1560. En Madrid a 16 de enero de 1590. *Que los concilios provinciales celebrados en las Indias se envien al consejo antes de su impression y publicacion, y los sinodales baste que los vean los vireyes, presidentes y oidores del distrito.*

Encargamos a los arzobispos que cuando celebraren concilios provinciales en sus arzobispados, antes que los publiquen ni se impriman, los envien ante Nos a nuestro consejo de Indias, para que en el vistos se provea lo que convenga, y no se ejecuten hasta que sean vistos y examinados en el . . .

Ley VII

D. Felipe II en S. Lorenzo a 18 de setiembre de 1591. Y en Madrid a 2 de febrero de 1593. Don Filipe III en Madrid a 9 de febrero de 1621.

Que se guarden los concilios Limense y Mejicano ultimamento celebrados en las provincias del Peru y Nueva España, en cada una el que le tocare.

Por cuanto los concilios provinciales, que conforme al decreto del santo Concilio Tridentino se celebraren en la ciudad de los Reyes de la provincia del Peru el año pasado del mil y quinientos y ochenta y tres, y en la ciudad de Mejico el de mil y quinientos y ochenta y cinco, en que se ordenaron diversos decretos tocantes a la reformacion del clero, estado ecclesiastico, doctrina de los indios y administracion de los santos Sacramentos en los arzobispados del Peru y Nueva España, y en los obispados sus sufraganeos, se vieron en nuestro consejo de Indias, por nuesta orden se llevaron a presentar ante su Santidad para que los mandase ver y aprobar, y tuvo por bien de dar su aprobacion y confirmacion, y mandar que los decretos se ejecutasen en la forma y como se entendera por los originales y traslados que por nuestra orden se han impreso, que todo se ha revisto en nuestro consejo y llevado a las dichas provincias. Y pues se han hecho y ordenado con tanto acuerdo y examen, y su Santidad manda que se cumplan y ejecuten, y mandamos a nuestros vireyes, presidentes y oidores de nuestas audiencias reales de las provincias del Peru y Nueva-España, corregidores y gobernadores de los distritos de todas las audiencias, a cada uno en su jurisdiccion, quc para que se haga asi den y hagan dar todo el favor a ayuda que convenga y sea necessario, y que contra el no vayan ni pasen en todo ni en parte en mansera alguna. Y encargamos a los muy reverendos en Cristo padres, arzobispos del Peru y Nueva-España, y obispos sufraganeos comprendidos en los dichos concilios provinciales por lo que les tocare segun sus distritos, que cumplan y hagan cumplir inviolablemente lo que esta dispuesto y ordenado como en ellos se contiene y su Santidad lo ordena y manda, sin los alterar ni mudar en cosa alguna.

Ley VIII

D. Felipe IV en Madrid a 8 de agosto de 1621. *Que los clerigos y religiosos doctrineros tengan los concilios de sus diocesis, y por ellos sean examinados.*

Conviene quo todos los curas y doctrineros seculares y regulares tengan en su poder los decretos y resoluciones de los concilios provinciales que se habieren celebrado y celebraren en sus diocesis. Y rogamos y encargamos a los arzobispos y obispos que les obliguen a ella, y ordenen que cuando fueren examinados lo sean tambien por los puntos mas particulares do cada concilio provincial.

Ley IX

El emperador don Carlos y la reina gobernadora en Valladolid a 16 de abril de 1538. Y los reyes de Bohemia gobernadores a 29 de abril de 1549. D. Felipe II en Madrid a 27 de febrero de 1575. Y don Felipe IV en esta Recopilacion.

Que en los concilios provinciales se hagan aranceles de los derechos que han de percibir los ecclesiasticas por sus occupaciones y ministerios.

Rogamos y encargamos a los arzobispos y obispos de las Indias que en los concilios provinciales ordenen se hagan aranceles de los derechos que los clerigos y religiosos deben percibir, y justamente les pertenezcan por decir las misas, acompañar los entierros, celebrar las velaciones, asistir a los oficios divinos, aniversarios y otros cualesquier ministerios eclesiasticos, y no escendan de lo que se puede llevar en la iglesia de Sevilla triplicado, y los vireyes, presidentes y gobernadores tengan cuidado de proponerlo en los concilios donde asistieren conforme a la ley 2 de este titulo.

CHAPTER II

PROVINCIAL COUNCIL OF MANILA 1771

ARTICLE 1. THE *Real Cedula*

Within a short time after the discovery of the Philippines by Magellan in 1521, Catholicism took firm root in the Filipino people. Inspired by the dauntless missionaries, they readily discarded their paganism and steeped themselves in the appealing doctrine of the true faith. On February 6, 1579, Pope Gregory XIII created the diocese of Manila, suffragan to the Metropolitan See of Mexico, with Fr. Domingo de Salazar of the Order of St. Dominic as its first Bishop. On August 14, 1595, Manila was raised to the status of an Archdiocese by Pope Clement VIII, with three suffragan bishoprics created in the same year (1595), namely, Cebu (Santisimo Nombre), Nueva Segovia (Vigan) and Nüeva Caceres (Naga).[1]

From the establishment of Manila as a Metropolitan See (1595) almost two centuries passed without the celebration of any provincial council. The fact that such a long period of time had passed without the celebration of a provincial council was of general incidence throughout the New World (Indies).[2]

But in 1769, under the pretext of ecclesiastical reform (which indeed was necessary, since no council had been held in the Indies for a long time), Charles III alleged the neces-

[1] *Annuario Pontificio* (1956), p. 306; "Erigio la sede de Manila sufraganea de Mejico el Papa Gregorio XIII en 21 de Diciembre de 1581; la elevo a Metropolitana, Clemente VIII en 14 de Agosto de 1591 asignandole por sufraganeos tres obispados, el de Cebu (Nombre de Jesus), el de Nueva Segovia (Ilocos), y el de Nueva Caceres (Camarines)..."—Javier Hernaez, *Coleccion de Bulas, Breves, y Otros Documentos Relativos a la Iglesia de America y Filipinas* (2 tomos, Bruselas, 1879), II, 342. The dates given by Hernaez are not the same as those given in the *Annuario Pontificio.*

[2] Vargas Ugarte, *op. cit.*, II, pp. V & VI.

sity of convoking a provincial council. He therefore issued a *Real Cedula* or *Tomo Regio* (so called from a phrase contained in the royal decree)[3] on August 21st of that year, ordering the Archbishops of the Indies and the Philippines to hold a provincial council without delay.[4]

In the *Real Cedula,* the king ordered the archbishops to make the necessary arrangements with the viceroy and captain-general of the province, and to fix the time and the duration for the holding of the provincial council with their suffragans, observing what the canons and the laws of his Kingdom disposed about the provincial councils. He charged them to propose, discuss, and decide all points pertaining to discipline, but principally the twenty points he set forth in the *Real Cedula.*

Among the matters contained in those twenty points set forth by the king in the *Real Cedula* were the following:

1. Any motive alleged for delaying the convocation of the council had to be investigated by the viceroy or the president of the respective Royal *Audiencia,* who in consonance with the archbishop's decision with regard to the necessity of the motive could permit the convoking of the council to be delayed.

2. A copy of the *Real Cedula* was to be sent to all the suffragan bishops in order that they might gain a clear idea of the several purposes of the council, and that they might ready themselves for deciding upon matters pertaining to the service of God and of special interest to the King.

3. The fixed ecclesiastical fees were to be revised and proper remedies introduced both in the ecclesiastical courts and in the parishes.

4. Catechetical instruction was to be given to the people and this was to be based on the abridged catechism according to the Roman or Tridentine Catechism.

5. A regulation was to be introduced with regard to

[3] "Por tanto, conformandome con el tenor de los puntos que van insertos, he acordado expedir esta mi cedula o tomo regio . . ." Vargas Ugarte, *op. cit.*, II, 211.

[4] Vargas Ugarte, *op. cit.*, II, 211.

preaching and the correct expounding of Christian doctrine.

6. The council and the bishops were to see to it that the expelled Jesuits were not allowed to teach.

7. Seminaries were to be established in every diocese where those who were being trained for priesthood could live together for at least six months, for which purpose the houses vacated by the expelled Jesuits could be utilized.

8. Restrictions were to be placed on pious foundations and chaplaincies.

9. Parishes were to be divided for the convenience of the faithful if the extension of the territory and the number of the people demanded it.

10. The divine worship was to be properly exercised and executed.

11. The assistance of the clerics at the parochial functions, especially on holy days of obligation, was to be introduced.

12. Recommendations were to be made concerning the spiritual life of the clerics, and regarding the needed correction and canonical punishments for the transgressors.

13. One-third or one-fourth of the seminarians were to be *mestizos* or Indians who would reside in the seminary.

14. Religious charged with care of souls were to be subordinated to the jurisdiction of the local Ordinary. In this connection, religious provincials and superiors were ordered to attend the council.

15. Means were to be established for the uprooting of idolatry, superstition and false beliefs.

After setting forth the twenty points, the king ordered that the *Real Cedula* be inserted in the *acta* of the provincial council, the original copy of which was to be sent to him. He further recommended to all prelates punctual assistance at the council, the greatest harmony in their deliberation, and the avoidance of disputes in their discussions and decisions regarding the matters treated therein. He charged the prelates to be in consonance with the viceroy, presidents, and royal ministers, and to assist at the council according to the disposition of the law.

When the *Real Cedula* (1769) of Charles III reached distant Manila, the Philippines were in a deplorable condition because of the British invasion and occupation (1762-1764) of the city, the war of reconquest, the uprising of various provinces against the civil authorities, the treacherous rebellion of the Chinese, and other similar disturbances which destroyed the peace of the nation.[5] Besides these factors there were the long bitter struggles between the authorities of the Church and of the State, between the Archbishops and Friars, and among the religious Orders themselves.[6]

Basilio Sancho de Santa Justa y Rufina was the Archbishop of Manila at that time. He was a man of unparalleled firmness and energetic character. He belonged to the Order of the Pius Schools (Piarists). He took possession of the Metropolitan See of Manila on July 22, 1767, and immediately undertook to subject the regular *curas* (pastors) to his diocesan visitation.[7]

The strife or controversy in the Philippines over the episcopal visitation of the regular *curas* (Pastors) began already with the first bishop, Domingo de Salazar, and continued for three centuries. As late as 1863, the Archbishop of Manila and two of his suffragan bishops joined in sending to the Spanish government complaints against the friars, complaints of substantially the same tenor as those made earlier by Bishop Salazar, Archbishops Camacho and Santa Justa. Papal and royal decrees were issued at intervals, insisting on the right of episcopal visitation; but in most of the cases these were practically nullified by the influence or opposition of the friars of the different Orders and the inadequate supply of secular priests. The friars threatened several times to abandon their curacies, and they actually

[5] Zaide, *Phil. Pol. Cult. Hist.*, II, 39ff.; Montero y Vidal, *Historia General de Filipinas*, II, 229.

[6] Zaida, *op. cit.*, *I*, BJG ff.; II, 39 ff.

[7] Blair & Robertson, *op. cit.*, IV, 29; XVII, 25-116 *passim;* Zaide, *op. cit.*, II, 44 ff.; Basilio Sancho de Santa Justa y Rufina, *Documentos Importantes para la Cuestion Pendiente sobre la Provision de Curatos en Filipinas* (Madrid, 1863) pp. 1-68 *passim.*

did so on some occasions. They claimed exemption from visitation on various grounds—claiming a privilege granted to them by Pope St. Pius V (which, however, was afterward annulled by Clement XI), giving them the right to be subject solely to the superiors of their respective Orders, and taking from them any obligation to serve their curacies, which they considered to be purely a work of supererogation.[8]

The Governor General was D. Simon Anda, who had just recently (1770) returned to the Philippine Islands. When he went to Madrid in 1767, he was warmly received by the king and enthusiastically applauded for his heroic conduct during the British invasion. He was raised to the peerage and was made a member of the Council of Castile; later the king offered him the governorship of the Philippines. Anda refused the honor several times, but he was finally persuaded to accept it. He arrived in Manila in July, 1770, amidst the applause of the people.[9] Anda succeeded to the office of Jose Raon. The most notable event during the governorship of Raon had been the expulsion of the Jesuits from the Philippines, executed in compliance with the order of Charles III of Spain. Raon was later prosecuted by his successor upon instruction of the king for violating the king's orders regarding the expulsion of the Jesuits. He

[8] Blair & Robertson, *op. cit.*, L, 149-151; 265 ff.; XVII, 25-116; Pero el Revmo. P. Vazquez, General de los Agustinos en una instruccion decia bien claramente "Nos Deo in Religione dicati, qui cum proximis nostris Angeli pacis esse debemus, potiori jure tenemur exemplarem harmoniam veramque concordiam servare cum saecularibus sacerdotibus, et Regularibus ac praesertim cum parochis, praestantes, quoque, subordinationem illustrissimis Dominis Archiepiscopis et Episcopis in iis quae ad sacramentorum administrationem, ad praedictionem Evangelii, et ad custodiam legis dioecesanae, in missionibus et doctrinis nostrae curae concreditis, cum nunquam recedere debeamus ab istis obligationibus constitutis a sacris canonibus a Concilio Tridentino, et concordibus legibus regii nostri Principis"—Bernardo Martinez; *Apuntos Historicos de la Provincia Agustiniana* (Madrid, 1909), p. 241.

[9] Montero y Vidal, *op. cit.*, II, 236.

died soon after the commencement of the trial.[10]

Archbishop Santa Justa and Governor Anda made the necessary arrangements for the convocation of the first provincial council of Manila (1771)[11] in compliance with the above-mentioned *Real Cedula.*

ARTICLE 2. THE COUNCIL

The Archbishop of Manila, Basilio Sancho de Santa Justa y Rufina, convoked the council for May 19, 1771. The three suffragan bishops, Antonio de Luna (a Franciscan) of Nueva Caceres, Espleta of Cebu, and Miguel Garcia of Nueva Segovia, were called to this council.

Having been indicated by Archbishop Sancho, president of the council, Ildefonso Garcia de la Concepcion and Joaquin Traggia, both of the Order of the Pius Schools (Piarists), were elected secretaries. Theologians who were to assist the council were designated—ten from the secular clergy, seven from the Dominicans, four from the Franciscans, three from the Augustinians, and two from the Recollect Order. Three jurisconsults, two notaries, two fiscal promoters, and a master of ceremonies were likewise designated. Governor Anda represented the King.[12]

[10] Montero y Vidal, *op. cit.*, II, 141 & 236, *passim.*

[11] Bernardo Martinez, *op. cit.*, p. 241.

[12] Los teologos del clero secular lo fueron el licenciado D. Esteban Aguiler, el licenciado D. Esteban Rojas y Melo, D. Miguel Cortes Arredondo, D. Joaquin Rubio, D. Jose Tomas Quesada, D. Ignacio Salamanca, D. Clemente Blanco Vernudez, Ldo. Luis Carro, D. Patricio Molina, D. Prudencio Gobuen. Los Teologos de la Orden de Sto. Domingo lo fueron eos Frailes Joaquin del Rosario, Santiago de la Portilla, Felipe Fabie, Pedro Martin, Nicolas Cora, Manuel de San Jose, y Miguel Diez; Los de la Orden de San Francisco—Casimiro Pitarque, Jose Masegra, Jose Casanas, y Juan Mata; Los de la Orden de San Agustin—Juan Bernaola o Eusebio Polo, Mariano Alafont y Cayetano Lopes; Los Recoletos—Juan de la Concepcion y Manuel de Santa Barbara; Los jurisconsultos del Concilio lo fueron D. Francisco Lopez Perea, y D. Domingo de Azara; D. Recaredo Villa, maestro de ceremonias. Los notarios—D. Clemente Enriquez, y D. Remigo Bayom; Los promotores fiscales—D. Jose A. Borrea y

This provincial council consisted of six sessions. The first was held on May 19, 1771, the Feast of Pentecost in that year. The council opened with the invocation of the Holy Trinity, after which followed the reading of the decree of the Council of Trent (Session XXIV, on Reform, Chapter 2).

Then the archbishop president of the council asked the following question:

> Does it please you, for the praise and glory of the Holy and undivided Trinity, Father, Son, and Holy Ghost, the protection of the discipline of the Christian religion, the regulation of morals, the correction of abuses, and the settlement of the controversies in the Philippines, to decree and declare that this provincial council of Manila, legitimately convoked by the Metropolitan, Basilio Sancho de Santa Justa y Rufina, begins and has begun? (Cf. Council of Trent formula, with some changes adapted to the Philippines.)

To this question all the members answered: *Placet* (it pleases us). Thus the provincial council was formally opened. Then followed other matters concerning the manner of living, *De modo vivendi,* and matters on the procedure to be observed during the council, such as *de praejudicio non afferendo, de modo subscribendi, de petendo regio assistente, contra conventicula,* and so forth. Before the termination of the session it was announced that the next session was to be held on August 15, 1771.

The second session of the council was held as announced, on the 15th of August. During this session there were treated such measures as chiefly concerned the bishops, namely, the bishop's home, the ministry, visitation and synods.

Alluding to a scriptural passage that runs: "For if a man cannot rule his own household, how is he to take care of the Church of God",[13] the council concerned itself with the drawing up of measures regarding the bishop's *famili-*

Antonio Fernandez de Cordoba.—Cf. Montero y Vidal, *op. cit.*, II, 245 ff.

[13] 2 Timothy, III:5.

ares and immediate personnel, stressing the needed good qualifications and the requisite number of the personnel.

Concerning the bishop's ministry, particular duties were emphasized: preaching; care for the poor, the needy and the sick; solicitude for the propagation of Christian doctrine; exercises of piety such as daily meditation, mass, divine office, spiritual reading, and solemn functions in the cathedral.

With regard to the bishop's visitation one of the most interesting measures to be considered concerned the solemn preparation not only in the parish or place that was to be visited, but also in the cathedral. In the cathedral a forty-hour devotion was to be held for the success of the episcopal visitation. Apart from the forty-hour devotion in the parish that was to be visited, a retreat or mission was to be held, the bells of the church were to be rung, and other functions were to be carried out to insure a cordial and respectful welcome for the bishop.

Among other practical matters concerning the bishop's visitation, the council treated of the means whereby the visitation was to be kept from becoming a burden to the pastor. In this connection there was stressed the prohibited acceptance, by the bishop or by his *familiares,* even of voluntary offerings from those whom they visited.

Provincial councils and diocesan synods were among other matters taken up for discussion in the second session. As to the synods, they were to be held yearly in every diocese, and the first was to be held within six months after the provincial council. The purpose of this first synod was to communicate to the people the decrees of the provincial council. It is interesting to note that in view of the scarcity of the ministers one or two pastors, if thoroughly acquainted with the status of the diocese, could suffice for the holding of a synod. If for some reasonable cause no pastor could attend, then public witnesses of the place, if they were equipped with a letter informing the bishop which things needed reform in the diocese, could suffice for the holding of a synod. Other subjects treated during the session included the monthly meeting of the priests in every vicariate (deanery), and a consultation regarding the life, conduct and ministry of the pastors.

On September 8, 1771, the third session was held. This session dealt with clerics.—Title: On the Seminary and on the Life and Manners of the Clergy.

At the outset the buildings vacated by the Jesuits were to be utilized as seminaries. It was decided that the care of the seminaries should be under the secular clergy, and not under the regulars, unless extreme necessity should demand it. In this latter case the care would be only temporary, and subject to the bishop's will the regulars could be removed from the care of the seminaries. Doctrines were to be taught within the pattern established by St. Augustine and St. Thomas. Professors were to take an oath against regicide or tyrannicide before entering upon their teaching position.

Matters of importance for the spiritual life, the preservation of holiness, the exchange of good social relations among the clergy were likewise treated. One item worthy of note was the ten-day spiritual retreat for priests, to be made annually in the seminary.

The fourth session was held on September 29, 1771. It dealt at length with pastors. Amongst many matters taken up in this session were the *concursus* for the gaining of an appointment to a parish, the knowledge of the dialect of the Indians—another requisite for obtaining a parish—and the desirable harmonious relationship between the pastors and the civil officers.

A very important point was taken up in this session, i. e., the regulars charged with care of souls—whether they labored in parishes or in the missions—were to be subject to the visitation and correction of the bishop, and they were bound *ex justitia* to administer the sacraments as long as the bishop had no secular priests to whose care the parishes or missions could be entrusted.

In the fifth session, held on October 27, 1771, the various

matters concerning the seven sacraments and disciplinary reform were treated.

Among the interesting measures relating to the sacraments one may point to the prohibition of the reception of baptism and confirmation more than once, which measure sought to eradicate the erroneous belief of the natives that there would be an increase of grace if baptism and confirmation were repeatedly received; to the prohibition against the natives' changing of the name the person had received at baptism, which measure strove to cancel the natives' belief that through a change of the name of the baptized person the malignant spirit would not be able to know him; to the establishment of a time limit within which as measured from the day of its birth the infant was to receive baptism, namely, within 9 days from the date of birth; to the prescription of punishment for confessors who proceeded with undue haste in the hearing of confessions; to the prohibition against bringing the sick to the church for Holy Viaticum; to the prohibition against stealing the Sacred Hosts as food for the cocks and cockerals in order to make them invincible; to the prohibition of the custom of having a man live in the service and in the house of his future wife, which custom had been the occasion for numerous abusive practices on the part of the man, not only with his future wife but also with his future sisters-in law.

Of vital importance to the Catholic religion were the matters taken up during the session on disciplinary reform. Among the many and miscellaneous measures drawn up on this matter were: the correction of the paganized way of celebrating religious feasts; the prohibition against the custom of shooting firecrackers at the *Gloria,* the *Sanctus* and the *Consecration* of the solemn Mass celebrated on the feast days; the legislation on modest dress for women. Other matters taken up were concerned with simony, prohibited books, heresy, monastic discipline, usury, and so forth.

The sixth session, held on November 24, 1771, was the final one, and was chiefly concerned with the conclusion of the council. In this session an expression of loyalty and adherence to the Spanish monarch was reiterated, and the necessity of submitting the *acta* of the council for correction and approbation to the Sacred Congregation of the Council was duly adverted to.

It should be noted that in this session it was ordered that the legislation of this council should immediately be promulgated.[14]

The Metropolitan, President of the Council, finally asked this question:

> Does it please you for the praise of God Almighty to declare that this first Provincial Council of Manila has been terminated and brought to its conclusion?

Placet (it pleases us) was the answer of the members, followed by the subscription of the Archbishop Basilio of Manila, Bishop Michael of Nueva Segovia, Procurator Clemente of Cebu. But Bishop Antonio de Nueva Caceres was not among those who signed the *acta* of this provincial council, for he had been expelled from the council. His expulsion was motivated by his strong opposition and protest against the appointment of secretaries. By virtue of a decree of the council supported by the Governor of the Islands, the expulsion from the council of Bishop de Luna was effected. (Sess. VI, *De Promulgatione Concilii,* decretum 1, § 4). He then retired to his diocese and rejected in advance whatever would be resolved in the council. On account of the death of Bishop Espleta of Cebu during the holding of the council, the government of the diocese devolved upon Bishop de Luna; but he immediately protested against the representation of the diocese in the council, and he opposed the proceedings of the council with protests, legal formalities and edicts.[15]

According to the letter of a Franciscan missionary, written at Manila on December 13, 1771, and communicated to Father Aloysius Knaupp, a Jesuit, Bishop de Luna of Nueva

[14] Montero y Vidal, *op. cit.,* II, 249.
[15] Montero y Vidal, *op. cit.,* II, 247.

Caceres rose in indignation and left the council upon the bold decision of Archbishop Santa Justa and Governor Anda to abolish both the solemn votive mass of the Blessed Virgin Mary and the *Salve Regina.* From the first christianizing of these islands it had been the custom to chant these every Saturday in honor of the Blessed Virgin Mary for the preservation and spread of the Catholic religion. It was decided to abolish them under the pretext that the Indians might not thereby be led into the idolatry of worshiping Mary as a goddess.[16] Thus the acts without Bishop Antonio de Luna's signature were subscribed to and attested by the notaries.

[16] Blair and Robertson, *op. cit.*, L. 317, ff.

APPENDIX

Real Cedula de 21 de Agosto de 1769

EL REY

MUY REVERENDOS en Christo Padres Arzobispos de las Indias, e Islas Philipinas, de mi Consejo. Bien sabeis la obligacion que me incumbe en consequencia de los dispuesto por las Leyes de mis Reynos, de los derechos de mi Patronajo Real, de la proteccion que debe a los Canones, y de la Regalia anexa y la Corona desde los principios de esta Monarchia a promover la Congregacion, y celebracion de Concilios Nacionales, o Provinciales, indicando los puntos que se han de tratar en ellos, y asistiendo mis Virreyes, o Presidentes de las Audiencias, y por su ausencia, o ocupacion, quien haga sus veces, para protejer al Concilio, y velar en que no se ofendan las Regalias, Jurisdiccion, Patronazgo, y Preheminencia Real. Si en otros tiempos ha sido necessaria su convocacion, en ningunos, mas propriamente que en los presentes, por lo tocante a esos mis Reynos de las Yndias, e Yslas Philipinas, para exterminar las doctrinas relajadas, y nuebas, substituyendo las antiguas, y sanas conformes a las fuentes puras de la Religion, y restableciendo tambien la exactitud de la disciplina ecclesiastica, el fervor de la predicacion a los que aun gimen bajo de la gentilidad, para atraerles al gremio de la Iglesia, y confortar, e instruir a los que ya estan en el. — La necessidad de Concilio Provincial me fue representada por algunos celosos Prelados de esas regiones, y al mismo tiempo se vio la decadencia de la disciplina monastica, no solo en lo interior de sus observancias, sino tambien en el exterior Porte, y en la falta de subordinacion a los Diocesanos, en todo aquello que los Canones y las Leyes disponen, a demas de lo que el estado presente de las cosas exige, conviniendo en lo mismo otras representaciones de Ministros mios muy authorizados, residentes en esos

Dominios. — Todo mande examinarlo; y arreglado el methodo practico con que el Concilio puede celebrarse en cada Provincia al thenor de la Cedula, o Tomo Regio, he venido en preveniros, que poniendoos de acuerdo con mi Virrey, y Capitan General de esas Provincias, fixeis el termino y tiempo de celebrar el Concilio Provincial, con vuestros suffraganeos, guardando en su convocacion, y celebracion lo que los Canones, y Leyes de mis Reynos disponen en el asunto; y os encargo propongais, trateis, y arregleis todos los puntos pertenecientes a disciplina, y principalmente los siguientes.

I. Que si algun motivo huviera que retardase la celebracion del Sinodo, se examinara por el Virrey, o Presidente respectivo de la Real Audiencia, y en tal caso no se pasara a ella, interin no esten vencidas, de acuerdo con el Metropolitano, cualesquier dificultades previas, que no sean afectadas o inventadas, para dilatar tan santa obra, lo que no es creible en el firme supuesto de que no conviene resulten disturbios de lo que se busca para consegir la mejor concordia, y harmonia en todas las clases del Clero entre si, y para estimular el sancto, y zeloso uso de sus edificativas funciones, a beneficio de los fieles, y de nuestra Santa Religion Catholica.

II. Que en las convocatorias que despace el Metropolitano a cada uno de sus sufraganeos inserte la Cedula, o Tomo Regio para que se entere del objeto de la convocacion, y pueda venir instruido de los hechos particulares de su Diocesis.

III. Que el Concilio Provincial examine los excesos, que cometan en la exaccion de derechos los subalternos de sus Tribunales ecclesiasticos y sobre ello se ponga el conveniente remedio atendiendose al arancel real, y escusando la exaccion de derechos en aquellos casos, y cosas que el Santo Concilio de Trento lo prohibe, y manda despachar graciosamente.

IV. Que los Parrochos tampoco hagan exacciones indevidas a sus feligreses y se corrija donde todavia exista el abuso de llevar los Curas Synodales acosta del Real Patrimonio en aquellas Parrochias que tengan emolumentos, y rentas suficientes por no ser justo gravar indevidamente al

Aerario Real teniendo contra si tantas cargas de justicia para la administracion de esta, y defensa de esas remotas Provincia.

V. Que se arregle teniendo presente el Cathecismo Romano, llamado del Concilio, un Cathecismo abreviado, escrupulosamente extractado del Romano, a fin de que los fieles reciban la pura y doctrina de la Yglesia con uniformidad y con la authoridad conveniente del Concilio Provincial, deputando theologos doctos, y timoratos que hagan este Cathecismo, y reviendole con dilijencia el Concilio Provincial pues de esta suerte no correran en materiar tan importante obras sueltas, destituidas de lejitima authoridad, y revision en materia tan grave.

VI. Que la misma dilijencia haya en reveer los Cathecismos puestos en las lenguas naturales de los Yndios, para hacerles reconocer, explicar, y evitar qualquiera equicocacion en lo que interesa tan de lleno la salud espiritual de los fieles, y neophotos de esos dominos.

VII. Que siendo tan estrecha la obligacion de los Parrochos a explicar el Evangelio e instruir en los rudimentos de la doctrina christiana a los fielos, el Concilio arregla con conocimiento de los descuidos que en esto haya, el tiempo y forma en que precisamente se cumpla en los dias festivos a lo menos.

VIII. Que al thenor de la Real Cedula de doce de Agosto del año proximo pasado de mil, setecientos, y sesenta y ocho, communicada por mi Supremo Consejo de las Yndias en dies y ocho de Octubre del mismo año, cuide el Concilio, y cada Diocesano en su Obispado de que no se enseñe en las Cathedras por Authores de la Compania proscriptos, restableciendo la enseñansa de las Divinas Letras, Santos Padres, y Concilios y desterrando las Doctrinas laxas, y menos seguras, e infundiendo el amor y respecto al Rey, y a los superiores como obligacion tan encargada por las Divinas Letras.

IX. Que tambien se establezca la asistencia del Clero de cada Parrochia en los dias festivos, a los oficios Divinos, con el cargo de ayudar todos sus individuos, ya en el altar, ya en el choro, a su celebracion, como va expresado por lo tocante a las explicaciones de doctrina; pues siendo el establecimiento de la Gerarquia, e institucion de los Ecclesiasticos, dirigido a formar ministros utiles a la Iglesia, ninguno de ellos puede quexarse de que el Concilio Provincial le recuerde la obligacion en que esta constituido todo Ecclesiastico, no pudiendo haver cosa mas edificativa a los fieles, ni mas util al proximo, que el cumplimiento de lo que va propuesto incumbiendo a los Reverendos Obispos en sus diocesis hacer conocer, por medio de Cartas Pastorales o de las Synodales al clero la importancia de llenar dignamente este encargo, como parte de su obligacion y vocacion al orden sacerdotal, sirviendo esta asistencia de merito, para los ascensos correspondientes.

X. Que se ponga limite en las fundaciones de Capellanias, y que no se permita perpetuar los bienes de Patrimonio, pues los que se ordenan a titulo de el por causa util y necessaria a la Yglesia, una vez que aseguren durante su vida la congrua sustentacion, han complido con lo que las dispocisiones Canonicas previenen, sin necesidad de enajenar de las familias estos bienes raices, ni sacarles del Patrimonio de los seculares.

XI. Que se dividan las parrochias donde su distancia, o numero lo pida, para la mejor asistencia, y administracion de sacramentos de los fieles, arreglando el Concilio los medios de executar esto, con intervencion del Vice-Patronato, y sin perjuicio del Patronazgo Real, ni del Aerario, prefiriendo en esta division, y comoda distribucion de parroquianos el bien espiritual de estos al interes bursatico de los actuales Parrochos, y entre tanto que esto se formalize, les obliguen los Diocesanos a dotar, y poner thenientes.

XII. Qe se recomiende, y establezca todo lo conveniente para la conducta del clero, y apartandole de comercios, y grangerias, y torpes lucros debiendo su conversacion ser espiritual, y encaminado a conducir a los fieles en el camino de la virtud, renovando las penas Canonicas contra los infractores.

XIII. Que en quanto a estas se procure proceder correcionalmente, atendida la verdad, y justificacion del hecho, ya con amonestaciones pastorales, y en defecto de emmienda, con reclusiones en alguna comunidad, segun el tiempo, y forma que se establezca, para que disipadas las malas costumbres del comercio y grangerias seculares, revivan los objetos propios de la vocacion clerical.

XIV. Que se establezca numero de sacerdotes en las diocesis, para que no se ordenen los que no sean precisos, o convenientes, pues la abundancia excesiva les hace menos apreciables.

XV. Que se establezca en todas las diocesis el uso de Seminario, en el qual residen todos los ordenandos por el tiempo de seis meses, o el que pareciere al Concilio, pues de esta suerte se acostumbran a la vida de comunidad; se les advierten por las directores, y maestros del Seminario sus defectos particulares; y moderados en la juventud, son utiles en adelante a la Iglesia, teniendo en el dia facultad los Ordinarios de establecer estos seminarios en las casas vacantes por el extranamiento perpetuo de los Regulares de la Compania, dotandose de sus rentas los Maestros de Theolojia Moral, Liturjia, o Ritos, y de Disciplina Ecclesiastica, que es en lo que deben perfeccionarse durante su mansion, costeandose los ordenandos su manutencion diaria con aquella frugalidad que pide el estado, y guardando la misma moderacion en el vestido con lo que seran menos onerosos a sus familias, debiendo ponerse en esto por el Concilio Provincial para tasar estos gastos a la justo, y hacer proficua la mansion en el Seminario, toda la attencion posible para establecer reglas oportunas y los medios de que se cumplan efectivamente, entendiendose los Sufraganeos, con su Metropolitano, para la execucion en los casos que corresponda.

XVI. Que en estos Seminarios se admita una tercera, o quarta parte de Indios, o mestizos, aunque tenga otras fundaciones particulares, para que esos naturales se arraiguen en el amor a la Fe Catholica, viendo a sus hijos, y parientes incorporados en el clero, y deberan cuidar mucho los ordinarios, de que se cumplan las fundaciones de esta especie, en que haya havido descuido.

XVII. Que en el mismo Concilio se arregle la subordinacion del Clero regular, tanto en su disciplina externa, como en la sujecion devida a los Diocesanos Ordinarios, en todo lo que mira a la administracion de sacramentos, o manejo de las missiones de su cargo, y en establecer regla para velar en que el numero no exeda de el que se fixe por los Religiosos reformadores, con acuerdo de los Virreyes, y Metropolitanos. Los Provinciales, o superiores regulares respectivos deberan asistir al Concilio, para que con ellos se traten, y se les oiga, en los puntos tocantes a la disciplina regular, previniendoselo desde aqui sus generales.

XVIII. Que se deben establecer al tenor de las Leyes Reales, y de la buena disciplina las reglas para las questuaciones de limosnas, no permitiendolas, sin que preceda, como es debido la licencia de los Magistrados Reales, y Ordinarios Diocesanos, y en tal caso cada Communidad Mendicante pida en su distrito.

XIX. Se debe establecer providencia por el Concilio en lo que asi toca, para no consentir que los Hermitañoz, no otros, sin profesar orden aprovada, usen trajes arbitrarios, con que en gran parte se substraen de la justicia ordinaria por deber arreglarse el traje comun de cada pais.

XX. Finalmente se deberan establecer todos los medios de desarraigar ritos idolatricos, supersticiones, falsas creencias, instruyendose el Metropolitano, y Sufraganeos de lo que pase en sus respectivas diocesis, para deliberar en el Concilio Provincial, condenando, y proscriviendo quanto sea de esta especie, y encargo la instruccion solida de los fieles en los misterios de ntra. saggrada relijion, y practica de las virtudes, y asistencia a las parrochias, y divinos oficios, como lo dispone la Yglesia escusando en lo posible todo trato duro a los neophitos, edificandoles mas bien con el ejemplo, y la continua enseñanza, indicando los medios practicos para que los parrochos, y demas individuos del clero secular, y regular cumplan tan necesaria obligacion suya.

Por tanto conformandome con el thenor de los puntos que van insertos, he acordado expedir esta mi Cedula, o Tomo

Regio para vos los referidos Metropolitanos, a efecto de que cada uno, haciendose cargo de la importancia, informandose por si, y remitiendo traslado authentico de esta Cedula a cada uno de sus Sufraganeos, se enteren respectivamente de su conthenido, e informen puntualmente de lo que pasa sobre otros puntos, y demas anexos, y vengan bien instruidos al Concilio insertandose esta Cedula en las actas, y deliberando a su thenor lo que convenga al servicio de Dios, y mio; cuyos Decretos, que se sacaran por duplicado se me embiaran originales, para que los mande reconocer por si algo contuvieren opuesto a mi Regalia, y Patronato Real; bien entendido, que en lo que mira a Doctrina, y correccion de costumbres, e instruccion del clero y subordinacion de los regulares en lo que va expresado, se deberan poner en execucion provisionalmente; y recomiendo a todos los Prelados la puntual asistencia, y la mejor harmonia en las deliberaciones, para apartar disputas entre si al tiempo de conferir, y determinar las materias, que se traten en el Concilio: Y asi mismo sera de su cargo, imitando a los antiguos Toledanos, advertir en sus Actas a los parrochos, y al clero la veneracion, y obediencia devida al Suberano, con obligacion de conciencia para que asi lo enseñen, y expliquen a los fieles, procediendose de acuerdo en todo con los Virreyes, Presidentes y Ministros Reales, asistiendo al Concilio, segun lo quc disponen las Leyes, los que conforme a ellas deben hacerlo y se previene en Cedula separada, para que de este modo la authoridad Real, y sacerdotal concurram respectivamente a promover la pureza de la Relijion y la practica de las virtudes; en el concepto de que tendre muy presente el desempeño, que en esto espero de los Religiosisimos Prelados de mis Yndias, e Yslas Philipinas, y les dispensare mi proteccion, y amparo real, para que lleven a execucion tan santas y justas deliberaciones. Fecha de San Ildephonso, a veinte y uno de Agoso de mil setecientos y sesenta nueve. Yo el Rey. Por mandado del Rey Nuestro Senor. Don Thomas del Mello.

Concuerda con su original, que queda en esta Secretaria Arzobispal de mi cargo, a que me remito: y de orden de su

Senoria Ilustrisima el Arzobispo mi Senor hize sacar, y saque el presente Testimonio el cual va fielmente sacado, corregido, y concordado con su original, siendo testigos Philoteo Bernardino de Borja, Santiago de Leon Esguerra, y Juan de la Fuentes, y es fecha en esta Ciudad de Manila en dies y seis de Agosto de mil setecientos, y setenta años de que, doy fee.

En testimonio de verdad lo firme
(Ill.) IGNACIO
Secretario

CHAPTER III

THE TEXT OF THE MANILA PROVINCIAL COUNCIL OF 1771

ARTICLE 1. PRELIMINARY REMARKS

The original Latin manuscript of the Acts of the Provincial Council of Manila of 1771 was recently found in the Manila Archives. It contains five or six thousand closely written pages covering the *Acta,* minutes, decrees, and correspondence of the council.

The manuscript is in an extremely poor condition. It was badly deteriorated by worms and insects, as also by the heat and dampness that took their slow but certain toll through the centuries. Added to these enemies were such others as earthquakes, fires, floods, and the man-made devastation of wars, which caused the Manila Archives to be evacuated from place to place.

The original manuscript of the acts and decrees of the council, preserved in the Archives of the Archdiocese of Manila, consists of forty-four numbered leaves or eighty-eight pages. The size of the leaves is eight inches by thirteen inches. The handwriting is regular, neat, and legible, except in those badly damaged areas which occur very frequently. The paper is so brittle and bug-eaten that photostating it would involve the danger of destroying the text.

There is also a contemporary manuscript copy of the original manuscript of the acts and decrees of the council preserved in the Manila Archives. It is in fairly good condition, but not quite complete, as *Actio IV* is lacking.

The only other copy of the decrees of this council is to be found in the Library of Congress in Washington, D. C. As described by Dr. Schafer Williams, the water-marked manuscript contains forty-four folios or eighty-eight pages with incorrect pagination. A small part of the text, written in a poor hand, is repeated in a better hand. Generally quite legible, the script has the peculiarities of the period.

The spelling is erratic, with the mistakes of a Spaniard who, while pronouncing Latin *hispanice,* proceeded to spell it phonetically. In places the paper is badly worn and flakes, and it is worm-eaten throughout.[1]

The repeated part of the manuscript described by Dr. Williams runs from *Decretum VI* to *Decretum XIV* of the *Actio IV* as examined by the writer. A microfilmed and photo-print copy of this manuscript was placed in the Library of The Catholic University of America at the request which the writer submitted to the Faculty of the School of Canon Law of this University. As noted in the foreword of this dissertation, the writer began his work by using the rough transcript of the manuscript which Dr. Williams kindly placed at the disposal of the writer. The other two above-mentioned manuscripts were discovered only after this work was begun. These discoveries were made during a search at the Manila Archives undertaken at the writer's request. The Rector of the Archdiocesan Seminary had the original manuscript copied for use in this dissertation. The writer received the copy in December of 1956.

The original manuscript has the following peculiarities:

1) Many words begin with capital letters though they do not occur at the beginning of a sentence or cannot be treated as proper names, e. g., Superiorem Episcopi Familiarum ex Clero accisci debet, quae quemadmodum Episcopalis Vitae Custos esse debet. . . ."[2]

2) Commas are frequently used, e. g., "Curent Episcopi, tum per se, juxta probabilem, tum etiam per alios divites, his, quae vere viduae sunt, et desolatae. . . ."[3]

3) The medieval and early modern Latin writing *ij* for *ii,* as in *concilij,* often appears.[4]

[1] Schafer Williams, "The First Provincial Council of Manila of 1771," *Seminar* (annual extraordinary number of *The Jurist*) XIII (1955-1956), p. 33, footnote 1.

[2] *Manuscript of the Manila Council of 1771,* Actio II, Titulus I, Decretum III, § 1 (hereafter cited as *MS*).

[3] *Ibidem,* Titulus II, Decretum IV, § i.

[4] *MS,* Actio II, Proemium; Actio VI, Decretum I, § i.

4) The *e caudatum* is used for *ae*, as in *sępe (saepe)*.[5]
5) The ligature *æ* is used for *ae*, as in *Puellæ*.[6]
6) Unusual spelling is not infrequent, e. g.,
   a) *ss* for *s*, as in *quadragessimo;*[7]
   b) *v* for *b*, as in *guvernator;*[8]
   c) *dd* for *d*, as in *traddit;*[9]
   d) *ch* for *c*, as in *nosochomia;*[10]
   e) *ph* for *f* as in *prophanis.* [11]

7) The use of abbreviations in the footnotes (marginal notes in the manuscript) is inconsistent, e. g.,
   a) *conc., concil., C.,* for *concilium;*[12]
   b) *Timot., Tim.,* for *Timothy;*[13]
   c) *Mediol., Med.,* for *Mediolanensis;*[14]
   d) *Eccl., Eccles.,* for *Ecclesiae;*[15]
   e) *Eccles.,* also for *Ecclesiasticus.*[16]

8) The letters of the Spanish alphabet are used as indexes for the footnotes.[17]

9) Footnotes are frequently incomplete, e. g.,
   a) *Eccles.* 39;[18]
   b) *C. Laodicen.,* C. 55;[19]
   c) *Mediol.* V;[20]
   d) *C. Rotomagen.*[21]

[5] *MS*, Actio V, Tit. I, Decretum II, § i.
[6] *Ibidem*, Decretum V, § xxxiii.
[7] *MS*, Actio II, Tit. II, Decretum I, § i.
[8] *Ibidem*, Decretum IV, § iv; Actio III, Tit. I, Decretum II, § i.
[9] *MS*, Actio II, Tit. I, Decretum IV, § iv.
[10] *Ibidem*, Tit. III, Decretum V, § v.
[11] *MS*, Actio III, Tit. II, Decretum IV, § i.
[12] Cf. *infra*, pp. 64, 65, & 66, footnotes b, h, & o.
[13] Cf. *infra*, p. 65, footnotes e & f.
[14] Cf. *infra*, pp. 65 & 66, footnotes h, m, & o.
[15] Cf. *infra*, p. 66, footnotes k, l, m, & n.
[16] Cf. *infra*, p. 66, footnote j.
[17] The letters *u* and *v* were mistakenly used. The letter *u* must come before the letter *v*. Cf. *infra*, p. 67.
[18] Cf. *infra*, p. 66, footnote j.
[19] Cf. *infra*, p. 67, footnote r.
[20] Cf. *infra*, p. 71, footnote k. The *pars* or *caput* is not indicated.
[21] Cf. *infra*, p. 73, footnote o.

10) The citation of Gratian's Decree in the footnotes follows the pattern employed in the work of Joannes A. Turrecremata, e. gr., Decr. Gratian., tit. 15, Rubr. 5, C. 11, si quis vult.[22]

The text of the decrees as it appears in this dissertation is based on the original manuscript as collated with the other contemporary manuscript copy and with the copy of the manuscript in the Library of Congress.

This is the first publication of these decrees. In order that the text may be easily read and understood, the writer has deemed it practical to use the modern Latin spelling instead of that of the original manuscript. Also, the excessive use of capital letters has been eliminated in the present work. But the original punctuations have, for the most part, been retained.

Most of the footnotes of *Actiò III* etc. of the original manuscript have been worn or eaten away. However, the footnotes of *Actio II* are in a good state of preservation and are recorded in this text according to their original form. The writer hopes eventually to obtain and evaluate these footnotes by means of a study of the documents regarding the Manila Council, very recently unearthed in the *Real Academia de la Historia* in Madrid.

The original manuscript in the Manila Archives is probably the only authentic document of the Manila Council. No copy of the document could be located in the Vatican Archives, according to a letter of the last Msgr. Angelo Mercati, prefect of the Vatican Archives, to Dr. Schafer Wil-

[22] Cf. *infra*, p. 67, footnote v; Joannes A Turrecremata, *Gratiani Decretorum Libri Quinque* (2 vols., Romae, 1726), I, 111. "Joannes de Turrecremata, Hispanus, Ordinis Fratrum Praedicatorum, doctor Parisiensis, magister Sacri Palatii Apostolici Cardinalis (1439) (Romae, 26 septembris, 1468). Ipsi tribuitur opus in quo materia Decreti Gratiani disponitur iuxta ordinem Decretalium; controvertitur tamen utrum ipse opus confecerit an in paucis mutavit scripturam iam saeculo XIV confectum."—Van Hove, *Commentarium Lovaniense in Codicem Iuris Canonici* (1 vol. in 5 tomes, Tom. I, Prolegomena, Mechliniae-Romae: H. Dessain, 1945), I, *Prolegomena*, pp. 502-503, footnote 11.

liams. Msgr. Mercati's report was further verified by his successor, the Rt. Rev. Msgr. Martino Giusti, in February of 1957.[23] Likewise no copy of the acts and decrees of the council which were sent to the Spanish King has come to light, according to the information of Sr. de la Peña, director of the *Archivo General de Indias.*

ARTICLE 2. SCHEMA OF THE DECREES

Actio I. Habita die 19 Maii 1771. DE SERVANDIS IN CONCILIO

Decretum I. De Inchoando Concilio. i.
II. De Modo Vivendi. i.
III. De Praejudicio non Afferendo. i.
IV. De Petendo Regio Assistente. i.
V. De Modo Subscribendi. i.
VI. Contra Conventicula. i.
VII. De Ordine in Congregationibus Servando. i.

Actio II. Habita die 15 Augusti 1771. DE EPISCOPIS

Proemium

Titulus Primus. De Domo Episcopi.

Decretum I. De Episcopi Familia Inferiori. i-vi.
II. De Supellectili et Mensa Episcopi. i-ii.
III. De Superiori Familia. i.

Titulus Secundus. De Ministerio Episcopi.

Decretum I. De Sacra Praedicatione. i-iii.
II. De Vigilantia. i, ii.
III. De Cura Pauperum. i-iv.
IV. De Cura Aliorum Miserorum. i, ii.
V. De Cura Doctrinae. i-iii.
VI. De Orationis Studio. i, ii.
VII. De Consultoribus et Confessario. i, ii.

Titulus Tertius. De Visitatione.

Decretum I. De Visitatione Annua. i-vi.
II. De Praeparatione Visitationis. i-v.
III. De Regulis Visitationis. i-vi.

[23] Cf. a letter obtained through the good offices of Ill. mo e Rev. mo Signore Giacomo Morelli, Consigliere di Nunziatura, Segreteria di State di S. S.

III. De Sacramento Poenitentiae. i-xxv.
IV. De Sacramento Eucharistiae. i-xix.
V. De Sacramento Extremae Unctionis. i-iv.
VI. De Sacramento Ordinis. i-xii.
VII. De Sacramento Matrimonii. i-xvi.

Titulus Secundus. De Reformatione.

Decretum I. De Celebratione Festorum. i-xiv.
II. De Veneratione Sanctorum Reliquiarum. i-v.
III. De Miraculis, et Eleemosynarum Questoribus. i-iv.
IV. De Jejuniorum Observantia. i-iii.
V. De Piis Legatis et Tutoribus. i-iii.
VI. De Simonia. i-iii.
VII. De Confraternitatibus. i-iii.
VIII. De Rebus Ecclesiae Alienandis Vel Non. i-vi.
IX. De Libris Prohibitis. i-ii.
X. De Maleficis, Sortilegiis, Calumniatoribus, Maledicis, et Concubinariis. i-vii.
XI. De Haereticis. i-iv.
XII. De Sententia Excommunicationis. i-ii.
XIII. De Abusibus Laicorum. i-x.
XIV. De Regularibus. i-iii.
XV. De Usuris. i-xxi.
XVI. De Decimis. i-iii.
XVII. De Observantia Dictorum.

Actio VI. Habita die xxiv Novembris 1771. DE PROMULGANDIS DECRETIS ET FINIENDO CONCILIO HABITA

Decretum I. De Concilii Promulgatione. i-iv.
II. De Obedientia Erga Regem. i.
III. De Subjectiendo Concilio Correctioni Ecclesiae. i.
IV. De Fine Concilii.

Article 3. Decrees

CONCILIUM PROVINCIALE MANILANUM

celebratum Anno MDCCLXXI sub Illustrissimo et Reverendissimo Archiepiscopo Manilano D.D. Basilio Sancho a SS. Justa et Rufina &.

ACTIO Ia

Concilii Provincialis habita die 19. Maii Anni 1771.

DE SERVANDIS IN CONCILIO

In nomine Sanctissimae et Individuae Trinitatis, Patris, et Filii et Spiritus Sancti. Amen.

Primo loco lectum est Decretum Tridentini de habendo Concilio Provinciali Sess. XXIV, de ref., c. 2.

DECRETUM I

De Inchoando Concilio

Placet ne vobis ad laudem, et gloriam Sanctae, et Individuae Trinitatis Patris, et Filii et Spiritus Sancti ad tuendam Christianae Religionis Disciplinam, ad moderandos mores, ad corrigendos excessos, et controversias finiendas Provinciae Philipinensis, Sacrum Manilanum Provinciale Concilium ab Illmo. et Rmo. Metropolitano D.D. Basilio Sancho a SS. Justa et Rufina, Archiepiscopo Manilano, legitime convocatum decernere, et declarare hodie in ipso Pentecostes festo, id est: decima nona die mensis Maii anni millessimi septingentesimi septuagesimi primi, incipere, et inceptum jam esse? Responderunt: Placet.

DECRETUM II

De Modo Vivendi

Sancta Manilana Synodus Provincialis legitime congregata, in ea Praesidente Archiepiscopo Manilano, agnoscens Concilii tempore enixius serviendum esse Deo, ab eoque, qui dat omnibus affluenter, et non improperat, exorandum esse scientiae donum, ut congregatis Episcopis oriatur lux ex alto, ad Cleri Populique reformationem, vehementer hortatur singulos Episcopos, ut sectantes justitiam, pietatem, fidem, charitatem, patientiam, mansuetudinem, in omnibus se praebeant exemplum bonorum operum, in doctrina, in integritate, in gravitate, stultas et sine disciplina quaestiones, quae, dicente Apostolo, ad nihil aliud utiles sunt, nisi ad subversionem audientium devitantes. Ut quoniam omnium fidelium, qui eisdem communicant Sacramentis, cor unum, et anima una esse debet, Episcopi non quaerentes quae sua sunt sed quae Iesu Christi, eo vota dirigant, ut pacem, fidem, & gloriam Divini Nominis, quae concilio, qua industria, qua zelo firment, stabiliant et augeant, commissosque populos, exemplo magis quam verbo studeant ad virtutis viam revocare. Rogat etiam sancta synodus concilii officiales per viscera misericordiae Dei, ut virtutum omnium specimina praebeant in cultu modestiam, in mensis sobrietatem, in incessu gravitatem, in lingua moderationem, sectantes. Quotidie sacris operentur, si sacerdotes sint, sin minus singulis saltem Dominicis Diebus sacram synaxim percipiant. Omnes, qui concilio interesse debent, audito primo signo, in locum congregationum conveniant. In congressibus, nullus loquatur nisi obtenta venia, nullus alterius sermonem abrumpat, nullus convitia, scommata, jocos, aut satyras misceat, nullus clamore obstrepat. Si quis tacere jussus recusaverit, arbitrio Patrum puniatur. Clerum etiam omnem rogat Sancta Synodus, ut caste, & pie Deo serviat, convivia fugiat, Divinis Officiis Dominicis festisque diebus in Cathedrali Ecclesia intersit, a ludis alearum abstineat, domicilia matronarum non frequentet, post primam horam noctis domo non exeat, orationi et lectioni assidue vacet in sacrificiis, et orationibus pro Domino Nostro Papa Clementi XIV, pro Congregatis Episcopis et pro salute Domini nostri Regis Caroli oret, ut inchoatum Concilium felicem sortiatur finem. Hacque de causa jubet Sancta Synodus ut tam in Ecclesia Metropolitana, quam in Ecclesiis Regularium, singulis quintis feriis Missa de Spiritu Sancto, Concilii tempore, vel si per ritum non licuerit, ejus commemoratio habeatur, et supplicatio cum litaniis maioribus, et precibus, et orationibus, pro Papa, pro Concilio, et pro Rege instituatur. Reliquos Vero Christi fideles etiam atque etiam hortatur Sancta Synodus ut diebus saltem festis, officiis Divinis, concionibusque intersint, conscientias expient, pauperes alant, et assidue orent pro bono exitu Concilii, deponentes odia, et induentes armaturam fidei. Et quoniam bona est oratio cum jejunio, omnibus cujuscumque status et conditionis sint, qui in pervigiliis congregationum jejunaverint, octoginta dies verae indulgentiae eadem Sancta Synodus liberaliter concedit.

DECRETUM III

De Praejudicio Non Afferendo

Decernit, et declarat ista Synodus, si cui contigerit ad hanc Provincialem Synodum non jure admissum esse, vel suo loco non sedere, sententiamve dicere, et alios quoscumque actus facere, durante Synodo, nulli propterea praejudicium generari, nullique novum jus adquiri. Deinde lectum est Decretum Regis Wambae, quod habetur in Conc. Trid. Sess. 2. de non discendendo.

DECRETUM IV

De Petendo Regio Assistente

Cupiens maxime Sancta Synodus conciliares actiones rite celebrari, illasque nullo modo perturbari a seditiosis hominibus, statuit et decernit ut Metropolitani studio a perillustri Gubernatore harum Insularum Assistens Regius, si ipsi per occupationes interesse non licuerit, postuletur, qui omnibus Congregationibus, tam publicis quam privatis, necnon solemnibus sessionibus intersit, quique ubi opus fuerit patrocinium, et auxilium Patribus impartiatur, ejusdemque Metropolitani opera rogari vult Sancta Synodus perillustrem Gubernatorem, ut invigilet super seditiosis hominibus, et perturbatores pacis, et concordiae procul ab urbe arceat, Concilii que tranquilitatis invidos cujuscumque sint dignitatis et conditionis, auctoritate Regia comprimat, et illorum nefariam temeritatem retundat.

DECRETUM V

De Modo Subscribendi

Animadvertens Sancta Synodus malitia hominum, et diaboli invidia multas disceptationes, controversias, et discordias oriri posse in subscriptionibus Decretorum, nisi certa aliqua regula stabiliatur jubet, et praecipit ut plurium suffragio stabilitis Decretis manu propria omnes Episcopi subscribant, licet in omnibus proprio nomine non consenserint nulla adjecta protestationis additione. Qua non obstante subscriptione, si in aliquibus quis se gravatum senserit, viam juris per appellationem ad Summum Pontificem, Provincialis Concilii Judicem ei patere declarat Sancta Synodus, dummodo non intelligat Decreta, plurium suffragio firmata hac via suspendi, et irrita fieri. Quod si quis pertinaciter plurium sententiae absque nulla additione subscribere recusaverit, e consessu expellatur, et arbitrio Patrum etiam anathemate feriatur.

DECRETUM VI

Contra Conventicula

Quoniam adversarius noster diabolus in jugi vigilia est, et nihil non agat, ut morum reformationi sese opponat malitia hominum, qui ipso daemone quandoque nocentiores sunt, utens legitimis praecipue conventibus malignantium synogogam objiciens, necessarium rata est sancta synodus ad aludendum insidias Principis tenebrarum omnibus fidelibus sive laicis sive Clericis, tam saecularibus quam Regularibus cujuscumque status & conditionis excommunicationem in quascumque personas, quae conventicula sive publica, sive privata, ad concilium quomodolibet pertinentia, quovis praetextu sine concilii licentia congregare vel illis interesse praesumpserint ferendam minitare, necnon admonere promotores hujus Concilii, ut per se et per alios vigilent, et inquirant, an praedicta Conventicula celebrentur, illorumque auctores et fautores Sanctae Synodo renuntient. Atque ut omnibus Sanctae Synodi voluntas constet jubet, Decretum hoc vulgari lingua inter Missarum Solemnia per tres Dominicas legi, et valvis Ecclesiarum aliisque locis affigi.

DECRETUM VII

De Ordine in Congregationibus Servando

Ut ordine omnia tractentur, praecipit Sancta Synodus, ut hi, qui in Congregationibus tam publicis, quam privatis, et in solemnibus sessionibus loqui possunt, in scriptis afferant quae proponere, et controverti digna judicaverint. Si quae autem ibi occurant ex tempore dicenda clare, breviter et distincte ad certa capita redigantur. Nullus alterius sermonem abrumpat, excepto Praeside, penes quem erit, stultas, et sine disciplina quaestiones finire silentiumque indicere iis, qui tumultuarie loquantur. Insuper jubet Sancta Synodus, ut quantum fieri possit latinus sermo in proponendis, dirimendisque quaestionibus adhibeatur. Denique lecta sunt Decreta, primo de Judicibus quaerelarum, accusationum, et excusationum quorum electio missa est, et causae ab illis, si electi fuissent, tractandae Concilio reservatae. Postea circa ferias Congregationum sancitum est, ut Illustrissimi Episcopi singillatim cum suis theologis privatos coetus haberent tertiis, et sextis feriis. Publicis autem, et privatis omnium Episcoporum dies certi praefixi non sunt. Mox alio Decreto publicatum est Concilium Tridentium, et anathematizatae tum antiquae hereses, tum recentiores Quietistarum, precipue Jansenistarum, Materialistarum et Deistarum, juratque Romano Pontifici Clementi XIV ejusque successoribus vera obedientia. Demum Lectum est Decretum Tridentinum Sess. 25. Cap. 2. Cogit temporum calamitas de professione fidei emittenda quae juxta formulam Pii IV. facta est, addito juramento de non defendenda doctrina damnata in Concilio Constantiensi, de Regicidio, et Tyrannicidio. Quibus factis futura sessio ad diem decimam quintam proximi Augusti indicta est.

ACTIO IIa

DE EPISCOPIS

habita die XV Augusti, Anni MDCCLXXI.

Proemium

Quoniam nihil ita fidelium animos percellit ac exemplum, et Pharisaicum est dicere, et non facere[a] Patres in Concilio Manilano legitime congregati, juxta veterem Toletanam Patrum sanctionem, arbitrati sunt ab Episcoporum Institutione Philipinensis Ecclesiae reformatione initium facere[b] ut hi, quorum vita ad aliorum exemplum tota informari debet, quemadmodum reliquos fideles, dignitatis fastigio,

[a] Math. 23. 3.
[b] Conc. Tolet. 9, in Proem.

longe antecellunt, ita eos antevertant vitae puritate. Monstruosa siquidem res est gradus summus et animus infimus, sedes prima et vitia ima.[c] Quod quum maturo animo perpendissent Manilani Patres, statuerunt[d] in ipso concilii aditu, Episcopalis vitae regulam proponere ut ea prius informati Antistites, libere adimplere possent Consilium Apostoli[e] dicentis: Praedica verbum, insta opportune, importune, argue, obsecra, increpa in omni patientia, et doctrina facti jam operarii inconfusibiles.[f]

TITULUS PRIMUS
DE DOMO EPISCOPI

DECRETUM I.
De Episcopi Familia Inferiori

§ i. Dicente Apostolo: qui domui suae preesse nescit,[g] quomodo Ecclesiae Dei diligentiam habebit: maxime invigilare debet Episcopus ne in familia sua eos admittat, qui aut necessarii non sint[h] aut bonae vitae testimonium non habeant.

§ ii. Quemadmodum providere debet, ne Domesticis suis necessaria desint ita etiam non patiatur, familiam suam sponsorum instar, ornari muliebriter.[i]

§ iii. Neque modo omnem luxum, vanitatemque ab Episcopi familia exulare oportet, sed virtutum omnium praxim induci ita ut solo etiam intuitu, familia Episcopi ab aliis dignoscatur, tum ob vestium honestatem, tum etiam ob gravitatem morum.

§ iv. Id vero cum obtineri non possit absque optima vitae institutione, curabit Episcopus, ut certa hora, familares sui, a strato surgentes, imitantes justum, qui cor suum (Eccl.

[c] D. Bern. de Consid. 2. cap. 6.
[d] ex Act. Congr. Publ. habitae die 1. Maii an. 1771.
[e] 2 Timot. 4. 2.
[f] 2 Tim. 2. 15.
[g] 1 Tim. 3. 5.
[h] Concil. Mediol. I. p. 2.
[i] D. Bernd. de Consid. Lib. 4. c. 4; Conc. Trid. Sess. 2. de modo vivendi.

39-6.) tradit ad vigilandum diluculo ad Dominum qui fecit illum[j] et in oratorium domesticum convenientes, postquam meditationi tantisper incubuerint[k] incruento Missae sacrificio devote intersint, vespere autem piae alicui meditationi, et Rosarii recitationi vacare faciat.

§ v. Semel, aut bis in hebdomoda, inferiorem familiam circa fidei rudimenta instrui curet, et salutaribus documentis imbui.[l] Praecipue vero satagat ut familia sua[m] ad sacramentum Poenitentiae et Eucharistiae frequenter accedat in solemnioribus festivitatibus et primis Dominicis cujusvis mensis, adhibita pridie pia aliqua instructione, ad recipiendum cum fructu sacramenta.

§ vi. Caveat ne in familia sua jurgia sint, et disidia nec detractiones aut colloquia minus casta, quod ut familia exequatur, constituat Episcopus e superiori familia aliquem, qui inferioris assidue curam gerat.[n]

DECRETUM II.

De Supellectili et Mensa Episcopi

§ i. Meminerit Episcopus sibi pauperum Apostolorum successori et Dominicae Crucis sectatori, haud expedire preciosam supellectilem, monilia aurea et argentea praeter levissima instrumenta, quae ori cibum admovendo serviunt[o] habere, neque pretiosis vestibus indui, tum quia dignitatis auctoritas, fidei et vitae meritis[p] quaerenda est, tum etiam ne inferiores clerici malo exemplo adducti, quam deposuerunt, ignominiam vestis saecularis iterum assumant.

§ ii. In mensa, eam frugalitatem servabunt Episcopi, quae Christi Ministros decet, ne vel deliciis assueti, vel crapula, aut ebrietate gravati, minus idonei, ad muneris sui functiones reddantur. Quapropter conviviis non intersint,

[j] Eccles. 39.
[k] Act. Eccl. Med. P. 2. Inst. Famil. Archiep. P. I.
[l] Act. Eccl. Med. P. 2: ubi sup.
[m] Act. Eccl. Med. ubi sup.
[n] Act. Eccles. Med. ubi sup.
[o] C. Med. I. P. 2.
[p] C. Carthag. 4. c. 15.

praecipue apud saeculares[q] neque ipsi celebrent magnificas epulas[r] quin potius pauperi mensae quae sacra benedictione condiri debet[s] sacra lectio, tum Scripturarum, tum eorum Patrum qui de officio Pastorali scripserunt adhibeatur, ne saturato corpore animus esuriat.[t]

DECRETUM III
De Superiori Familia

§ i. Superiorem Episcopi Familiam ex clero accisci decet, quae quemadmodum Episcopalis vitae custos esse debet, et testis, ita etiam piae Praesulis conversationis imitatrix sit oportet.

TITULUS SECUNDUS
DE MINISTERIO EPISCOPI

DECRETUM I
De Sacra Praedicatione

§ i. Duo sint Pontificis opera: a Deo discat legendo scripturas sacras, et saepius meditando, quae a Deo didiscerit; Populum doceat[v] Unde Concilium Tridentinum declaravit, praecipuum Episcoporum munus esse praedicationem verbi Dei.[u] Quapropter totis viribus incumbere debet Episcopus, in Quadragessima praecipue, Adventu, et solemnioribus festivitatibus desseminationi verbi Dei, per seipsum, ubi id licuerit.

§ ii. Sed quoniam ob linguarum varietatem et confusionem fieri saepe non potest, ut Antistites huic muneri incumbant, occurrere satagant huic malo per Epistolas Pastorales. Vult autem haec Provincialis Synodus, ut Episcopi ter saltem in anno ad Populum suum, captui, et necessitati ovium accomodatas epistolas vulgari lingua prius a peritis vertendas, mittant, quibus oves suas salutaribus imbuant docu-

[q] Conc. Maguntin. an. 813.
[r] Conc. Laodicen. c. 55.
[s] C. Rhemens. an. 813. cap. 17.
[t] Ex Decr. Euseb. Pap.; Trid. Ses. 2. de modo vivendi.
[v] Decr. Gratian. Tit. 15. Rubr. 5. c. 11. si quis vult.
[u] Conc. Trid. Ses. 5. c. 2 et Ses. 24. c. 4.

mentis, et arctam viam, quae ducit ad vitam, ingredi doceant, "non in persuasibilibus humanae sapientiae verbis, sed in ostensione Spiritus."[x]

§ iii. Neque modo aliquando ad Populum pie et graviter scribent Episcopi sed etiam ad Parochos, confessarios et concionatores, illos maxime hortantes commissam sibi gregis partem sanis doctrinis pascant, fidelium auribus semper inclamantes, quam angusta porta, et arcta via est quae ducit ad vitam, et pauci sunt, qui inveniunt.[z]

DECRETUM II
De Vigilantia

§ i. Christus Dominus pastoris officium describens apud Joannem, inquit: Ego sum Pastor bonus, et cognosco oves meas, et cognoscunt me meae et animam meam pono pro eis.[y] Unde excusatio Pastoris bona non est, si eo nesciente, lupus ovem rapiat. Quapropter haec Provincialis Synodus vehementer inculcat omnibus Episcopis, ut assidue invigilent super custodia gregis, ut errantes oves reducere possint ad ovile.

§ ii. Ut autem oves suas agnoscant Episcopi, habeant libellum in quo describant nomina omnium ecclesiasticorum suae Dioecesis, cum expressione aetatis, generis, scientiae, opum, indolis, zeli morum, officii, et tituli ordinationis. Habeant alium libellum, in quem referant nomina peccatorum, quae ex Vicariis Foraneis discere oportet, ut si oportuerit, exemplo Pauli, monere unumquemque possint cum lacrimis,[a] ut revertatur a via sua prava: bonus enim Pastor, si una ex centum ovibus erraverit, dimissis nonaginta novem, amissam quaerit et suis humeris impositam ad ovile reducit.

DECRETUM III
De Cura Pauperum

§ i. Avaritia, quae simulacrorum servitus ab Apostolo

[x] 1 Cor. 2. 4.
[z] Math. 7. 14.
[y] Joan. 10. 14.
[a] Act. Ap. 20. 31.

dicitur[b] adeo alte fidelium animos occupavit ut ipsi pauperes mendicantes ex eleemosynis, usuras quaerant, quod maximo dolore animadvertens Provincialis Synodus, rogat Illmos. Metropolitanos, ut accito etiam si opus fuerit, auxilio brachii saecularis, invigilent, ne veris pauperibus illi admisceantur, qui, cum in sudore vultus sui victum quaerere possint, subterfugiunt.

§ ii. Praeficiant ergo aliquem ex seminario clericorum bonae vitae et quoad fieri possit provectae aetatis, qui pauperum curam gerat spiritualem nullusque mendicare ostiatim permittatur, nisi prius nomen suum designato sacerdoti dederit.

§ iii. Sacerdotis autem sit diligenter exquirere pauperum patrias et vitas, et prohibere, ne aut vagabundi, aut qui possunt laborare, in damnum vere pauperum mendicent. Curet etiam ut omnes pauperes diebus festis certa aliqua hora ad se confluant, ut eos, et rudimentis fidei, et salutaribus monitis instruant, maxime invigilans, ut praeceptis communionis, et confessionis annuae satisfaciant.

§ iv. Rogat autem Provincialis Synodus Perillustrem Gubernatorem ut aliquod Hospitium in hac urbe ad pauperum utilitatem erigi curet, ubi veri mendici congruis laboribus dediti, Reipublicae utiles evadant.

DECRETUM IV
De Cura Aliorum Miserorum

§ i. Curent Episcopi tum per se,[c] juxta possibilitatem, tum etiam, per alios divites, his, quae vere Viduae sunt et desolatae, et aliis miseris personis subvenire; inertes, et otiosos, qui malorum omnium sentina sunt, coercentes.

§ ii. Aegrotorum in valetudinariis jacentium, et carceribus mancipatorum, paternam curam gerant, providentes, ut aliquot clerici, diebus saltem festis, illorum confessiones excipiant, et in rudimentis fidei, et vitae christianae praeceptis erudiant. Quam diligentiam circa collegiorum puellas multo

[b] Colos. 3. 5.

[c] Decret. Gratian. tit. 15 rub. 5 cap. 18 & 19.

magis adhibebunt, curantes, tamen, ne quis sine socio ad eas accedat.[d]

DECRETUM V

De Cura Doctrinae

§ i. Ne ob catechismorum varietatem errores irrepant, prohibet Provincialis Synodus sub poena excommunicationis maioris latae sententiae Episcopis reservatae, et privationis officii, et beneficii, ne quis Parochus Secularis vel Regularis seu alius quicumque in tradenda Doctrina alio catechismo, utatur, quam edendo a Concilio, ut uno ore omnes glorificent Patrem Caelestem.

§ ii. Curabit autem Concilium, ut quam primum duo catechismi adornentur, quorum alter rudium captui accomodatus, necessaria necessitate medii, et praecepti continebit; alter vero pro ingeniosioribus fusior uberiorem Doctrinam amplectetur.

§ iii. Si quis vero his catechismis plene imbutus, altiora quaerere contendat, ei non interdicit Provincialis Synodus alios Misteriorum nostrae fidei explanatores, probatos tamen, adire.

DECRETUM VI

De Orationis Studio

§ i. Cum sine Orationis studio in via Dei parum, aut nihil profici possit, Provincialis Synodus summopere hortatur omnes Episcopos, ut mane surgentes, per horam saltem, cum superiori familia orationi vacent in Oratorio Domestico,[e] qua finita, vel sacrificium offerant vel Missae intersint. Persoluto deinde attente, et devote Divino Officio, reliquum tempus Divinarum Scripturarum, Patrumque lectione, aliisque utilibus negotiis absumant ab inutilibus salutationibus abstinentes. Noctu, antequam cubitum eant, diligenti examine semetipsos dijudicent, attenta consideratione discutientes quid in illa die in bonum sui gregis, aut fecerint, aut omiserint, et pro eo Divinam implorent clementiam exemplo s.

[d] C. Carthag. 3. 25.

[e] Act. Eccl. Med. ubi sup.

Job qui singulis diebus pro peccatis filiorum hostiam Deo offerebat.[f]

§ ii. Officiis Divinis in Ecclesia Cathedrali in Quadragesima precipue, Adventu, et solemnioribus festivitatibus per annum intersint, ne clerici exemplum Praelati in excusationem suae negligentiae afferant.[g]

DECRETUM VII
De Consultoribus et Confessario

§ i. Cum scriptum sit, ne innitaris prudentiae tuae[h] oportet Episcopum aliquot habere Consultores viros probos, et libertate Evangelica praeditos, quorum consilio, et opera in magnis negotiis utatur.

§ ii. Sed in primis Episcopo necessarius est optimus confessarius, et prudens, qui Episcopum negotiorum magnitudine oppressum, dirigere valeat, et si erraverit libere[i] dicat: non licet tibi.[j]

TITULUS TERTIUS
DE VISITATIONE

DECRETUM I
De Visitatione Annua

§ i. Cum fieri non possit ut amplas Dioeceses et invias Ecclesias quotannis aut singulis bienniis visitent Episcopi, oportet declarare satis esse, si Episcopi visitantes quotannis aliquam Dioecesis suae partem per semetipsos, alias per Vicarios Foraneos, singulis annis semel, aut iterum visitaverint.

§ ii. Itaque decernit Provincialis Synodus, ut Vicarii Foranei[k] per duas Dominicas ante Quadragesimam, Paroeciarum sui Territorii Visitationem quotannis instituant, una tantum die in quavis Ecclesia commorantes, & nulla jura,

[f] Job. 1. 5.
[g] C. Aurelian. C. 13-; Med. 4. p. 3.
[h] Prov. 3. 5.
[i] C. Med. 4. p. 3.
[j] Math. 14. 4.
[k] Mediol. V.

praeter cibum exigentes. At vero priusquam visitationem aggrediantur, proprium Episcopum certiorem faciant, ut si velit, aliqua monita dare possit.

§ iii. Meminerint Vicarii Foranei sibi nullam fieri potestatem ad innovandum aliquid, vel ad puniendum Parochos, sed tantum ad inquirendum, tam de synodalium statutorum observantia, quam de Parochorum vita ut expleta visitatione proprium Episcopum moneant de his, quae correctione digna videantur.

§ iv. Vicarii Foranei in Visitatione de his omnibus inquirant, quae in Visitatione Episcopali inquiri solent. In primis autem summam diligentiam adhibeant ne Ecclesiae sordidae sint & ruinosae. Quod si aliquam minus mundam invenerint, ex toto vel ex parte, Parocho certum praefiniant tempus ad reparationem, quo expleto, si reparata non sit, Parochi sumptu id fiat, nulla circa id admissa excusatione. Atque in hoc maxime gravat Provincialis Synodus Visitatorum Conscientias.

§ v. Liberum Episcopis reliquit Provincialis Synodus Vicarii Foranei loco alium visitatorem designare, tum alicujus Vicariatus, tum etiam totius Dioecesis dummodo e Capitulo non sit.[I] Canonici enim nec plena sede, nec ea vacante, visitatores institui debent.

§ vi. Secunda vicariatuum visitatio fieri, vel omitti poterit, prout expediens in Domino, Episcopi judicaverint. Si autem fiat, ea paulo ante pluviarum exordium instituatur.

DECRETUM II

De Praeparatione Visitationis

§ i. Visitaturi Episcopi, sive per se, sive per visitatorem Generalem, edicto admoneant visitandas Ecclesias, & aliquam Pastoralem epistolam dirigant[II] de scopo Visitationis tractantem, necnon si per se visitaturi sint, de Sacramento Confirmationis.

§ ii. Antequam ab urbe exeant, & Visitationis exordium faciant orationem quadraginta horarum in Cathedrali insti-

[I] Ced. R. desp. en Madr. a 3 de Abr. de 1627.

[II] C. Med. 4. p. 3.

tuant pro bono exitu visitationis, ipsamque institui faciant in visitandis ecclesiis.[m]

§ iii. Praemittant etiam, si fieri potest, aliquem Missionarium, qui verbi Dei praedicatione fidelium animos disponat, tum ad visitationem tum etiam ad sacram Eucharistiam[n] pro lucranda indulgentia plenaria.[n]

§ iv. Pridie, aut paulo ante quam Episcopus adveniet in aliquam Paroeciam, si expedire videbitur praemitat aliquem Ecclesiasticum, qui leviores causas explicet, ne ipsi diu immorari cogatur[o].

§ v. Nocte, quae praecedat visitatoris adventum[p], Parochus pulsare faciat campanam, ut populus ad devotionem excitetur, & sequente die Pastori suo obviam procedat, non in choreis, non saltationibus, non in ludis, sed in Hymnis, & Canticis Pastorem excipiat, et ad Ecclesiam commitetur, ubi fine praecandi atque benedicendi facto, ad suas Domos compunctus potius quam hilaris revertatur. Si quis Parochus in adventu Episcopi vel Visitatoris choreas permiserit, ludosve exhibuerit decem argenti unciis seminario applicandis, mulctetur.

DECRETUM III

De Regulis Visitationis

§ i. Visitaturi Episcopi, aut eorum nomine alii quicumque necesarios tantum in comitatu habeant, qui in sacra visitatione usui esse possint, non impedimento[q].

§ ii. Caveant, ne cum se cognoscendos ovibus suis praebent, illas, quas pasturi exeunt verbo, exemplo occidant; ideoque omni diligentia studeant visitationis tempore omnium virtutum, charitatis praecipue erga miseros specimina exhibere.

[m] C. Med. 4. p. 3 et Synodicon. Bened. 13. p. 2 Appar. ad tit. 21. de Visit. Edict. Visitat. § 3.

[n] Bened. 14, Inst. 19.

[n] Ex Solit. Episcopor. Ind.

[o] C. Rotomagen.

[p] Synodic. Benedict. 13 ubi Conc. Mediol. 4. P. 3.

[q] C. Med. 4. p. 3.

§ iii. Sacram Lectionem in mensa adhibeant & bonas noctis horas discutiendis Clericis insumant, illos de materiis moralibus, de methodo praedicandi, & administrandi Sacramenta, de Rubricis, & materiis spiritualibus interrogantes.[r]

§ iv. Bonos ad meliora excitent, pigros vero prout necesitas postulaverit, acriter reprehendant, memores tamen communis fragilitatis.

§ v. Neque modo Parochos, sed etiam Laicos erudient, publicos peccatores ad virtutis viam revocantes, tum publice, tum private, et si expediens judicaverint,[s] eos publicae poenitentiae subjiciant, ut caeteri terrorem habeant vel in Urbem adduci faciant, ut solemni penitentiae eos addicant.

§ vi. Magistros scholarum, et Ministros Parochorum zelatores, testes publicos, et similes, per interpretem discutiant; nihilque omittant, quod utilem reddere Visitationem possit.

DECRETUM IV
De Non Gravandis Parochis

§ i. Ne Parochi Visitatione graventur, districte jubeat Episcopus sub poena decem aureorum, testibus publicis applicanda, ne Parochi Visitatori, & ejus sociis, ultra quinque fercula[t] quovis praetextu etiam sponte oblata, in mensa apponant, neque Primores, et seniores, neque Plebeios, durante visitatione, etiam ad secundam mensam excipiant, nec eos admittant etiam titulo serviendi Episcopo, vel Visitatori, sed suo, & visitatoris famulitio contenti, Episcopo vel Visitatori in sobrietate ministrent. Quapropter cibi in mensa apponendi, ex illorum genere sint, qui facile in oppido comparari possunt.

§ ii. Musicos, & cantores, nullus Parochus Visitationis tempore in domum suam inducat, etiam si nullos sumptus ob id faciat.

§ iii. Prohibeat[v] Episcopus vel Visitator, ne Parochis visitandis, vel visitatis, quantumvis pusillum donum, etiam

[r] C. Brachar. 2. c. 1.
[s] Thomasin, vet. et nov. Eccl. disciplin. tom. 2. p. 2.
[t] C. Med. I. P. 2.
[v] Bened. 14. Inst. 6.

sponte oblatum aut ipse, aut familiares sui accipiant: quo circa Provincialis Synodus maxime gravat visitatorum conscientias, quibus Sacrorum Canonum poenas, ultra restitutionem dupli intra mensem, in memoriam revocat.

§ iv. Ne diuturna Episcopi aut Visitatoris immoratione, Parochi aere alieno opprimantur Visitatores in parvis oppidis uno die, in magnis vero ultra triduum non detineantur[u] nisi Parochi negligentia in causa fuerit ut amplius immorentur. At vero, si ultra id tempus moram traxerit Episcopus, non ob culpam Parochi sed confirmandorum causa, suis sumptibus cum suo comitatu alatur.

DECRETUM V
De Visitandis Conservatoriis Puellarum

§ i. Cum Manilae et in eius suburbiis aliquot reperiantur feminarum Collegia & Beateria, quorum Visitatio, sine dubio, ad Episcopum spectat, Provincialis Synodus hujusmodi collegiorum curam, et visitationem vehementer commendat Illustrissimis Metropolitis, quorum conscientias in hoc onerat.

§ ii. Scrutentur ergo hujusmodi Collegiorum, et Beateriorum Institutionem, eorumque regulas et statuta. Invigilent etiam, ne Puellae ibi degentes, desidem vitam ducant, sed eis exsequenda exercitia praescribant, illisque provideant de optimo confessario, et quantum fieri possit, sene qui eas instruat in rudimentis fidei, et via perfectionis.

§ iii. Quapropter praeter annuam visitationem aliquoties per annum ad eas accedat Antistes, honesto Clericorum stipatus comitatu, et inquirat, an ea serventur quae in praecedenti visitatione statuta fuerint.

§ iv. Quae autem domus sub Regis fuerint Patronatu, & ejus immediata protectione, salvis in omnibus juribus Regis, quae nunquam, vel in minimo violare Provincialis Synodus intendit, sed potius eorum observantiam exigere, quoad spiritualia tamen visitentur ab Episcopis, poenis, et omnibus juris remediis contra reluctantes utendo.

[u] C. Tolet. 6. c. 4 et C. Brachar. 2. c. 1.

§ v. Nosocomia autem, sub Regio Patronatu constituta, visitent Episcopi, Regio tamen adhibito Assistente. Adjiciant etiam in primo actu visitationis se valetudinariorum visitationem ob specialem Regis commissionem instituere.[x]

§ vi. Demum prae oculis habeant Episcopi Cap. 8. de Reformat. Sess. 22. Concil. Trid. et ea omnia, quae ibi Episcopis visitanda praecipiuntur, diligenter invisant.

TITULUS QUARTUS
DE SYNODUS

DECRETUM I
De Concilio Provinciali

§ i. Concilia Provincialia in his Regionibus celebrari vix posse animadvertit felicis recordationis Urbanus VIII Pontifex Maximus, ideoque haec Provincialis Synodus, magna Dei miseratione, post duo secula ab inventione harum Insularum congregata, tametsi hortatur Illmos. et Rmos. Metropolitas, ut si qua detur occasio celebrandi provincialem synodum, ea utantur in commodum, et utilitatem hujus Ecclesiae; eis tamen certum tempus non praefinit.

DECRETUM II
De Synodis Dioecesanis

§ i. Synodi Dioecesanae[y] quotannis ab Episcopis celebrentur per se, vel per alium eo tempore, quo commodius haberi possint, vocatis tamen prius per edictum Parochis totius Dioecesis.

§ ii. Sed quoniam ob Ministrorum inopiam fieri non potest ut omnes conveniant, declarat Concilium Provinciale ad Synodi celebrationem sufficere si ex remotis Provinciis unus, aut duo Parochi accedant bene instructi de Provinciarum statu.

§ iii. Si ex aliqua Provincia ob aliquam causam, Episcopo significandam, nullus Parochus convenire possit, sufficit, ut

[x] Ced. Rl. despac. en Mad. a 18 de Dic. de 1768.

[y] Trid. Ses. 24, c. 2, de Reform.

testes publici illius Provinciae veniant et Episcopus certior fiat per epistolam de his, quae in ea Provincia reformatione egent.

§ iv. Decernit Provincialis Synodus ut intra sex menses fine hujus nostri concilii, singuli Episcopi synodum celebrent Dioecesanam, ut Plebi suae Decreta Provincialia referant: quod si quis haec parvipendenda crederit, sententia suspensionis duorum mensium curriculo persistat usquequaque mulctatus.

§ v. Declarat Provinciale Concilium Synodos Dioecesanas[z] haberi posse extra urbem, quinimo expedire ut visitationis tempore in illis ecclesiis congregentur, quibus hoc saluberrimo remedio egregie praeter alias opus sit.

DECRETUM III
De Kalendis Seu Coetibus

§ i. Prima Die cujusvis mensis non impedita festo aliquo de praecepto, convenient Parochi cujusvis Vicariatus in Foranei Vicarii domum et emissa ab omnibus Confessione sacramentali decantabitur Missa pro defunctis Parochis, et concio habebitur de magnitudine officii pastoralis vel de via perfectionis. Post Missam cui omnes intereunt cum superpelliceis Processio Defunctorum circa Coemeterium pro Defunctis illius territorii instituatur.

§ ii. Finitis his Officiis superpelliceis induti Parochi in sacristia vel alio commodo loco conveniant, dum Vicarius Foraneus secreto coram suo Notario vel eius vices gerente, testes publicos, qui accedere debent, examinat circa vitam, et honestatem Parochorum.

§ iii. Inquirat ergo Vicarius a testibus, an Parochi singulis festis diebus concionem habeant et quomodo: an exercitia Dominicalia servent; an moribundis per se, aut per alios auxilia spiritualia praestent; an aliquis sine sacramentis decesserit; an aegroti ad Ecclesiam deferantur; an funeribus pauperum praesentes sint; an frequenter celebrent; an familiaritatem habeant cum feminis; an crudeles sint in

[z] Bened. 14. de Synod. Dioec. 2. 1 c. 5.

jurium exactione; an vinolenti; an chartarum ludo dediti; an vestem clericalem deferant; an post primam horam noctis e domo exeant sine causa; an resideant in suo territorio, et bene vivant sine quaerela; an templa, aut altaria sordida sint, et hujus generis alia.

§ iv. Expleta privata hac inquisitione testes publici in congressum adducantur, et coram omnibus a vicario interrogentur de publicis peccatoribus, ebriosis, concubinariis, veneficis, superstitiosis, vagabundis, discordibus, et similibus de quibus statim ac rationem reddiderint, excludantur, et Parochi inter se consulant quid facto opus sit.

§ v. At vero nisi delictum grave nimis sit et notorium, prima vice juxta salvatoris praeceptum a propiis Parochis corripiantur peccatores, qui si hac via emendati non sint, in sequentibus Kalendis coram omnibus publice arguantur. Quod si nec ita emendati adhuc in peccato perseverent, certior fiat Episcopus, ut de necessario remedio provideat. Atque hic ordo in Parochorum correctione, nisi criminis aut gravitas, aut scandalum aliud postulaverit, a Vicariis servetur.

§ vi. Finitis delationibus et correctionibus consulant inter se Parochi de negotiis suarum Ecclesiarum vel ad utilitatem ovium spectantibus adhibito etiam, si opus sit, Primorum consilio.

§ vii. His gestis omnes Parochi et Clerici exhibeant quatuor casus morales a se resolutos juxta principia theologiae moralis edendae a Concilio in scriptis Latino sermone. In proponendo autem casus omnino abstineant Vicarii a subtilibus et speculativis quaestionibus, quinimo casus practicos, et dubia quae accidere solent in administratione sacramentorum sectentur. Curent etiam ut vertente anno omnes tractatus morales debent, et semel, aut iterum de theologia Mystica et de Rubricis aliquid attingant.

§ viii. Lecta casuum resolutione designandus ex tempore a Vicario respondebit ad duo argumenta per dimidiam horam, posito primum in materia, ut ajunt, statu quaestionis. Quibus factis Vicarius interrogabit singulos an habeant aliquod dubium, ut consilio Fratrum adjuventur.

§ ix. Denique lecto aliquo titulo hujus nostrae Provincialis Synodi ad Parochos, Confessarios, Concionatores, vel Clericos spectante & positis casibus pro sequenti coetu, conventus solvetur et Acta Kalendarum eo ordine quo facta sint, in librum ad id destinatum redigentur a Notario vel ejus vices gerente cum expressione loci, diei, mensis, anni, et eorum qui interfuerunt vel abfuerunt. Primae autem contra Parochos delationes in libro separato describentur.

§ x. Confectis actis omnes qui interfuerunt subscribant antequam discedant si fieri potest, sin minus in sequentibus Kalendiis. At vero ante Parochorum discessum, epistola fiat ab omnibus subscribenda, et ad Episcopum vel vacante sede ad Capitulum per quam certior fiat de his quae in Kalendis acta sunt et de casuum resolutione, mittatur.

§ xi. Qui Kalendis non interfuerit sine legitima causa, una argenti uncia testibus applicanda mulctetur, eademque poena afficiatur, qui in coetu clamosis vocibus obstrepuerit, aut convitium dixerit, aut casus non resolverit.

§ xii. Si pluviarum aut pesti causa, coetus congregari nequeant, casuum tamen resolutio non omittatur, et cum primum licuerit coetus instaurentur. Interim tamen Episcopus certior fiat de Kalendarum intermissione.

§ xiii. Qui mare trajicere opus habet ut intersit Kalendis ad id non cogatur, nisi eo tempore quo navigatio facile institui possit et sine periculo.

§ xiv. Si vicarialis domus sit in loco parum accommodato illa domus pro coetibus eligatur, quae in centro Provinciae sita sit. Quae domus si ob paupertatem sumptus ferre nequeat, singuli Parochi aut Clerici confluentes unum regale Parocho domus solvant, mensa sutem etiam si Parochus dives sit, ultra tertium ferculum et aliquod fructus genus non extendatur.

§ xv. Vicarius qui sine legitima causa Episcopo probanda coetum convocare omiserit, decem argenti uniciis mulctatur quarum quinque seminario, quinque vero testibus publicis applicabuntur, eademque poena puniatur si propositionem casuum omiserit in quo, si negligens extiterit, etiam officio privetur.

§ xvi. Casuum solutione facta a Parochis singulis mensibus ex Kalendis ad Magistrum Theologiae Moralis Seminarii, vel ad eum, quem huic muneri praefecerit Episcopus, ubi non est seminarium, mittetur et postquam ab illo probata, aut correcta transmissa fuerit, in libro separato juxta ordinem tractatuum Theologiae Moralis edendae describetur, cujus libri exemplar unusquisque Parochus habeat in sua Paroecia.

§ xvii. Declarat Provincialis Synodus non modo Parochus, sed etiam coadjutores, et alios quosqumque Clericos in territorio existentes teneri ad casuum resolutionem et interesse Kalendis. Quod si Vicariatus ampli sint, et Parochi vel Clerici sine magno labore aut longa absentia convenire nequeant, curent Episcopi eos dividere in plures Vicariatus ad hunc saltem effectum.

§ xviii. Manilae vero ubi numerosior est Clerus domum Parochialem oppidi Sanctae Crucis pro coetibus Parochorum et Clericorum designat Provincialis Synodus et insuper jubet ut conferentiae morales prima et quintadecima die cujusvis mensis hora quinta vespertina per horam habeantur cui intersint omnes Parochi, et Clerici extra seminarium existentes quorum indicem habeat Parochus Sanctae Crucis. Si aliquo designato die lyceus habere nequit, in proximo celebretur.

§ xix. Iisdem diebus, aut si impediti sint, in proximis, Canonici, Cappellani, Parochi, Coadjutores et alii Clerici Ecclesiae Cathedralis mane per horam integram, conferentiam moralem in sacristia habeant, in qua duo casus practici discutientur. Conferentiae autem praeerit Canonicus Magistralis, quousque Penitentiarius creetur, vel eo legitime impedito, Canonicus Doctoralis.

§ xx. Quicumque sine legitima causa, sive Canonicus, sive Parochus, sive Clericus ab hujusmodi coetibus abfuerit dimidia argenti uncia mulctetur pro prima vice; pro secunda vero una argenti uncia; pro tertia autem Parochi, et Clerici in Seminario per decem dies recludantur. Canonici vero in aula capitulari per totidem dies detineantur.

§ xxi. Pecunia ex mulctis Canonicorum et Parochorum

respectivis Ecclesiarum fabricis applicabitur; aliorum vero Clericorum, Seminario adjudicetur.

§ xxii. Praeses autem conferentiarum habeant librum in quo notentur conferentiae, et illi, qui abfuerunt, vel interfuerunt, et curet ut mulctae numerata pecunia solvantur. Ubi autem opus sit aliquem Seminario includere, Episcopum certiorem faciat.

§ xxiii. Declarat Provincialis Synodus causae legitimae nomine eam tantum intelligi qua quis vel lecto aegrotus decumbit vel aliqua gravi occupatione, Episcopo significanda, detinetur impeditus. Ne autem Praeses negligentium excusationes facile excipiat, ejus conscientiam in hoc gravat Provincialis Synodus. Sunt enim hujusmodi coetus, si, prout decet, non perfunctorie fiant, magnae in Ecclesia utilitatis.

§ xxiv. Ut autem Praesidibus omnis occasio tollatur gerendi se in his coetibus otiose et oscitanter, Provincialis Synodus hortatur Episcopos, ut aliquando se repente coetibus ingerant aut aliquem mittant qui quomodo fiant, diligenter observet.

§ xxv. Severe in Domino praecipit Provincialis Synodus, ne Kalendarum aut coetuum occasione chartarum alearumque ludi, aut comessationes misceantur atque in hoc maxime gravat, tum Vicariorum tum Episcoporum conscientias.

DECRETUM IV
De Testibus Publicis

§ i. In qualibet Provincia, duo aut plures testes publici eligantur in Synodis dioecesanis, quorum officium praestito prius juramento fidelitatis, erit investigare vitiorum latebras et inquirere vitas Parochorum. Ad id vero Parochi proponant duo ex qualibet Paroecia viros probos bonae famae et melioris vitae; sint etiam magnae auctoritatis apud indigenas et habeant mediocres divitias, ne si pauperes sint, muneribus facile corrumpantur.

§ ii. Ex his vero Episcopus in Synodo eligat duo, aut plures in testes publicos quibus subiaceant zelatores majores et minores qui ad illorum praescriptum inquirant in vitia et peccatores publicos, ebriosos, concubinarios, Patres familias negligentes, Magistros scholarum deficientes ad montes et hujusmodi ut in Kalendis, et Synodis renuntient quidquid mali per se, aut per alios repererint, nihil amicitiae nihil odio tribuentes.

§ iii. Ut vero occultandi veritatem, aut calumniandi locus non detur, Vicariis occultissimos zelatores constituant, qui invigilent in vitam testium publicorum, quos private saepe examinabunt et instruent de suo officio, ut eo rite fungantur.

§ iv. Si quis testis calumniator extiterit aut veritatis occultator, talionem subeat, aut eam poenam quam verus peccator ab illo occultatus subire debebat.

§ v. Si aliqua de causa intermittantur Synodi, testes publici eligantur in Kalendis.

ACTIO IIIa.
DE CLERI INSTITUTIONE
Habita die VIII. Mensis Sept. Anni MDCCLXXI

TITULUS PRIMUS
DE SEMINARIO

DECRETUM I
De Utilitate, et Necessitate Seminarii

§ i. Ea est humanae naturae lapsae conditio, ut homines proni ad malum ab adolescentia nisi in tenera aetate in via Dei pie, et sancte educentur, nihil ab eis in matura aetate sperandum relinquatur. Quamvis enim potentia Dei a via sua prava Saulus revocatus sit quum provectae esset aetatis et ex persecutore Ecclesiae vas electionis factus sit, tamen hoc et similia exempla non infringunt legem illam Spiritus Sancti: Adolescens juxta viam positus etiam quum senuerit non recedet ab ea.

§ ii. Hac de causa jam inde ab initio Ecclesiae a pluribus conciliis statutum est, ut juvenes Clerici probati alicujus senis educationi commendati pie, et sobrie in lubrica aetate, et litteris, et virtutibus imbuerentur, eo nempe consilio ut a teneris annis pie informati, optimi postea mysteriorum Deo dispensatores evaderent.

§ iii. Itaque Provincialis Manilana Synodus Philippinensi Ecclesiae consulere cupiens illique de optimis sacerdotibus providere, praecipit per hoc Decretum, ut Seminarium ab Illmo. et Rm. Metropolita inchoatum in perpetuum stabiliatur ad Cleri institutionem.

§ iv. Et quoniam in suffraganeis Dioecesibus, tum ob Magistrorum inopiam, tum etiam ob paupertatem juventus litteris imbui vix potest Provincialis Synodus declarat, Seminarium Manilanum omnibus suffraganeis Dioecesibus commune esse futurum, donec Dioeceses peculiaria seminaria habere nequeant.

DECRETUM II

De Seminarii Erectione

§ i. Quum Religiosus noster Princeps Carolus III per Regium Tomum facultatem fecerit Episcopis erigendi seminaria in Jesuitarum domibus, Provincialis Synodus rogat Illmum. Gubernatorem nomine Majestatis Catholicae, ut pro suo zelo Collegium Maximum pro seminarii erectione, Illmo. et Rmo. Metropolitae tradat expeditum.

§ ii. Metropolitae autem studio ab eodem Illmo. Gubernatore secundum Regium Tomum postuletur, ut ex reditibus piis Jesuitarum vel, iis non suficientibus, ex profanis juxta Regiam voluntatem in commodum, et utilitatem Philippinensis Ecclesiae Cathedras dotet, a quarum Moderatoribus Clerici praeter morales disciplinas, sacra Rhetorica, scriptura, liturgia, et ecclesiastica historia imbuantur.

§ iii. Cathedrae autem omnes praevio accurato examine dignioribus dentur, et caeteris paribus Parochi reliquis omnibus praeferantur.

§ iv. Praecipit Provincialis Synodus, ut Praeceptores Seminarii juxtam sanam et inconcussam Div. Augustini, et Div. Thomae Doctrinam alumnos erudiant, laxam, et novam opinandi libertatem ab evangelica Doctrina prorsus alienam omnino execurantes clericos instruant probabilioribus opinionibus tum circa propriorum actionum regulas, tum praecipue circa obedientiam Regi, et Magistratibus debitam, juxta illud Apostoli omnis anima Potestatibus Sublimioribus subdita sit.

§ v. Provincialis Synodus optans maxime populos in officio erga Principem continere, jubet ut Magistri, antequam Cathedras adeant, et Clerici priusquam sacris initientur, juramentum praestent de improbanda Doctrina damnata in Concilio Constantiensi de Regicidio et tyrannicidio.

§ vi. Ut Magistri sedulo suo officio incumbant, rogat Provincialis Synodus Illmos. Metropolitas, ut vacantibus semiportionibus, portionibus, aut Dignitatibus Ecclesiae Metropolitanae, Praeceptores, qui per decem annos suo munere cum laude functi fuerint, Vice-Patrono presentent, salvis tamen Ecclesiae juribus et statutis.

§ vii. Ad seminarii sustentationem, Provincialis Synodus applicari jubet omnes cappellanias aut beneficia, que iuxta Concilium Tridentinum Sess. XXIII cap. 18. applicari possunt, sine praejudicio tamen eas obtinentium, nec piarum dispositionum.

§ viii. Praecipit Provincialis Synodus, ut omnes qui reditus habent Ecclesiasticos etiam Regulares, ex reditibus Paroeciarum tres argenti uncias Seminario ex centum quibusque solvant.

§ ix. Seminarii curam ad Clericos Saeculares perpetuo spectaturam declarat Provincialis Synodus et insuper prohibet, ne Seminarii regimen ullo tempore, et ulla de causa ad quosvis transeat Regulares, nisi ob summam necessitatem ad tempus, cum amovibilitate ad nutum, illis ab Episcopis commendetur.

§ x. Ad vitandas in posterum lites quae inter Episcopos et Metropolitas oriri possent circa Magistrorum electionem, Provincialis Synodus, cuicumque ex suffraganeis Episcopis permittet duos Manilae habere examinatores, qui una cum Metropolita, et ejus examinatoribus suffragium habeant:

§ xi. Quum Religiosus Rex Carolus Seminarii Fundator sit ad eum jus Patronatus spectare sine controversia quum exploratum habeat Provincialis Manilana Synodus ad Directoris munus praevio concursu tres ab Illmis. Metropolitis Majestati Catholicae praesentandos declarat.

§ xii. Curabit Provincialis Synodus pro optima Seminarii gubernatione tam in spiritualibus quam in temporalibus, salubria condere statuta.

Titulus Secundus
De Vita et Honestate Clericorum

DECRETUM I
De Vestibus Clericalibus

§ i. Dicente Apostolo: habentes quid edamus, et quibus tegamur his contenti simus, facile intelligi potest quam indecorum sit Christi Domini sacerdotibus pretiosas vestes aut deferre aut statui congruentes deponere.

§ ii. Iubet ergo Provincialis Synodus ut nullus Clericorum Canonicis exceptis (quos tamen ad inferiorem exemplum sericas vestes deponere hortatur), sericis vestibus exterius, vel interius, utatur quum non desint aliae vestes honestae, et calori regionis accommodatae: omnes enim de tenuitate redituum quaeruntur quin tamen luxui modus imponatur.

§ iii. Ut autem factae vestes consumantur declarat Provincialis Synodus hoc decretum non nisi post annum ab ejus publicatione effectum suum sortitum ire; Interim tamen, moneri jubet omnem Clerum ne ultra novas vestes sericas sibi comparet. Exacto vero anno, si quis sericam vestem deferat, eam amittat.

§ iv. Si quis Clericus cujuscumque sit dignitatis extra domum sine clericali veste nigra, et oblonga, deambulaverit poenis a Concilio Tridentino statutis coerceatur.

§ v. Neque sericas tantum vestes prohibet Synodus, sed multo magis aureas fibulas et globulos aureos, tam in indusiis quam in thoracibus, et quidquid aureum sit vel argenteum sub amissionis poena in omni cultu, exceptis fibulis calceorum, quae ex argento fieri permittuntur, simplicis tamen, et rotundae. Equorum sellae et ornamenta simplicia sint, nec bombice, nec auro vel argento ornata: sudariola honesti coloris sint; non rubri, nec viridis et fimbriis careant. Nullus pretiosa habeat monilia, horologia, capsas, scipiones cum capis aureis sed omnis clericorum supellex paupertatem, et modestiam redoleat.

DECRETUM II

De Cohabitatione Mulierum

§ i. Universis Clericis, Canonicis, etiam et Dignitatibus domi habere, inhibet Provincialis Synodus feminas, matre, sororibus innuptis, et amitis exceptis, nisi de licentia Episcopi in scriptis obtinenda.

§ ii. Ut autem Episcopi Clericis permittant alias feminas domi habere prae oculis habeant ut feminae provectae sint aetatis, quadraginta ad minus annorum, et pie et sobrie, in Domino vixerint non in luxu, non in saltationibus et impudicitiis quod ex testimonio Parochi diligenter inquiri debet. Postquam autem de aetate et vita constiterit, ea tantum lege permittantur Clericis, ut dum in suo fuerint contubernio, vestes sericas aut pictas aut rubras omnino dimittant, et coloris subobscuri modesto vestitu ornentur. Nullum matrimonium, paterno excepto in clericali domo inveniatur, quod si ob paupertatem aliquis has regulas servare nequeat, in seminario vivat.

§ iii. Misero et orphano succurrere pietas est, omnesque hortatur Provincialis Synodus id ut faciant juxta possibilitatem. Unicuique enim mandavit Deus de proximo suo, sed ordo charitatis servandus est, et modus subveniendi necessitati, non indulgendo luxui, et quidem sine scandalo.

§ iv. Quapropter Provincialis Synodus districte prohibet, ne Clerici, vel Canonici, etiam Dignitates domi habeant clientulas, vulgo crianzas, quovis titulo, vel praetextu si qui autem, aut expositis, aut orphanis, succurrere velint, consulto quamprimum Episcopo, id facere permittantur sub sequentibus conditionibus: videlicet clientulae in aliquo collegio, vel decenti domo ad praescriptum Episcopi collocentur; ut eas aut nunquam, aut rarissime invisant et quidem de licentia Episcopi; ut eis ad ornatum nihil aureum, aut argenteum, suppeditent, nec vestes sericas, aut pictas, aut coloris rubri, sed subobscuri et modesti.

§ v. Quoniam Clericis, Indis praecipue, innumeri propinqui nascuntur, qui laborem fugientes, ecclesiasticis reditibus fovere suam optant socordiam; Provincialis Synodus hortatur universum Clerum, ut pietatem erga consanguineos juxta Charitatis regulas exercens otiosorum turbam, qui labore victum quaerere valent, procul a se arceat, ut vere miseris subvenire possit.

DECRETUM III
De Officiis Divinis

§ i. Omnes Clerici diebus Dominicis et festis de praecepto officiis divinis mane, et vespere, et Missae conventuali intersint. Clerici intra Urbis maenia viventes in Cathedrali Ecclesia, alii in respectivis Paroeciis quorum catalogum habeant Parochi Ecclesiarum quibus addicti sint.

§ ii. In suburbiis Manilae ubi aliquot Clerici reperiuntur, diebus festis decantentur Vesperae, quibus non minus ac Paroechiali Missae praesentes sint Clerici, illi Paroeciae addicti superpelliceis induti.

§ iii. Neque modo Parochiali Missae et Vesperis intererunt Clerici in suburbanis et ruralibus Paroeciis, si qui praeter Parochum Clerici inveniantur quovis titulo ordinati, sed diebus festis Parochum in administratione sacramentorum comitabuntur, et in tradenda Doctrina Christiana ad illius praescriptum exercebuntur.

§ iv. Ex Clericis qui ad divina officia in Cathedrali convenire debent, eligatur punctator, qui in libello notet negligentes, ut singulis mensibus Episcopum certiorem faciat. In aliis Ecclesiis Parochorum curae id relinquitur.

DECRETUM IV
De Exercitiis Clericis Prohibitis

§ i. Qui Deo militat implicare se negotiis saecularibus prohibetur, idcirco Provincialis Synodus edicit ne Clericus sacris initiatus aut ecclesiastico beneficio praeditus coram judice saeculari advocati, aut Procuratoris nomine causas agat, nisi ab aliis in judicium vocatus suam vel Ecclesiae suae, propinquorum etiam si necesse erit, et miserabilium personarum causas, ab episcopo facultate prius scripto concessa, tueatur. Ne in profanis negotiis officium tabellionatus exerceat. Ne artem medendi faciat. Ne in negotiationibus et mercaturis se interpretem, et medium interponat. Negotiationem etiam omnis generis omnino prohibet Provincialis Synodus sive per se sive per alium exerceatur sub capitalis, et sortis amissione, ex quibus illud pauperibus ecclesiis, haec vero seminario applicabitur.

§ ii. Negotiationis nomine intelligi Concilium Provinciale contractum qui *corresponder* vulgo dicitur, sive propria, sive aliena pecunia fiat, cujus usum omnino Clero universo, Canonicis etiam, et Dignitatibus interdictum declarat.

§ iii. Clerici aliena praedia lucri causa non conducant nec aliorum tutelam suscipiant sine Episcopi licentia, quae in casibus tantum necessitatis concedetur, Clerici pro aliis non fidejubeant, nec negotiorum sint procuratores, nisi prius per litteras, facultas ab Episcopo obtineatur.

§ iv. Venatio cum canibus, et strepitu Clericis censeatur interdicta, non minus ac saltationes, et choreae, quarum non actores modo, sed spectatores, Clerici acriter ab Episcopo corripiantur. Comediis quae in oppidis fieri solent, et lubricis spectaculis non intersint, nec conviviis se ingerant praecipue ubi viri, et feminae convivantur, aut periculum dedecoris timetur. In primis interdicit Provincialis Synodus omnibus Clericis, ne proecursores, aut asseclae feminarum sint aut illis discumbentibus adsistant aut ancillentur.

§ v. Provincialis Synodus universo Clero, Canonicis etiam, et Dignitatibus interdicit ludos tum alearum tum tesserarum, talorum, et chartarum tollens circa id omnem interpretandi libertatem. Non enim desunt alii honesti ludi, quibus animus recreari possit.

§ vi. Honestis autem ludis multum non incumbant Clerici, praecipue in Adventu, Quadragesima, et solemnibus festivitatibus. Si animi gratia ludo aliquando indulgeant, id aut cum aliis clericis faciant aut cum honestis viris. Cum feminis autem, quantumvis ludus honestus sit, ludere omnino prohibet Provincialis Synodus.

§ vii. Quum ludi ad animi relaxationem inventi sine culpa ars lucrandi nequeant, Provincialis Synodus hortatur universum Clerum cujusvis sit Dignitatis ut nihil, aut certe parum pecuniae ludo quantumvis licito exponat. Prohibet, autem sub poena excommunicationis majoris latae sententiae Episcopis reservatae ne quis Clericus quacumque fulgeat dignitate ludo exponat, ultra viginti quinque argenti uncias.

§ viii. Clericorum arma quum sint orationes, et lacrimae interdicit Provincialis Synodus universo Clero arma cujusvis generis sive ad offensionem, (sive ad defensionem) praecipue sclopeta, et parvulas bombardas in equorum sellis, nisi forti per suspecta loca iter faciendum sit et tunc obtenta prius, si fieri potest, ab Episcopo licentia.

§ ix. Qui vero Clericus cujusvis etiam gradus, ordinis, dignitatis in aliqua re ex iis non obtemperaverit, quae in titulo hoc de vita et honestate clericorum expressa sunt, aut salutari poenitentia, aut pecunia, aut suspensione ab ordinum munere, et beneficiorum administratione, aut ipsis etiam beneficiis, aut carcere, aut exilio, aut pluribus simul ex his poenis, aut etiam gravioribus pro modo culpae Episcopi arbitratu mulctetur; qui iterum in eadem re peccaverit duplicata is poena pro ratione criminis ab eodem plectatur.

§ x. Optaret Provincialis Synodus, ut Manilae erigerentur pia exercitatio, quae schola Christi nuncupatur in qua Clerici orationis, et pietatis exercitia adimplerent ad aedificationem populorum.

§ xi. Omnes Ecclesiasticos cujuscumque sint dignitatis quotannis per decem dies in seminario exercitiis spiritualibus vacare maxime decet, quo tempore altitudinem sacerdotii perpendentes attenta consideratione ad virtutum praxim excitentur. Qui autem ab urbe absunt, vel in suis Paroeciis, vel in alio loco ad praescriptum Episcopi id exsequi conentur, tum ob plenariam indulgentiam, tum etiam ob summam utilitatem.

§ xii. Denique Provincialis Synodus universum Clerum hortatur, ut memor suae vocationis vitam suam componens habitu, gestu, incessu, sermone, omnibusque rebus nihil nisi grave, et religionis plenum prae se ferat. Quum enim Ecclesiasticorum vita ad aliorum posita sit exemplum, id praestare debent ut quemadmodum reliquum populum sacerdotis fastigio, et status celsitudine longe superant, ita etiam a saecularibus in mensa, vestibus, colloquiis, et aliis actionibus ob morum integritatem, et sanctimoniam secernantur.

ACTIO IVa
DE PAROCHIS
habita die XXIX. Septembris. Anni MDCCLXXI

Titulus Unicus
De Paroeciarum Regimine

DECRETUM I
De Reductione

§ i. Parum certe a feris illorum mores differunt, qui tametsi rationis sint participes nulla societate devincti sine legum metu, et absque ulla politia sparsim inter montes, et silvas vitam agunt. Religio quoque in eorum animis altas radices nequaquam agere potest, tum quia ii, qui agratim vivunt, Pastorum vocem rarissime audiunt, tum etiam quoniam nullis exemplis ad virtutes Christianas excolendas excitantur.

§ ii. Impunitas denique quam solitudines faciunt, et infidelium consuetudo et commercium silvestres illos homines adeo professionis Christianae immemores reddit, ut eorum plurimi non mores modo, sed nomen etiam Christianum abjicientes otiose, barbare et sine ulla Religione vivant, quod jam olim venerandae memoriae Illmus. D. Michael Poblete Archiepiscopus Manilanus, et caeteri Antistites harum Insularum lacrimati sunt.

§ iii. Quapropter Provincialis Manilana Synodus auditis plurimorum Parochorum quaerelis ob nondum civili vita sociatam Indorum gentem et populorum informitatem, rogat Illmum. Gubernatorem ut omnibus viribus perfectam populorum reductionem, quam religionis causa exigit, et Rex Catholicus enixissime inculcat, sublatis omnibus impedimentis aggrediatur.

§ iv. Quamvis enim aliquam rei familiaris jacturam experiantur Indi e silvarum latebris aut solitudine extrahendi gaudere potius debent quam dolere Dominicam sententiam considerantes: Quid prodest homini si mundum universum lucretur, animae vero suae detrimentum patiatur.

§ v. Provincialis Synodus praecipit universis Parochis, ut accito etiam, si opus fuerit, brachii saecularis auxilio, diligentissime invigilent ut omnes oppidani suae curae commissi simul in oppido vivant, ut eis melius in spiritualibus providere possint. Et quoniam Ecclesiae quae vulgo *visitas* dicuntur, impedimento etiam sunt quominus reductio fiat, jubet Provincialis Synodus, ut hujusmodi Ecclesiae, quae sine licentia Episcopi et Vice-Patroni erectae sunt, omnino destruantur ad vitandum multa inde nascentia incommoda, vel in novas Paroecias, si ultra trecenta sint tributa, erigantur.

DECRETUM II

De Paroeciarum Regimine

§ i. Venerandae memoriae primus Episcopus Manilanus D. Fr. Dominicus Salazar ex inclita Praedicatorum Familia in sua Dioecesana Synodo nulli Ministro ultra sexcentos ad summum Indos commendare posse existimavit. Strictius circa hanc materiam, sed cum de rudioribus Indis Peruanis ageretur, Concilium Limanum sensit. Tamen hoc licet sentiat Provincialis Manilana Synodus, oppidorum paupertas, et Ministrorum paucitas aliud postulat. Quapropter statuit Provincialis Synodus, ut qui quingentis tributis praepositus est, Coadjutorem habeat; Majora oppida servata proportione, praeter Parochos, necessarios habeant Coadjutores. In vicis magnorum oppidorum, si prope quatuor centa sint tributa, novae Paroeciae juxta Tomum Regium ab Episcopis quam primum erigantur, cum consensu Vice-Patroni, praecipue si vel ob distantiam, vel laboriosum iter, aut interjecta flumina difficilis evadat administratio. Minores vici ad respectivos populos reducantur, vel si ob itinerum securitatem id fieri non possit, Vicarium ibi alere perpetuo cogantur.

§ ii. Paroeciae in tres Classes dividantur, nullusque praeficiatur Paroeciae secundae Classis, qui per tres annos Paroeciae primae Classis Curam non gesserit; nec ad tertiae Classis Paroecias quis promoveatur nisi in secunda Classe per triennium cum laude ex testimonio sociorum versatus fuerit, regulasque de vita, et honestate clericorum ad unguem servaverit.

§ iii. Caeteris paribus in collatione Paroeciarum secundae, et tertiae Classis ii praeferantur, qui tenuiores, et prope montes Paroechias administrarunt. Ne autem praescriptus ordo invertatur Provincialis Synodus maxime hac in re Episcoporum gravat conscientias. Nullus etiam ad paroeciarum regimen admittatur nisi per annum coadjutorem egerit laudabiliter, quod ex testimonio Parochi, cui inservierit, constare debet.

§ iv. Nulli Paroecia aliqua conferatur, nisi praevio accurato examine quod ad formam Concilii Tridentini et Legum Indiarum fieri debet, ita ut de omnibus fere doctrinis moralibus interrogatus probabiliores, et saniores doctrinas tenere reperiatur.

§ v. Admonet Provincialis Synodus examinatores strictam obligationem referendi de vita et moribus examinandi, ita ut de ejus prudentia, scientia, zelo, moribus, et vita, judicium ferre possint.

§ vi. Quum examinatores extra Synodum eligi nequeant, nisi in illorum defectum, qui intra annum obierint, curent Episcopi in Dioecesanis Synodis eos quotannis, designare quod si ob aliquam causam synodi haberi nequeant de consensu Capituli ab Episcopo eligantur et consulatur sacra congregatio.

§ vii. Necessarium est, ut hi qui inter Indos Parochum agunt eorum linguam calleant, dum Hispana ignoratur. Ideoque praecipit Provincialis Synodus, ut nullus ad Paroecias censeatur approbatus, nisi in Indorum idiomate, a peritis examinatoribus bene instructus inveniatur.

§ viii. Non sit in potestate Parochi Coadjutorem eligere, sed Episcopi sit Parochis doctos et pios Clericos in adjumentum pastoralis officii designare. Coadjutores in Parochialibus domibus vivant, eisque juxta possibilitatem subveniant Parochi. Meminerint Parochi sibi coadjutores non concedi ad otiamdum, neque posse tuta conscientia in Coadjutorem omne pondus rejicere; sed sibi plus omnibus laborandum existiment.

DECRETUM III

De Seminatione Verbi Dei

§ i. Inter magna officii pastoralis munia primatum tenet sacra praedicatio, in quam licet hactenus constanter incubuerint Parochi, fere omnes tam Saeculares quam Regulares, ne tamen humana fragilitas ab ea desistat, praecipit Provincialis Synodus, ut singulis Dominicis et festis de praecepto Parochi inter Missarum solemnia, concionem ad populum habeant rudium captui accommodatam. Si quis sine legitima causa concionem omiserit, si monitus non emendatur, substractione fructuum hebdomadae, aut tempori respondentium mulctetur. Pecuniae vero tertia pars Ecclesiae fabricae applicetur; aliae vero duae partes delatori et fisco Regio. Quam divisionem in omnibus mulctis fieri jubet Provincialis Synodus.

§ ii. Illi tantum de suo concionari permittantur qui pie et graviter facere id possunt, alii vero etiam Parochi, ne vel risum moveant vel aliquid dicant minus aptum recitatores potius homiliarum sint quam auctores. Quod si ob aliquam causam concionari nequeant, curent Parochi, ut aliquis pius Liber, vel Epistolae Pastorales populo legantur.

§ iii. Explicent semper concionatores initio concionum aliquod caput doctrinae Christianae, non perfunctorie aut obscure, sed fuse, et perspicue, ita ut omnes, intelligere valeant.

§ iv. Fugiant in concionibus nimiam prolixitatem, quae taedium generat audientibus et multo magis satiras, scommata, aut jocos, qui spiritum extinguunt, et lacrimas potius quam plausus contendant excitare. Caveant a ridiculis, vanis, inutilibus, aut sublimibus ideis et prodesse potius cupiant, quam placere.

§ v. In panegiricis, hyperboles, et comparationes praetermittant totique sint in ostendendo media practica, quibus laudandus Sanctus ad apicem perfectionis pervenit, et in excitando auditores ad imitationem proponendo modum, quo id fieri possit, in quolibet statu.

§ vi. Moneant saepe fideles de gravissima obediendi Magistratibus, etiam si mali sint, obligatione secundum illud Apostoli; Subditi estote in omni timore dominis non tantum bonis et modestis sed etiam discolis. Multum temporis impendant in declamando adversus abusus superstitionis, et idolatrias de quibus mentio fiet in hac Synodo et quae in ea Regione grassantur; caveant tamen ne dum imprudenter ignoratas superstitiones, aut abusus reprehendunt, eos doceant.

§ vii. Frequenter Patres familias excitent ad curam filiorum gerendam, ut illos ad scholam, et Ecclesiam mittant et in timore Dei caste educent. Commendent etiam, quam gravissime, frequentiam sacramentorum, virtutum praxim, et vitiorum fugam.

§ viii. Ut autem in concionando aliqua methodus servetur statuit Provincialis Synodus ut a Septuagesima, Parochi toti incumbant in explicandis necessariis ad fructuosam confessionem, et sumptionem Corporis Dominici. A Dominica Sanctissimae Trinitatis incipiant explanare fidem unius Veri Dei, Creatoris, et Remuneratoris, nec non Trinitatem Personarum et reliquos articulos ad divinitatem pertinentes. In Adventu Misterium Incarnationis, Passionis, et Redemptionis explanent.

§ ix. In omnibus concionibus semper populum hortentur ad eliciendum crebro actus virtutum theologicarum, Latriae et Contritionis. Assidue tractent de necessitate orationis et Divinae gratiae ad pie et meritorie operandum. Frequenter etiam agant de Sacro-sancto Sacrificio Missae quo nihil acceptabilius Deo offertur in Ecclesia, tam pro vivis quam pro defunctis, ad exorandam Divinam Clementiam, et abluendas peccatorum sordes.

§ x. Aliquoties explicent dogma catholicum de Intercessione B. V. Mariae et Sanctorum, illorumque cultu, et veneratione, admonentes spem unice in DEO per Jesum Christum ejus filium ponendam esse, cujus misericordia Sanctorum orationibus, intercessione praecipue Genitricis Dei erga homines inclinatur. Saepissime denique adversus antiquas Indorum pravas traditiones, quae apud ipsos magno sunt in honore, orationem convertant annunciantes Jesus Christum, et hunc Crucifixum.

DECRETUM IV

De Doctrina Christiana Tradenda

§ i. Experientia Magistra compertum est Indos, tametsi memoriter sciant catechismum, summa tamen ignorantia intelligentiae laborare. Quapropter jubet Provincialis Synodus, ut brevis Catechismus a Concilio edendus vulgari lingua, singulis festis diebus in Ecclesia, duobus pueris praeeuntibus, ab omnibus alta voce recitetur, quod pueri scholares quotide hispana, et vulgari lingua praestabunt. Parili modo elicientur actus virtutum theologicarum, utque diversa phrasi tradita doctrina non memoriae modo, sed cordi etiam infigatur, septem salutationes per gyrum a Parochis in singulis concionibus recitandae, quibus Doctrinae summa contineatur, edentur.

§ ii. Diebus festis omnes pueri, et puellae usque ad quatuordecim annos in Ecclesia, praesente Parocho, ordine dispositi, alta voce a signo crucis incipientes recitabunt orationem Dominicam, Salutationem Angelicam, Symbolum, praecepta Decalogi et Ecclesiae, Sacramenta, Confessionem Generalem, et Actum Contritionis. Quibus finitis per dimidiam Parochus in forma Dialogi explicet Doctrinam Christianam, ea facilitate ut puerorum rudissimus intelligere valeat. Dein recitabunt Rosarium B. V. Mariae, et elicitis actibus virtutum theologicarum, pueri dimittantur.

§ iii. Quoniam ea quae in tenera aetate instillantur, altius imbibuntur, semper Parochi pueros hortentur ad peccati fugam, et honestatem vitam instituendam adhibitis ad rem Divinae justitiae exemplis. Innumerato habeant peccata quae a pueris inconsiderate patrari quum soleant, magnorum vitiorum in adulta aetate seminarium sunt, illorumque foeditatem describant. Commendent quam saepissime devotionem erga B. V. Mariam, et invocationem sanctissimorum Nominum Jesu, et Mariae in omnibus periculis et tentationibus, usum frequentem Crucis Dominicae ad superandas Diaboli insidias, nec non firmam in Deo per Jesum Christum fiduciam.

§ iv. Moneant illos creberrime fugam pravarum societatum, obligationem convertendi se ad Deum, quum ad annos discretionis pervenerint, et obediendi majoribus. Circa id tamen (quum senes sint superstitionum conservatores, eosque maiori veneratione quam ipsos Parochos prosequantur Indi, ipsisque magis credant) doceant nullam fidem, aut obedientiam senibus, aut parentibus deberi, quum *Nono, Tianac,* et similium metum incutiunt, aut populorum *ugali* seu consuetudines contra Parochorum monita defendunt.

§ v. Caveant Parochi, ne pueros, aut puellas aspera voce aut aliis motibus deterreant, sed suaviter et fortiter in eorum animis instillent sanctum Dei timorem qui verae sapientiae initium est.

§ vi. Quum Parochi sine aliorum adjumento in magnis Paroeciis omnes docere nequeant salutis viam, piorum laicorum opera ad id utantur. Iubet ergo Provincialis Synodus, ut in omnibus Paroeciis, instituantur Confraternitas Doctrinae Christianae, in quam ex utroque sexu ii tantum cooptentur qui necessarii sint, provectae aetatis, optimorum morum et in Catechismo bene instructi, qui per turmas, per id temporis quo pueri in Ecclesia instruuntur, eadem methodo in patentibus locis suae curae comendatos erudiant. Coadjutores, si qui erunt, ab hoc onere non sint immunes, Parochi autem aliquoties per annum alterius curae commendatis pueris, de aliis turmis periculum faciant.

DECRETUM V
De Scholis et Collegiis

§ i. Monstruosa Respublica illa est, in qua pueritiae educatio negligitur. Quapropter Provincialis Synodus animadvertens hac in re incuriam irrepsisse, vehementer rogat Illmum. D. Gubernatorem, ut Praetoribus Provinciarum, et oppidorum Rectoribus districte praecipiat, propositis etiam poenis, in singulis Paroeciis scholas aut erigere, aut conservare, efficereque ut Patres-familias filios suos ad eas mittant.

Scholae vero ad educationem non puerorum modo, sed etiam puellarum instituantur.

§ ii. Ad Magisterium vero illi tantum admittantur, qui provectae aetatis, et optimae vitae quum sint, ita calleant linguam hispanicam ut eam docere possint, pueros, et puellas, quibus omnino usus vernaculae linguae in profanis interdicatur. Comediae etiam, quae fieri solent in oppidis et cantilenae in nuptiis vel ludis non nisi hispanae permittantur, circa quod summam vigilantiam et Magistratibus, et Parochis inculcat Provincialis Synodus.

§ iii. Doctrina Christiana pueris hispana, et vernacula lingua tradatur juxta brevem Catechismum a Concilio edendum.

§ iv. Ludi Magistris autem, dum ars hispanica adornatur, curent Parochi aliquot regulas in scriptis ad docendum hispanum sermonem tradere per aliquem nomenclatorem, aut dialogos utraque lingua elaboratos, quibus communes loquendi modi, contineantur. Exemplaria vero scripturae pueris imitanda proponenda utraque lingua elaborentur pia tamen, et utilia.

§ v. Parochi tam Saeculares quam Regulares non modo non impediant usum hispanae linguae, sed eam quantum possint, et per pastorales liceat occupationes, promoveant, non hortando tantum sed etiam docendo ob summam inde tum Religioni, tum Reipublicae, tum Status felicitati et conservationi nascentem utilitatem. Ad id vero bis saltem in hebdomada scholas visitent et de Discipulorum profectu et Magistrorum diligentia periculum faciant. Magistris stipendium non solvatur, nisi ex testimonio Parochi constiterit, et Doctrinam Apostolicam, et hispanam linguam promovisse.

§ vi. Tractent saepe Parochi in Kalendis de scholis, Ludimagistris, et de mediis, quibus puerorum educatio, tam in spiritualibus, quam in politicis promoveri possit, adhibito etiam, si opus sit primorum consilio.

§ vii. Rogat Provincialis Synodus Illmum. D. Gubernatorem ut in singulis Provinciis unam aut plures domos prope Ecclesias erigi curet, in quibus tam pueri quam puellae usque ad duodecimum annum sub optimorum Magistrorum cura melius in bonis moribus, in politia, in lingua hispanica, et aliis artibus instruantur. Atque idipsum saepe in Kalendis Parochis discutiendum proponit.

§ viii. Provincialis Synodus quum intelligat ex optima pueritiae institutione populorum felicitatem pendere, decrevit aliquam Ludimagistris circa id regulam proponere. Mane hora septima pueri, et puellae cum suis Magistris in Ecclesiam convenient ad Missam Parochialem; qua peracta ab Ecclesia ordinati, praeeunte aliqua Cruce, in scholas pergent, aliquid pium hispana lingua cantantes. Hora decima cum dimidia ordinati, et praeeunte cruce ad Ecclesiam confluent, et brevem Catechismum ex integro vernaculo sermone recitabunt. Vespere hora tertia signo dato scholae aperiantur, qua finita hora quinta, praeeunte cruce ad Ecclesiam accedent Catechismum Hispanum, et Rosarium B. V. Mariae recitaturi, et elicitis actibus virtutum Theologicarum discedent.

DECRETUM VI
De Ecclesiarum Fabrica et Nitore

§ i. Saepe accidit, ut Dei cultui dedicata Templa sordida sint, et immunda quod tametsi aliquando ob paupertatem evenit, aliquoties etiam ob Parochorum incuriam contingit. Sunt etiam aliquot templa adeo spatiosa, et magnifica ut in honore conservari nequeant a miseris oppidanis. Iubet ergo Provincialis Synodus, ut nulla Ecclesiae fabrica inchoetur inconsulto Episcopo, et Vice-Patrono. Episcopi vero partes erunt attenta oppidi qualitate, eam mensuram, et fabricae formam et altarium numerum praescribere, quae sine labore nitida conservari facile possint.

§ ii. Optaret Provincialis Synodus, ut genus illud aedificiorum in Dei cultum, quae ex arundine, culmo et palmis fiunt, omnino tolleretur, tum quia incendiis obnoxia sunt tum etiam quia Dominicum Corpus in aegrotorum commodum servari nequit. Ideoque hortatur in Domino universos Parochos, ut templa Dei lateritia, aut lapidea faciant opere simplici, nec multum elevato, ad quod in Kalendis excogitent aliquod fabricae genus facile, et Indis haud multum onerosum.

§ iii. Omnes Parochi habeant Arcam tribus clavibus diversi operis fabrilis munitam, quarum una penes Parochum, altera penes populi Capitaneum, tertia denique penes Ecclesiae oeconomum, qui singulis annis Kalendis Januariis creari debet, servetur. In ea Arca Ecclesiae pecunia tam ex octavis sepulturam, quam ex *ambagan* et eleemosynis, vel aliis reditibus custodiatur, una cum libro dati et accepti, qui tertio quoque mense in Kalendis visitari debet a Vicario Foraneo. Nihil pecuniae ex Arca etiam ad necessarios sumptus, qui diferri nequeant, extrahatur nisi de Vicarii licentia.

§ iv. Ut Dei Templa nitida serventur singulis annis initio Januarii a Parochis visitentur Ecclesiae, et si vel pavimentum, vel tectum, aut altaria reparatione egeant aut parietes sint dealbandi, monito Vicario, statim resarciantur. Vicarii non habeant facultatem concedendi Parochis licentiam extrahendi ex Arca nisi decem argenti uncias, etiam pro necessariis reparationibus. Si vero majori summa opus sit, inconsulto Episcopo, nihil innovetur. Coemeteria ita sint clausa ut bestiis aditus non pateat. Arbores si quae sint etiam ad ornatum statim evellantur, nec lignorum strues nec sordes ibi reperiantur.

DECRETUM VII
De Ordine Exercitiorum

§ i. Diebus festis de praecepto hora commoda triplici signo ad Missam convocato populo antequam illa inchoetur, recitetur Rosarium B. V. Mariae, quod solemnis Missa sequetur, et concio post Evangelium. Finito Sacrosancto Sacrificio, duobus pueris praeeuntibus, Catechismus brevis recitetur vernacula lingua, caeteris repetentibus. Quo finito factis aliquot a Parocho interrogationibus, et elicitis actibus virtutum theologicarum populus in pace dimittatur.

§ ii. Vespere autem ultra exercitium Doctrinae modo dicto instituendum, hora quinta, signo dato, Antiphona Salve Regina in Ecclesia decantetur, et Rosarium B. V. Mariae recitetur; curentque Parochi fideles admonere de obligatione non modo audiendi Missam diebus festis, sed eos etiam per virtutum opera sanctificandi.

DECRETUM VIII
De Notitia Gregis, Vitiorum Superstitionumque Extirpatione

§ i. Nulla sane ratione a Parochis melius gregis sui notitia comparabitur, quam si librum Status animarum exacte habeant dispositum ita ut inter familiae et familiae descriptionem tantum relinquant spatii, quantum sufficiens sit pro re quas expedire judicaverint annotatione. Quem si diligenter, et crebro evolvant, facile deprehendent quinam bonae sint vitae, et quinam malae.

§ ii. Multum etiam ad id juvabit Zelatorum opera, qua Parochi non ad suum, hospitumque servitium uti debent, sed ad detegendum peccatores, concubinarios, discordes, vagos, ebriosos, lusores, et hujus generis alios; sic enim fiet, ut notitia parta morbidarum ovium eis juxta salvatoris praeceptum remedium adhibere possint suaviter, et benigne unumquemque cum lacrimis monendo, ut a via sua prava revertatur. Si qui vero moniti non resipiscant, ad Vicarium Foraneum deferantur, aut pro modo culpae in Kalendis puniantur, etiam publica poenitentia.

§ iii. Tametsi omnium vitiorum extirpationi incumbendum sit, illa vero maiorem exposcunt curam et vigilantiam, quae fidei puritati opponuntur. Hujus generis est cultus, qui maiorem animabus quae *Nono* dicuntur in arundinetis, arboribus, fluminibus et terrae tumulis ab Indis exhibetur. Curent ergo Parochi loca harum superstitionum rescire, et illa omnino destruant, graviterque declament contra *Nono, Tigbalan, Tianac,* et caeteras antiquas superstitiones, traditiones, et Crucis virtutem ostendant.

§ iv. Multae etiam inter Indos reperiuntur superstitiones, quam Indicem, dabit Provincialis Synodus ad usum Parochorum, inter quas frequentissimae sunt *Pagbibilao* et *pagsasananton,* quibus res furto ablatas inveniri putant; multas etiam in partibus observant obstetrices quas proinde crebro examinent Parochi. Medicastri quoque Indorum et illi qui *Tavac,* seu salutatores dicuntur adhibent ridicula, et crudelia remedia, et exoticas preces, et barbaras voces, et quum saepe, ne ignorantiam suam prodant, aegrotationes maleficis tribuant, magnarum calamitatum causa exstitisse constat.

§ v. In Provincia Cagayan reperiuntur quidam milites, qui nec Regis, nec oppidorum stipendiis militant vulgo *Mengal* genus hominum valde superstitiosum, barbarum, et truculentum. Nudi etiam in Processionibus incedunt variis insignibus ornati, quorum deliciae sunt ad cranium occisi a se hominis saltare, et inebriari. Rogat ergo Provincialis Synodus Illmum. Gubernatorem, ut hujusmodi hominum genus gravissimis poenis coerceat. Parochis autem praecipit ut hujusmodi milites etiam ab Ecclesia repellant, et altari, si moniti non emendantur.

§ vi. Sunt etiam, qui ut invincibiles evadant multa a collo pendentia habeant amuleta tum sacra, tum profana, quandoque etiam (horrendum dictu) hostias consecratas. Curent ergo Parochi in hujusmodi homines inquirere, et sublatis et publice combustis amuletis, eos ad Episcopum, seu Judices cum summario processu transmittant.

§ vii. Si quis his, aut similibus superstitionibus irretitus inveniatur pro modo culpae, publice, etiam imposita cuculla in signum ignominiae, verberetur. Rogat etiam Provincialis Synodus Illmum. Gubernatorem, ut hujusmodi homines infames, et inhabiles ad munia publica declaret.

§ viii. Indis, quorum pedes veloces sunt ad effundendum sanguinem, ut ferinos mores deponant interdicit Sacra Synodus, in nuptiis, et publicis festis saltationes, cantilenas, et comedias, et ludos, quae antiquo ritu cum lanceis, barbaro motu, aut in modum Aetiopum, Nigritum, aut infidelium a larvatis fiunt, circa quod Parochorum, et Magistratuum gravat consciencias.

§ ix. Utile admodum esset ad horum vitiorum extirpationem, ut Episcopi quandoque aliquot Missionarios Saeculares vel Regulares per provincias mitterent.

§ x. Sed quoniam per Ministrorum inopiam id saepe non licebit Episcopis, curabunt Parochi ut prima Dominica Quadragesimae quotannis populo in Ecclesia vulgari lingua legatur Decretum a Concilio circa abusus, et superstitiones edendum.

DECRETUM IX
De Residentia Parochorum

§ i. Parochos praecepto divino teneri ad jugem, et vigilem super commisso grege custodiam certum quum sit, Provincialis Manilana Synodus in memoriam revocat poenas a sacris canonibus, et a Concilio Tridentino contra non residentes statutas.

§ ii. Statuit insuper ut nullus per biduum a Paroecia sua absit nisi juxta de causa, et obtenta prius ab Episcopo, vel Vicario Foraneo, in scriptis licentia, et relicto idoneo vicario. Nullus etiam expiandi conscientiam causa Paroeciam deserat, nisi prius ei constiterit nullum esse in oppido graviter aegrotantem, ne aliquis sine sacramentis decedat, aut aliqua calamitas eveniat.

§ iii. Episcopi prae oculis habeant Ministrorum paucitatem, ut rarissime licentiam pro bimestri absentia concedant, quam non aliter, gravi etiam urgente necessitate, facient, nisi idoneum prius relinquant Vicarium.

§ iv. Damnat Provincialis Synodus illorum praxim, qui diebus tantum festis in suis resident territoriis, de caetero autem in vicinis Paroeciis commorantur, quos graviter arbitrio Episcoporum puniendos declarat.

DECRETUM X
De Concordia cum Magistratibus

§ i. Quemadmodum concordia duarum potestatum spiritualis et temporalis vitia reprimuntur, ita illarum divisione mala omnia dominantur. Quapropter Parochis universis in primis commendat Provincialis Synodus ne cum Provinciarum Praetoribus, Oppidorum Capitaneis caeterisque maioribus, aut inferioribus justitiae ministris lites habeant, et contentiones, sed si aliquid contigerit remedio dignum, per privatas correctiones cum illis benigne, et suaviter procedant, et Episcopum, nisi emendatio sequatur, certiorem faciant.

§ ii. Quum novi Magistratus creantur eos private admoneant de suscepta obligatione consulendi publicae utilitati et vitiorum extirpationi ostendendo ad id media practica. Eadem monita saepe repetant private tamen, et magno in honore tam in publico, quam in privato Magistratus habeant, ut non verbis modo, sed etiam exemplo reliquum populum ad debitam justitiae Administris venerationem inflamment.

§ iii. Nulla alia ratione concordia cum Magistratibus vigebit, quam si Parochi, quae ad se spectant sollicite exsequentes, oppidorum gubernationi temporali, quod plurimi faciunt, non se immisceant, nec contra rectores obloquantur. Inde enim lites et gravia scandala nascuntur.

§ iv. Reorum ad Ecclesiam confugientium occultatio magnorum scandalorum causa fuit, quibus in posterum consulere cupiens Provincialis Synodus praecipit universis Ecclesiarum Rectoribus cujusvis sint dignitatis et conditionis etiam superioribus Regularibus ad praescriptam Regiae schedulae, ut si contigerit reum aliquem ad Ecclesiam confugere, accepta cautione juratoria de non procedendo contra reum, donec a Judice Ecclesiastico declaretur, eum asyli immunitate gaudere, vel non, illico Justitiae Saeculari tradant custodiendum.

§ v. Monet enim Provincialis Synodus omnes Ecclesiasticos, ne atrocium criminum reos ad Ecclesiam confugientes aut occultent, aut dimittant. Ecclesia enim, tametsi sanguinis effusionem perhorrescat, malorum tamen impunitate non delectatur.

DECRETUM XI
De Gravandis Oppidanis

§ i. Iubet Provincialis Synodus ut in omni Provincia taxa a Concilio edenda servetur, ultra quam nihil exigi liceat sub poena restitutionis in duplum. Taxa vero hispana, et vulgari lingua in conspicuo loco appensa habeatur. In Provinciis, in quibus taxae usus non est, et pro Parochorum sustentatione alios vigent consuetudines, his omnino sublatis, taxa inducatur.

§ ii. Oppidani a Parochis non graventur nec servitio, nec remigibus, nec horti cultura, nec balnei fabrica, nec ovorum, pullorum, gallinarum, lignorum, funium, aut similium exactione, quas et similes consuetudines, etiam immemoriales abolet Provincialis Synodus, et insuper jubet, ut Parochi de hoc decreto oppidanos suos admoneant. Mos est, ut a puellis innuptis oriza in Parochorum usum pinsatur, et Ecclesia mundetur. Provincialis autem synodus utramque abolet consuetudinem quocumque obtineat sive apud saeculares Parochos sive apud Regulares.

§ iii. In oppidis quae quingenta tributa aut superant aut attingunt, domos Parochiales Parochorum sumptu conserventur et resarciantur. In minoribus oppidis, in quibus difficile Parochi sustentantur, ab oppidanis, ut moris est, id fiat. Sed in domorum Parochialium constructione, aut notabili reparatione, vel voluntaria non animus Parochorum, sed populi paupertas, Episcopi, et Vice Patroni monita pensanda sunt.

DECRETUM XII
De Pauperum Cura, et Operibus Misericordiae a Parochis Exercendis

§ i. Parochi rescire curent quot sint vere pauperes in sua Paroecia, et an hi a divitibus opprimantur, eisque quantum valeant paterne subveniant pestis praecipue et egestatis tempore.

§ ii. Funeribus pauperum, quae gratis fieri debent, praesentes sint et officium sepulturae pro illis persolvant. Parochi gratis pulsari faciant campanam tam in agone quam in funere pauperum.

§ iii. Quum humani generis hostis contra morti proximos eo tempore a quo pendet aeternitas, omnem tentationum aciem moveat, videre licet quanta obligatione constringantur animarum Pastores illis subvenire spiritualibus auxiliis non modo sacramentorum, sed etiam piarum considerationum. Ideoque praecipit Provincialis Synodus, ut Parochi saepe visitent aegrotos eosque ad patientiam, conformitatem cum divina voluntate, peccatorum contritionem, firmam spem in Dei misericordia per Jesum Christum Filium ejus et coeteras virtutes hortentur, non solum in decursu aegrotationis sed multo magis in agone. Hacque de causa pios aliquot laicos in quovis Vico bene instructos habeant de modo succurrendi moribundis, ut si Parochi per se morituris auxilia praestare nequeant spiritualia, justa aliqua de causa non desint pii laici, qui id pietatis opus exequantur.

§ iv. Nec modo erga morti vicino charitatem exercere debet Parochus sed etiam omnes miseros, tristes consolando, rudes docendo, hospites excipiendo, et caetera misericordiae opera explendo ita ut Ministrum, et servum se potius putet, quam Dominum.

DECRETUM XIII
De Infidelium Conversione

§ i. Pauci forte aut nulli in his Insulis infideles invenirentur, si Regulares, qui convertendi Infideles causa Regiis stipendiis huc advehuntur, relictis Paroeciis Christianorum, ad montes convolarent. Sed dum in Paroeciis terminum figant, desperandum est de Infidelium conversione.

§ ii. Quamvis enim aliqui in Missionibus Infidelium occupantur, et non desint viri magni spiritus, magna tamen ex parte aut inepti his sunt, et Praelatis suis invisi, quodque maxime dolendum est, ii qui ad Missiones mittuntur aliquando exules, et puniti traducuntur. Id vero regiis auribus insinuare erit operae pretium.

§ iii. Quum Europeis Ministris noxia sit montium habitatio, Infideles vero in illis degentes magno cum labore in plana loca reducantur, quo fit, ut eorum salus non ita facile procurari possit, oporteret, ut nullus Missionarius sine necessariis sociis Clericis Indis mitteretur, quorum opera uti posset in conversione Infidelium, tum quia Indi facilius ediscunt Infidelium linguas, tum etiam quia barbari eos plus diligant necesse est ob generis similitudinem.

§ iv. Missionarii summo delectu seligantur viri docti, et zelo propagandae Religionis in primis pleni, circa quod tum Episcoporum tum Praelatorum Regularium conscientias gravat Provincialis Synodus.

§ v. Curent Missionarii politicam vitam, et civilem inter barbaros inducere, et ferinos mores evellere, ne si forte sine delectu baptizent multiplicent gentem, sed non laetitiam. Ideo Missionarii observabunt instructiones hac de causa edendas.

§ vi. Oportebit, ut ex ipsis conversis ad fidem Catechistae eligantur in Doctrina Christiana bene instructi, et quorum vita, et mores, spem afferant quam plures ab infidelitatis tenebris revocandi.

DECRETUM XIV

De Parochis Regularibus

§ i. Nullus est sive Saecularis sive Regularis, qui sine titulo Paroecias possit obtinere, ideoque praecipit Provincialis Synodus, ut nullus etiam Regularis ad Paroeciarum Regimen accedat sine Vice-Patroni praesentatione et Episcopi institutione.

§ ii. Quum Episcopi idem valeant a Parochis Regularibus exigere, quod a Saecularibus, eadem Provincialis Synodus ad praescriptum Apostolicarum Bullarum et nuperrimi Regii Tomi, praecipit universis, et singulis Regularibus, qui quomodolibet, sive in oppidis sive in Missionibus animarum curam gerunt, ut Episcoporum, in officio officiando, visitationi et correctioni subjiciantur. Episcopis vero praecipit ut quam primum Regularium visitationem aggrediantur.

§ iii. Declarat insuper Provincialis Synodus, Regulares non ex charitate, sed ex justitia teneri ad sacramentorum administrationem, donec Episcopi non habent Clericos Saeculares, quibus Paroeciarum regimen committant, ideoque non posse tuta conscientia Paroecias aut Missiones ad vitandam Vice-Patroni praesentationem, aut Episcoporum visitationem, aut alia de causa dimittere sub poenis in Clementina *Cum Sicut* contentis, nec subditos teneri obedire Praelatis suis talem desertionem suadentibus, aut praecipientibus.

§ iv. Declarat denique Provincialis Synodus, Parochos Regulares, quantum ad sacramentorum Paroeciarum, aut Missionum ministrationem spectat teneri, et obligari ad executionem eorum omnium quae in hac Synodo circa saeculares Parochos sancita sunt aut in posterum sancientur.

ACTIO Va
DE SACRAMENTIS

Habita die XXVII. Octobris. Anno MDCCLXXI

Titulus Primus
De Sacramentorum Administratione

DECRETUM I
De Baptismo

§ i. Relatum est Provinciali Synodo ab Indis genus circumcisionis, seu incisionis usurpari quod licet in se forte tanquam consuetudo permitti posset, tamen quum id fiat vel ad majorem in venereis captandam voluptatem, vel vitandam sterilitatem falso metu, tolerari nequit. Quapropter Parochi contra hunc morem fortiter declament illiusque auctores ad Vicarios Foraneos puniendos transmittant.

§ ii. Ea libertate hactenus usi sunt Parochi in condendis vulgari lingua Baptismi formis non expectat Episcoporum approbatione, ut quandoque etiam irritas formas ob linguae imperitiam adornaverint. Quapropter jubet Provincialis Synodus ut Episcopi in Synodis Dioecesanis adhibito peritorum consilio, pro diversis linguis formas immutabiles componant, et Catechismo vulgari inserant. Qui aliam formam usurpaverit, quantumvis illa valida sit, arbitrio Episcopi puniatur.

§ iii. Parochi diligenter instruant obstetrices, et alias pias personas de modo administrandi sacramentum Baptismi, ut in casu necessitatis baptizare possint.

§ iv. Doceant etiam aliquot laicos incidere gravidarum cadavera, ut foetibus de salutari remedio provideri possit. Et quoniam Indi persuasum habeant foetum si per abortum ante tempus nascatur, anima carere rationali, ideoque baptizari non posse, curent Parochi ab hoc pernicioso errore illos abducere.

§ v. Usus invaluit ut Baptizati ab Indis iterum sub conditione indiscriminatim baptizentur. Iubet ergo Provincialis Synodus, ut tunc solum iteretur baptisma sub conditione, quum de illius valore post diligens examen probabile dubium perseverat, juxta declarationes Sacrae Congregationis.

§ vi. Quoniam aliquot Indi in eo sunt errore ut ex Baptismi et Confirmationis reiteratione gratiae fieri incrementum ignoranter putent, aut etiam virtutem Sacramentorum a Ministri bonitate pendere, Parochi semper contra hos errores declament.

§ vii. Quum aqua harum regionum corruptioni nimis obnoxia sit, jubet Provincialis Synodus ut qua pro Baptismi administrationi testa sinensi diligenter clausa custodiatur.

§ viii. Accidit ut quum alio praeter designatum diem aliquis infans valetudinis causa Parochis baptizandus offertur, contenti hi sint vel una aquae infusione, etiam si tempus suppetat ad caeteras caeremonias. Jubet ergo Provincialis Synodus, ut urgente aliqua necessitate, nisi periculum mortis urgeat, caeremoniae suo ordine fiant, vel si mors timeatur, prius aqua salutaris infundatur, et si supervixerit infans, reliquae suppleantur solemnitates.

§ ix. Ad tollendos abusus qui circa Compatres, et Commatres tam in Baptismo, quam in Confirmatione invecti sunt, jubet Provincialis Synodus, ne Parochi sine delectu quovis ad suscipiendum infantes admittant, sed eos tantum, quos ex utroque sexu certo numero designaverint. Sint autem ii viri probi et in doctrina christiana bene docti, et tales ut filios suos docere possint virtutis viam. Si quis praeter designatos admitti velit praevio de Doctrina Christiana accurato examine id fiat. Malae vitae homines a suscipiendis infantibus excludantur, et illi qui in alio oppido vivunt.

§ x. Clerici cujusvis sint dignitatis nec de sacro fonte levent, nec in Confirmatione teneant, commatres, et compatres nullos habeant, sine speciali Episcopi licentia.

§ xi. Baptismus nulli infanti ultra nonum diem differatur, et curent Parochi ne occasione custodiendi infantes, juvenes extranei apud recens nati domum pernoctent, aut ebrietates, et saltationes misceant.

§ xii. Quum Indi a Patrinis, aut etiam pro lubito agnomina mutuentur, fit inde ut magna in dignoscendis cognationibus confusio oriatur, quapropter praecipit Provincialis

Synodus ut Parochi suos cogant Parochianos parentum agnomina retinere.

§ xiii. Docente humani generis hoste crebro accidit, ut Indi Sanctorum nomina sibi in Baptismo ad imitationem posita mirum in modum ridicule corrumpant, aut etiam superstitionis causa illa mutent, ne a maligno spiritu agnoscantur. Itaque Parochi contra hunc perversum morem declament, et nominum corruptores acriter reprehendant.

DECRETUM II
De Confirmatione

§ i. Quum recitatio orationis: Omnipotens Sempiterne Deus, qui regenerare dignatus es, etc. coram confirmandis e substantialibus caeremoniis sit, et maxima digna veneratione, statuit Provincialis Synodus, ut Episcopi confirmaturi attente provideant, ne quis confirmetur qui praedictae orationi praesens haud fuerit.

§ ii. Sacra olea quum saepe ab Indis ad acuendas gallorum novaculas sacrilege subripiantur, ita diligenter a Parochis custodiantur ut nulla de causa, nec ad minimum tempus laicis, etiam sacristis, relinquantur, quin potius illorum claves a Parochis serventur.

DECRETUM III
De Sacramento Poenitentiae

§ i. Populorum reformatio quum ex selectis pendeat confessariis, Provincialis Synodus vehementer hortatur Episcopos, ut maxime animadvertant, quosnam sacerdotes dirigendis animabus praeficiant. In confessario enim non modo doctrina pensanda est, set etiam vita.

§ ii. Quapropter Episcopi nullum ad audiendas confessiones admittant, qui laxis doctrinis imbutus plus nocumenti, quam fructus allaturus praevideatur. Caveant, ne junioribus sacerdotibus facultatem faciant feminarum audiendi confessiones. Mercatoribus vero, advocatis et similibus, doctissimos tantum, et peritissimos Confessarios designet.

§ iii. Ut autem Confessarii omnes earumdem opinionum nexu copulati morum corruptione melius obsistant jubet

Provincialis Synodus ut Compendium Theologiae Moralis P. Danielis Concine, hispane redditum in usum hujus Ecclesiae edatur, et cum eo instructiones S. Caroli circa confessarios illudque unice tam in seminario quam in scholis explanetur et per id etiam examina instituentur.

§ iv. Graviter Provincialis Synodus illorum morem reprehendit, qui uno die centum, aut plures confessiones excipiunt; declarat ergo vix tute et sine gravi peccato ab uno sacerdote uno die quadraginta confessiones expediri posse, etiam si per septem horas integras illis audiendis incubuerit. Si quis posthac tanta celeritate, et ignavia divinissimum munus expleverit, arbitrio Episcopi gravissime puniatur.

§ v. Quamvis nullo tempore liceat illorum audire confessiones, de quorum in Doctrina peritia certi moraliter non sint confessarii quadragesimae tamen tempore nullius confessio excipiatur, nisi prius ostendat schedulam Parochi, vel Examinatoris Clerici de illius scientia testificantis.

§ vi. Abusus inolevit, ut confessarii saepe non pueros modo, sed etiam adultos mentis compotes sub conditione absolvant, quoniam de paenitentium dolore dubitant. Declarat ergo Provincialis Synodus non licere conditionata absolvendi formula uti, excepto casu extremae necessitatis, vel quum oblitus sit confessarius an absolverit, extra quos si de dolore, aut dispositione dubitent, paenitentes accuratius instruant, vel ut iterum accedant, moneant confessarii.

§ vii. Multi ex iis, qui ad praestandum moribundis auxilia vocantur, moris habent super infirmum absolutionem continuo repetere, quandoque etiam adstantes confessarios, si forte sint rogare ut idem faciant, etiamsi non postulet aegrotus, nec conscientiam expiet. Prohibet itaque Provincialis Synodus ne quis id de caetero audeat attentare.

§ viii. Sunt qui consuetudinarios, et recidivos excepto turpi crimine sine ulla absolvant haesitatione quibus edicit Provincialis Synodus sine gravi crimine id fieri non posse. Consuetudinarii enim in qualibet materia absolutionis capaces non sunt, nisi a pravo more desistant.

§ ix. Iubet Provincialis Synodus ne quis Confessarius feminarum confessiones extra sedem confessionalem, aegrotis exceptis, audiat, nec ante solis ortum, nec post ejus occasum excepta necessitate. Sedes confessionales duplicatis cancellis qui inter se quattuor ad minus digitorum intercapedine distare debent utrimque muniantur. Foramina vero adeo sint parva, ut vel digitorum minimo pervadi nequeant.

§ x. Indorum plurimi ad confessionem annuam accedere recusant ob paupertatem qua *ambagan* solvere non valeant. Iubet ergo provincialis Synodus ad tollendum locum hujusmodi excusationi ut ad aliud commodium tempus *ambagan* exactio rejiciatur.

§ xi. Provincialis Synodus Parochis, qui in confinio duarum dioecesum sunt, facultatem facit audiendi mutuo confessiones tum sui ipsorum, tum etiam suarum ovium.

§ xii. Animadvertens Provincialis Synodus sacerdotum inopiam, et messis magnitudinem, declarat initium quadragesimalibus confessionibus fieri posse urgente necessitate, et consulto Vicario in Dominica Septuagesima, finem vero Dominicae secundae Pentecostes. Ut autem fideles agnoscant obligationem confitendi peccata, et sumendi Dominicum corpus, initio Quadragesimae legatur in Ecclesia vulgari lingua Caput *Omnes utriusque sexus.*

§ xiii. Praedicent etiam, minus accurate eam fieri paenitentiam quae semel tantum in anno fit, et rem esse maxime dificilem sine multis criminibus vitam duci ab iis, qui semel tantum confitentur. Propterea saepissime Parochi, initio Quadragesimae inculcent Sacramentorum frequentiam, et magnam, qua opus est dispositionem ad fructuosam paenitentiam, quam tum lacrimae, tum jejunia, eleemosynae, diligens conscientiae discussio, periculorumque fuga, et novae vitae inchoatio praecedere debent.

§ xiv. Eo devenit hominum temeritas, ut faedissime pro suis peccatis paenitentiam agentes quoties peccare libuerit, toties se a Presbyteris reconciliari expostulent. Ii etiam quorum in absolvendo facilitas peccandi maxima illecebra est, omni cubito pulvillos consuentes maximam in Ecclesia Dei recidivorum, et consuetudinariorum turbam alunt, cum magno populi Christiani detrimento. Scrutentur ergo confessarii paenitentium vitam anteactam, et mores, et attente perpendant, an superiores confessiones emendatio aliqua successerit, an ablati, vel male parti restitutio, an occasionis fuga, an consuetudinis pravae emendatio, et quos ex fructibus dispositos invenerint absolvant, quos vero minus aptos repererint, eis vel negent omnino vel differant absolutionem. Certe non aliunde hujus Ecclesiae tepiditas, et scelerum lues provenit, quam ex male suada confessariorum benignitate qui contra id quod oculis patet, nullum reperiunt quem absolutione indignum arbitretur. Vae ergo his Confessariis, et iterum Vae! quia caeci sunt et duces coecorum; mactatores gregis, non Pastores; homicidae, non medici, seductores animarum, non doctores.

§ xv. Quum relatum sit Provinciali Synodo aliquot Confessarios super complice in venereis sciscitatos esse, in sacra exomologesi, prohibet Provinciale Concilium sub poena excommunicationis maioris latae sententiae Episcopis reservandae, et privatione officii, et beneficii ne quis de caetero super complice, in quovis etiam crimine, ejus domo, nomine, aut aliis indiciis interroget juxta constitutiones Bened. XV. *Ubi primum* et *Ad eradicandam.*

§ xvi. Solent aliqui adeo imprudenter de auditis in confessione loqui nonnumquam etiam cum expressione loci et temporis, ut violandi sigillum periculo se exponant, quod quum odiosam reddat confessionem peccatorum, Provincialis Synodus universis Confessariis cujusvis status et conditionis praecipit, ne quis de auditis in confessione, etiam si periculum adhuc remotissimum prodendi peccatorem non adsit, sine necessitate tantum consulendi, et quidem caute ad praescriptum cap. *Omnis utriusque* loqui audeat. Contraventores vero pro modo culpae acriter ab Episcopo corripiantur.

§ xvii. Intellexit Provincialis Synodus aliquot Confessarios in ea esse opinione, ut complicem in turpibus absolvere se posse arbitrentur quoniam constitutio Bened. XIV. *Sacramentum Poenitentiae* Kalend. Junii 1741, et alia data 8. Februar. 1745. ad has Insulas ex jure transmissa ignoratur. Fuerit tamen quodcumque Provincialis Synodus auctoritate sua, si opus sit, adimit omnibus Confessariis cujuscumque status, et conditionis facultatem absolvendi complicem in turpi crimine in foro interno, quovis praetextu, non obstante quacumque in contrarium consuetudine etiam immemoriali. Si quis ergo, excepto casu extremae necessitatis, temerario ausu complicem in venereis absolvere praesumpserit, sciat se ipso facto excommunicationem maiorem latae sententiae Episcopis reservatam incurrisse; et absolutionem in interno foro nullam et irritam esse.

§ xviii. Praecipit Provincialis Synodus universis Parochis Saecularibus et Regularibus, ut quotannis per se ipsos, et suos Coadjutores cunctos fideles examinent in Doctrina Christiana, quam diligentissime, parumque aut nihil fidant examini per Zelatores facto. Manilae vero ubi numerosior est plebs, et in ejus suburbiis omnes Clerici ad examinandum cogantur, et per Ecclesias dividantur. Examinatores autem admonet Provincialis Synodus, ut nullius vultum revereantur, sed servatis mansuetudinis, et Christianae politicae regulis, hispanos, et Indos accurate interrogent de Religionis Christianae dogmatibus, sciantque illorum animas de suis manibus requirendas esse.

§ xix. Pueri quum primo ad confessionem, vel sacram Eucharistiam admittuntur, diligenter prius examinentur et instruantur a Parochis de virtute, et necessitate illorum sacramentorum ad eorumque frequentiam eos hortentur, ostendentes qua via animus praeparari oporteat ad eorum fructuosam susceptionem.

§ xx. Nullus Confessarius quovis praetextu schedulam prius confessionis tradat paenitenti, quam confessio facta sit. Ex contraria enim praxi evenit, ut aliqui ad Eucharistiam non confessi accedant.

§ xxi. Nullus medicinam facere praesumat nisi prius coram Vicario Generali, aut rurali juramentum praestet ad praescriptum Apostolicarum Bullarum se aegrotos non invisuros etiamsi morbus gravis non sit, nisi ante tertiam visitationem conscientiam expiaverint et de peracta confessione testimonium Confessarii ostendant. Multi enim sunt, qui ob Medicorum adulationes sine sacramentis decesserunt.

§ xxii. Gravidae, ne sine sacramentis moriantur, doloribus subito praeoccupatae, instante nono mense conscientias expient et Sacra Synaxi reficiantur.

§ xxiii. Ut frequentiae sacramenti Poenitentiae assuescerent Indi nihil utilius esset, quam si pueri, et puellae scholares aliquoties per annuam in magnis saltem festivitatibus ad sacram confessionem Eucharistiam accederent. Curent ergo Parochi ad id teneram juventutem suavibus verbis allicere.

§ xxiv. Sunt qui extra Quadragesimam raro ad confessionalem sedem accedunt, ideoque sacramenta non frequentantur. Jubet ergo Provincialis Synodus ut omnes Parochi, et Coadjutores sabbatis et vigiliis festivitatum per tres horas mane et duas ad minus vespere in confessionali sede parati sint ad confessiones audiendas, et quamvis nullus accedat, ibi expectent, tempus illud lectione vel oratione absumentes, nisi ad aliquem infirmum vocentur. Expediret etiam ut fideles magna veneratione hoc sacramentum prosequerentur, ut nullus Sacerdos ad audiendas confessiones sine superpelliceo, et stola violacea accederet.

§ xxv. Denique Provincialis Synodus hortatur universos Confessarios ut assidue reconciliandis cum Deo hominibus incumbant, et paenitentes ad se accedentes benigne excipiant, illosque salutaribus instruentes, a vitiis revocent, horrorem peccati infundant, ad contritionem excitent, et piam vivendi methodum praescribant juxta verae paenitentiae regulas.

DECRETUM IV
De Sacramento Eucharistiae

§ i. Ut homines a salutari mensa arcerent communis hostis multa semper molitus est. Inter ea autem Indis persuasit, eum, qui primo ad sacram mensam accedit per triduum sputum reddere non posse, nec carnes edere, nec balneo uti; quo fit ut hoc metu pueri a communione retrahantur. Illis vero, qui saepius Sacra Synaxi refecti sunt, eam legem per integrum diem servandam induxit humani generis hostis, non minus ac obligationem jejunandi in pervigilio.

§ ii. Quoniam vero ob Parochorum vigilantiam nec his

artibus a coelesti mensa omnino excludi possunt Indi, tamen, ne fructum ex ea perciperent, persuasit diabolus, in die communionis jejunari non posse, quo fit, ut quandoque praecepta Ecclesiastica parvipendantur. Curent ergo Parochi, et confessarii Indos ab his, et similibus erroribus abducere eosque hortari ad salutaris Sacramenti frequentiam.

§ iii. Praedicent etiam contra pravum morem ornandi se plusquam decet in die Communionis, commodatis etiam vestibus, et monilibus unde non levia mala nascuntur. Doceant itaque Parochi suos oppidanos munditiam corporis non in vanitate, et luxu positam esse satisque mundum coram Deo apparere, qui statui suo congruentes vestes defert, quantumvis pauperculas dummodo anima spiritualibus virtutum monilibus ornata sit; Beati enim sunt mundi corde quoniam ipsi Deum videbunt.

§ iv. Barbara, et immanis illa est consuetudo, et Apostolicis sanctionibus contraria, qua infirmi pro Sacramentorum perceptione ad Ecclesias deferuntur. Nec sufficit vulgata excusatio, domos nempe Indorum valde esse viles et Majestati Dei indignas, Christus enim Dominus nec praesepe horruit, nec crucem. Iubet ergo Provincialis Synodus, ut nullus posthac sive Saecularis, sive Regularis permittat aegrotos ad Ecclesias deferri pro Sacramentorum susceptione, sed potius ad aegrotorum domos quantumvis pauperes Sacramenta deferantur, non obstante quacumque in contrarium consuetudine etiam immemoriali. Quod si aliquis post hoc Decretum, conciliari sanctioni non paruerit, si tertio monitus non resipuerit, officio pariter et beneficio privetur.

§ v. Inhibet pariter Synodus alium pravum morem deferendi Viaticum in lectis vulgo *examacas*, qui modus indecens valde est, et jubet ut quamprimum ex bonis Ecclesiarum lecticae, seu sellae gestatoriae fiant ad hunc effectum.

§ vi. Viaticum ad infirmos, qua possit veneratione deferatur, ideoque ultra lampadem bene clausam ita, ut extingui lumen non possit, duo ad minus cerei, et si fieri possit, quatuor, aut plures Dominicum Corpus comitentur necnon campanula. Parochi saepe oppidanos suos hortentur, pium maxime, et salutare, esse Dominicum Corpus ad infirmos comitari ob plurimas hac de causa concessas Indulgentias.

§ vii. Caveant Parochi, ne simul cum Viatico Extremam Unctionem infirmo praebeant, sine necessitate, ex contraria etiam praxi fit ut Parochi ultra infirmos non invisant iique forte cum periculo aeternae salutis Pastoris auxilio destituantur, hacque de causa infirmi, qui alias denuo confiterentur sine hoc auxilio migrant, cum ob suam pusillanimitatem Parochum vocare non audeant. Infirmis quorum aegrotatio aut habitualis, aut prolixa nimis est, saepius sacra Eucharistia porrigatur eosque hortentur Parochi, ut tam salutare Sacramentum concupiscant.

§ viii. Dicente Domino: Nolite sanctum dare canibus, attente perpendant Parochi quinan in sua Paroecia peccatores sint publici, ebriosi, aleatores, lusores, festorum profanatores, concubinarii, et similes, quibus omnino negent sacram Eucharistiam, etiamsi confessi, et absoluti fuerint, nisi publice egerint paenitentiam-Dolendum enim sane est quod multi Parochi faciunt, qui nihil magis optant, quam peccatores suae Paroeciae alio divertere ad expiandum conscientias, et nulla alia attenta ratione eos ad Sacram Synaxim admittunt, infideles profecto Mysteriorum Dei dispensatores.

§ ix. Magna sane libertas in adimplendis praeceptis Confessionis et Communionis annuae hanc Provinciam pervasit ita ut fideles quo velint, his praeceptis satisfaciant. Jubet ergo Provincialis Synodus sub gravi poena arbitrio Episcoporum, ut Parochi sine gravi necessitate, nulli facultatem faciant extra propriam Paroeciam sumendi Dominicum Corpus, quinimo antequam Eucharistiam in Quadragesima distribuant, inquirant, an sint alieni parochiani, eisque vel negent communionem, vel si devotionis causa accedere velint, eis nullo modo schedulam Communionis distribuant, nisi eos praevideant ad propriam Paroeciam intra statutum tempus pro annua communione redire non posse. Si quos etiam ex sua Paroecia in Quadragesima discessuros noverint, curent maxime, ut antequam exeant praeceptis Confessionis et Communionis satisfaciant.

§ x. Quoniam plurimi sunt, qui debito tempore praecepta Confessionis et Comunionis non adimplent, Parochi Dominica in Albis, Hispanis, si qui sunt, inter Missarum solemnia declarent graviter deliquisse eos, qui adhuc ad Paenitentiam et Eucharistiam non accesserunt et nisi intra septimanam praecepta adimpleverint, eos de facto interdictos ab ingressu Ecclesiae, et sepultura Ecclesiastica annuncient. Quod si non resipuerint, Vicarium vel Episcopum certiorem faciant. Idem respectu Indorum fiat Dominica secunda Pentecostes, aliis poenis loco interdicti appositis.

§ xi. Declarat Provincialis Synodus exteros Parochianos non satisfacere praecepto Communionis annuae in Metropolitana Ecclesia, non obstante quacumque in contrarium consuetudine etiam immemoriali.

§ xii. Decernit Provincialis Synodus, ut singulis Dominicis renovetur Sanctissimum Eucharistiae Sacramentum pridie factis hostiis et populo ostendatur. Dum autem renovatio fit quatuor ad minus ex primoribus populi, si fieri potest, accensis facibus adsistant.

§ xiii. Caecus amor, quo Indi in gallos suos feruntur eo pervenit, ut plurimi temerario ausu consecratas hostias gallis suis edendas porroxerint, aut illorum novaculis agglutinaverint, ut invincibiles fierent. Alii inter linteum et aram Altaris collocasse hostias deprehensi sunt, ut a sacerdotibus consecrarentur ad cumdem effectum. Ad vitandum ergo in posterum tam gravia sacrilegia, jubet Provincialis Synodus, ut nulli laicorum, etiam sacristae, clavis Tabernaculi tradatur, sed eam penes se habeant Parochi sub excommunicationis poena. Curent etiam scire quot in sacra Pyxide hostiae serventur, et quot fidelibus distribuantur ut hac via sacrilega furta innotescant.

§ xiv. Quoniam vero aliqui perceptas hostias ab ore extrahunt ut gallos suos pascant, invigilent ii, qui populo distribuunt Angelicam Escam, ut citissime fideles sacram Eucharistiam deglutiant. Inquirant etiam, quam diligentissime in eorum vitas, qui vel prae coeteris gallorum pugnae indulgent, vel fortitudinis famam assequi contendunt. Ii enim ad sui custodiam corporis hostias, et sacrarum vestium, aut librorum particulas adhibere solent. Quapropter summa diligentia omnis sacra supellex custodienda est.

§ xv. Omnes sacerdotes cujuscumque sint dignitatis et conditionis Missas celebrent attenta consideratione, in eisque tertiam ad minus horae partem insumant, quamvis eas citius expedire possint, servatis adhuc omnibus caeremoniis sub poena suspensionis. Nullus Missam audeat celebrare, sine debita praeparatione, hacque de causa in omnibus Sacrariis disponatur locus commodus in quo disponantur sacerdotes, ibique necessariae tabulae praeparationis ad Missam et gratiarum actionis, juxta Missale Romanum, appendantur.

§ xvi. In omni Altari sit Crux cum imagine Jeus Christi Crucifixi; duo ad minus candelabra et tabula secretorum. In omni Ecclesia, etiam Metropolitana, sint albae pro confluentibus sacerdotibus, et caetera ornamenta.

§ xvii. A gravitate divini cultus longe sunt albae et amictus plurimorum ex fimbriis magis quam ex lino facti. Casulae etiam adeo parvae fiunt, et circa humeros contractae ad pretiosissimarum albarum, et defluentium cingulorum ostensionem ut magna egeant reformatione. Cingula suas habent defluentes ad latera extremitates. Iubet ergo Provincialis Synodus, ut albae ex simplici linteo fiant, et fimbrias, ad summum, unius palmi latitudinis habeant: ex cingulis defluentes assutae extremitates omnino auferantur. De coetero curent Episcopi, ut sacrae vestes non pro cujusvis lubito fiant, sed prout rubricae praescribunt.

§ xviii. Avaritia omnium malorum radix multos induxit plura stipendia Missarum accipere, quam celebrare sufficiant. Nullus ergo juxta declarationes Sacrae Congregationis qui Missarum habet accepta stipendia, alia accipiat, nisi intra mensem omnibus valeat satisfacere.

§ xix. In privatis Oratoriis laicorum nullus audeat Missam celebrare sine speciali ad id Episcopi licentia, etiam si Regularis sit. In illis autem, non nisi unica Missa celebretur; imo nec unica dicatur nisi ii qui interesse possunt, publicis vestibus, non domesticis decenter sint ornati. Nullus nisi infirmus habitualis in privatis oratoriis aut communicet, aut conscientiam expiet. Moneant etiam ii, qui in Oratoriis celebrant, ibi non satisfieri praecepto audiendi Missam ab iis, qui in privilegio non exprimuntur.

DECRETUM V

De Sacramento Extremae Unctionis

§ i. Nullus sine superpelliceo et stola infirmos inungat, nec prius quam mortis periculum immineat. Attamen id auxilii aegrotis praestetur, antequam de eorum salute conclametur, vel rationis ii usum amittant. Virgula in administratione hujus Sacramenti nisi morbus contagioni sit obnoxius, non adhibeatur.

§ ii. Current Parochi Indos instruere de vi, et utilitate Extremae Unctionis erroremque illum, quo credunt infirmos eo Sacramento, aut debiliores reddi, aut etiam mori, removere studeant.

§ iii. Decernit Provincialis Synodus, ut pueris qui Sacramento Paenitentiae sunt capaces, tametsi de sacra mensa non participaverint, Sacramentum Extremae Unctionis conferatur, illisque si tempus suppetis, ejus virtus explicetur.

§ iv. Sacra olea diligenti asserventur custodia pro quorum securitate in Sacristia, vel Baptisterio intra parietem arcula firma, et bene obserata collocetur. Olea ad aegrotos ipsi Parochi, vel alii sacris initiati deferant, nulloque titulo pueris vel laicis asportanda committantur.

DECRETUM VI

De Sacramento Ordinis

§ i. Quindecim ante Ordines diebus nomina ordinandorum in Ecclesiis publicentur, et valvis Ecclesiarum affigantur, ut si quis sive Sacerdos, sive Laicus cujusvis status, et conditionis aliquid sciat quod aliquem ex candidatis, ordinibus indignum reddat, directori seminarii, Vicario Generali, aut ipsi Episcopo, per se, aut per alium significet.

§ ii. Nullus ad ordines admittatur nisi ex testimonio Parochi, Magistrorum, sociorumque de ejus vita et doctrina constiterit. Eos, qui titulo Operariorum ordinantur, priusquam ad Subdiaconatum admittantur, per duos annos Theologiae Morali incumbere oportet, et per idem temporis spatium Theologiae Scholasticae, priusquam Sacerdotio ordinentur. Qui ex testimonio Magistrorum laudabiliter in praedictis studiis, definito tempore, versatus non fuerit, nullo modo ad sacros maiores ordines admittatur. Idem a caeteris, qui alio titulo ordinantur intelligendum est, ita tamen ut cum his ex justa causa dispensari queat.

§ iii. Statim ac aliquis ordines postulaverit, secretae inquisitiones de ejus vita, moribus, scientia, fama, genere, et similibus, fiant eoque in libro, ad id destinato, in chancellaria notentur.

§ iv. Ii qui titulo Capellaniae, aut Beneficii ordinari cupiunt, ostendere debent authenticum titulum, et per idonea instrumenta probare Beneficii, aut Cappellaniae reditus centum argenti uncias attingere eosque revera possidere, cum ad subdiaconatum accedunt.

§ v. Novae Cappellaniae perpetua ex bonis immobilibus laicorum cautissime admittantur, praecipue si fundatores pauperes habeant consanguineos. Liceat tamen titulo patrimonii ordines suscipere ita tamen ut defuncto sacerdote bona immobilia ad laicos haeredes redeant.

§ vi. Ii, qui titulo Beneficii, aut Cappellaniae ordinantur, juramentum praestare debent inserviendi alicui Ecclesiae ad praescriptum Episcopi, quod in Charta ordinum notari debet.

§ vii. Ex iis, qui in Collegiis, vel extra Seminarium educati sunt, nullus titulo Beneficii, aut Cappellaniae ordinetur, nisi per sex menses in Seminario versatus fuerit. Qui vero titulo operariorum ordines suscipiunt, ultra sex menses, qui ad subdiaconatum praecedere debent, in Seminario tamdiu degant quousque alicui Paroeciae destinentur.

§ viii. Quoniam vero in his Insulis fere omnes titulo operariorum seu Indorum ordinantur, caveant Episcopi, ne plures sacris initient, quam utilitas exigit Paroeciarum, ne pauperes clerici contra dignitatem sui status mendicare turpiter cogantur.

§ ix. Quoniam ex Suffraganeis Dioecesibus studiorum causa, Manilam multi veniunt absque animo figendi domicicilium, qui tamen ibi promoti ad suas postes Dioeceses minime redeunt caveant Metropolitae ne eos etiam praetextu Cappellaniae, aut Beneficii (salvo tamen jure Patronatus) ad ordines excipiant ne Suffraganeae Ecclesiae suorum clericorum servitio priventur.

§ xi. Ne inferiores Sacerdotio ordines sine causa in Ecclesia Dei conferri videantur, nullus ad superiores ordines admittatur, nisi prius constet eum in inferioribus fuisse versatum, in ea Ecclesia cui addictus sit, vel in alia arbitrio Episcopi.

§ xi. Episcopi nullum ad ordines admittant sine praevio diligenti examine, et in ordinum collatione, ea omnia observent, quae a Sacrosancta Tridentiana Synodo Sess. 23 a Cap. 3 usque ad 17 de Reformat. sancita sunt.

§ xii. In dispensandis irregularitatibus, bigamiae praecipue et natalium cautissime se gerant Episcopi et considerantes monitum Pauli: Manus cito nemini imposueris, diligenter invigilent ne indignos ob scientiae, aut virtutis defectum ad ordines admittant, sed eos tantum, quorum vita, et doctrina spem afferat populorum instructioni, et aedificationi utiles fore.

DECRETUM VII
De Sacramento Matrimonii

§ i. Adeo altas radices in Indorum animis egit servitium personale quo ii qui uxorem ducere volunt in futurae sponsae domo gratis, per plures quandoque annos, servire coguntur, ut etiam hi, qui interdiu, vel ob Ministri metum, vel aliam ob causam servitium praestare non audeant, noctu id fecisse compertum sit. Persuasum ergo habeant Parochi, hanc consuetudinem adhuc vigere, non minus ac alios abusus.

§ ii. Tot autem malorum causa est hujusmodi servitium, ut non modo plurimi cum futura uxore illicitum habeant commercium, sed etiam cum ejus sororibus, unde fit ut multa matrimonia nulla reperiantur. Eo accedit parentum incuria, qui lucri causa domi vivere patiuntur futurum sponsum, eique liberum ad filias accessum faciunt.

§ iii. His ergo malis mederi cupiens Provincialis Synodus jubet, ut omnes Parochi summa diligentia per se et per alios observent, an servitium personale vigeat, et si aliquem invenerint id praestantem, eum, et parentes puellae et ipsam puellam loco securo collocabunt, donec inquirunt, an inter juvenem, et puellam legitima sint sponsalia, quibus inventis, nullo alias obstante impedimento, eos quam primum matrimonio copulabunt. Parentes puellae juveni restituent id quod servitio ejus respondeat juxta taxam regiam. Utque hic mos extirpetur, ipsius puellae parentes per tres dies festos publice in Ecclesia poeniteant, et coram omnibus a Parochis arguantur.

§ iv. Alius mos inter Indos viget, qui *pasusu* dicitur, quo puellae matri a futuro sponso certa pecuniae summa ob nutricium lac solvenda est; hacque de causa matrimonio cum periculo animarum differi solent. Curent ergo Parochi adversus periculum hunc morem saepius declamare, et si quos invenerint huic feritati obnoxios, publicae poenitentiae in Ecclesia addicant, non minus ac servitium personale exercentes, et pecuniae summam sponso restitui faciant. Huc mos a ditioribus praecipue Sinensium filiis sub aliqua tergiversatione sub voce *bigay caya* usurpatur, ideoque statutis poenis maneat obnocius.

§ v. Nullus matrimonio jungatur sine praevio de Doctrina Christiana examine, et domum separatam in oppido facere cogatur ab oppidorum Rectoribus. Domus suas habeant divisiones pro filiis, filiabus, et nuptis ut hac via Indi modestiae assuescant, et Patres familias in primis satagant, ne filii sui, etiam pueruli turpiter nudi incedant. Circa id negligentes viginti plagis mulctentur.

§ vi. Parochi diligenter explorent voluntatem contrahentium, eosque admoneant de impedimentis matrimonii, ex contraria enim praxi fit, ut multa postea Matrimonia irrita inveniantur. Satagant Parochi rescire quinam habeant sponsalia, hortenturque fideles ut ea publice contrahant, doceantque sponsalia esse veluti quodam tyrocinium; quo fideles per virtutis opera ad Sacramentum Matrimonii disponuntur. Invigilent, ut hi, qui sponsalia habent, ad sponsam non accedant.

§ vii. Pudet commemorare abusus, qui Provinciali Synodo relati sunt in nuptialibus conviviis Indorum reperiri, ideoque praecipit, ut convivia nuptialia non in agro, sed in oppido celebrentur, eaque usque ad vesperam exclusive ad summum protrahantur. Noctu vero si quis in sponsorum domo reperiatur, gravissime puniatur. Curent Parochi a nuptialibus conviviis pravos, et antiquos mores ebrietatemque continua praedicatione auferre.

§ viii. Quum viri dotent uxores, seu potius juxta antiquum ritum, eas a parentibus emant, fit inde, ut parentes plus dantibus eas tradant in matrimonium, nolentibus quandoque uxoribus, aut antiquiora iis habentibus sponsalia; quapropter Provincialis Synodus rogat Illmum. Gubernatorem, ut hunc morem juxta leges Indiarum extirpet; Parochis autem praecipit, ut creberrime contra hunc abusum, et reliquos, qui circa Matrimonium inveniuntur gravissime declament, persuasumque habeant nihil Indos in virtute profecturos, nisi matrimonia caste ineant et filios christiane educent.

§ ix. In oppidis, quae excursionibus Maurorum obnoxia sunt, nullus ad secundas nuptias transeat nisi de morte conjugis captivi certum habeat nuntium, qua in re, ne vigente primo conjuge matrimonia cum alio ineantur cautissime procedatur.

§ xi. Sunt qui ab uxoribus sine causa separantur et alio discedunt, quos Parochi ad uxorem redire cogant, accito etiam, si opus sit, auxilio brachii saecularis.

§ xi. Ex aliena dioecesi, vel oppido nullus prius matrimonio jungatur, etiam a Vicariis Foraneis, quam in propria Paroecia factis denuntiationibus, solutus et sine impedimento inveniatur. Vagi vero ad contrahendum matrimonium, non nisi ad praescriptum Sacrosancti Concilii Tridentini Sess. 24 cap. 7. De Reform. recipiantur.

§ xii. Quoniam vagantes, qui plurimi sunt, aliquando uxoriam vitam ducunt quum matrimonio juncti non sint, peregrini mariti, etiam si certam tandem sedem figant, separentur donec de contracto matrimonio testimonium ostendant. Parochis autem praecipit Provincialis Synodus ut pauperibus gratis hujusmodi exhibeant testimonia, utque id praestare possint data occasione, libros Ecclesiae bene habeant dispositos. Hortatur etiam Magistratus saeculares, ut pestem Rei Publicae vagantes homines coerceant.

§ xiii. In denuntiationibus nullus audeat dispensare, exceptis Episcopis. Regulares vero monet Provincialis Synodus ut in dispensandis impedimentis caute procedant, considerantes prius an sua privilegia expiraverint.

§ xiv. Matrimonium in facie Ecclesiae ad januam Templi contrahatur post solis ortum. Sunt enim quos pudet publice matrimonio jungi, ideoque secreto id faciunt. Inde etiam fit ut multi per plures annos sine benedictionibus nuptialibus cohabitent et filios suscipiant, cui corruptelae omnibus viribus obsistant Parochi.

§ xvi. Matrimonia inter infideles harum partium inita, valida cum sint, quamvis inter eos locum habeat lex divortii, Provincialis Synodus jubet ne quis Minister Saecularis vel Regularis temere audeat infidelium matrimonia irrita declarare, sed si aliquis ad fidem convertatur, qui plures conjuges habuisse noscatur, cum prima, si recordetur, vivere cogatur. Si vero memoria exciderit, quamnam prius duxerit, liberum ei sit cum alia quavis femina inire matrimonium, dummodo nullo ad id impedimento inhabilis inveniatur. Quod si alicubi, ita matrimonia contracta inter infideles reperiantur, ut de eorum valore dubitetur, eveniente casu, consulatur Episcopus cujus consilium exposci etiam debet quum alter conjugum in infidelitate permanens sine contumelia Creatoris, post semestre spatium, quod ad deliberandum ei concedi oportet, cohabitare nolit, ut facultatem converso ad fidem faciat matrimonium contrahendi.

§ xvi. Sunt Parochi adeo negligentes, qui quovis praetextu Ritualis caeremonias praetereunt, tum in Sacramento Matrimonii, tum in aliis omnibus, uti sunt professio fidei in administratione Eucharistiae moribundis, absolutio censurarum in absolutione sacramentali, praescripti ritus in Baptismo adultorum. Jubet ergo Provincialis Synodus, ut omnes Parochi cum magna gravitate omnes, quantumvis minimas Ritualis Romani caeremonias tam in Sacramentorum ministratione, quam in aliis Parochialibus officiis ad unguem observent, easque aliquando in Kalendis discutiant. Si quis Parochus scienter aliquam, quamvis minimam, caeremoniam omiserit, jura sibi debita amittat quae ipso facto Ecclesiae fabricae applicata censeantur.

Titulus Secundus
De Reformatione

Decretum I
De Celebratione Festorum

§ i. Inter multa, et gravia scelera, quae hanc Philippinensem Ecclesiam maxime deturpant haud infimum locum tenet festorum violatio. Etenim quasi ii dies ad otium, et corporis relaxationem facti essent, comessationibus, saltationibus, ludis, et caeteris oblectamentis ex integro fere absolvuntur. Inde fit ut Templa vacua sint, paucique reperiantur, qui divinis officiis intersint, conciones audiant, orationi insistant, nosocomia perlustrent, tristes consolentur, legem Dei meditentur, caeteraque pietatis erga Deum, et proximum opera expleant, quibus dies festi sanctificantur.

§ ii. Doceant ergo Parochi, Confessarii, et Concionatores Christianum populum duo esse circa festorum sanctificationem praecepta, unum Ecclesiasticum circa Missae auditionem, alterum divinum circa eorum sanctificationem. Primum, integrae Missae attenta et devota auditione expletur; secundum vero servilium operum cessatione, et virtutum latriae, contritionis, fidei, spei, charitatis, misericordiae operum actibus, Verbi Dei auditione, chorearum, conviviorum, ludorum, vitiorumque fuga adimpletur. Moneant etiam fideles a viro Christiano alienum esse diebus festis Missam tantum et quandoque omnium brevissimam audire, et reliquas diei horas amicorum salutationibus, et otio perditissime adjicere.

§ iii. Quoniam vero aliqui dies festos publice violare servilibus operibus non reformidant, obliti sententiae capitalis, quam in colligentem ligna die sabbati ipse Deus dixit, Provincialis Synodus per viscera misericordiae Jesu Christi rogat Magistratus Saeculares tam Manilae, quam extra, ut festorum transgressores auctoritate sua coerceant, illorumque impudentiam justis poenis retundant. Ex festorum enim contemptu egestates et calamitates nascuntur.

§ iv. Parochi fideles suos ab eo errore abducant, quo existimant diebus festis, post Missam, vespere, aut nocte laborare licere, et assidua praedicatione ad sancte, et pie transigendos festos dies inducant. Quoniam vero in Indorum oppidis aliquot festivitates votivae fiunt, hacque occasione augentur exactiones, seu contributiones, curent Episcopi, ne de caetero sine sua licentia hujusmodi festivitates fiant, et quae institutae sunt sine auctoritate, tollantur, non minus ac exactiones.

§ v. Declarat Provincialis Synodus Hispanos diebus sibi festis, ad quorum observantiam Indi non tenentur, non posse servos suos ad laborem cogere.

§ vi. Provinciale Concilium saeculares Magistratus vehementer in Domino hortatur ne diebus festis publicos ludos, gallorum praecipue ante Missae maioris finem, aut etiam antequam exercitium Doctrinae Christianae ad vesperam finiatur, permittant.

§ vii. Provincialis Synodus universis Parochis in memoriam revocat obligationem applicandi Missam pro populo diebus festis, a qua non excusantur pauperum Ecclesiarum Rectores.

§ viii. Mercatus, qui vulgo *Tianguis* dicuntur, diebus festis non permittantur, praecipue antequam Missae maiori finis fiat. Vendentium tabernae diebus festis clausae sint, et quae praeter esculenta aliquid vendiderint, graviter puniantur.

§ ix. Mos est Manilae ejusque suburbiis, necnon in aliis oppidis ut quum aliqua festivitas celebranda sit, usus nitrati pulveris adhibeatur, non solum in pervigilio sed etiam ad Gloriam, ad Sanctus, ad Elevationem Hostiae, et Calicis inter Missarum solemnia. Quum autem Ecclesiasticae solemnitates castrorum more celebrandae non sint, prohibet Provincialis Synodus sub poena aliquot librarum pyrii pulveris arbitrio Episcopi, ne quis sive Saecularis, sive Regularis de caetero usum nitrati pulveris, quovis modo sive in pervigiliis, sive in diebus festis permittat, non obstante quacumque in contrarium consuetudine, etiam immemoriali.

§ x. In pulsandis campanis, circa quod magnus abusus irrepsit, Provincialis Synodus modum, et regulam praescribere cupiens, statuit et decernit, ut tam Saeculares, quam Regulares in vigiliis festorum etiam primae classis, ter tantum pulsent campanas, meridie nempe, ad vesperas, si cantentur, et ad primam horam noctis, et quidem sine prolixitate. Ipso vero festivitatis die non nisi paulo ante Missam solemnem ad convocandum populum, et ad Elevationem Hostiae et Calicis, post Consecrationem. Contrarias quascumque consuetudines, etiam immemoriales, tollit Provincialis Synodus. Ad vespertinas conciones, si quando habeantur, unico signo convocetur populus.

§ xi. In Altari, dum Missa celebratur, exceptis Cathedralibus, feriatis diebus duae tantum candelae accendantur. Dominicis et minoribus festis, quatuor: in solemnioribus festivitatibus sex ad summum in altari, quatuor vero prope Imaginem Sancti, cujus festum celebratur. Extra altare, sex maiores faces, praeter ceroferarios, Manilae; extra vero, quatuor ad summum, permittuntur. Omnes enim quum de paupertate querantur, Provincialis Synodus tot sumptus in festivitatibus, quomodo fieri possint non animadvertit, sine extortis magis, quam oblatis eleemosynis. Quum sanctissimum Eucharistiae Sacramentum publicae venerationi exponitur, ultra viginti quatuor candelas non accendantur, et hae quidem prope Sacram Pyxidem. Utque fidelium mentes unice ad Sanctum Sanctorum dirigantur, dum sacra Eucharistia exponitur, Sanctorum omnium Imagines cooperiantur nec in aliquo altari lucernae accendantur.

§ xii. In processionibus, larvati nulli reperiantur, nec pueri instar Angelorum vestiantur. Nullus sit, qui per vias, aut templa, etiam in hebdomada Sancta publice se flagellet, aut poenitentis habitum deferat. In Ecclesia, aut Cemeteriis nullae representationes sive profanae, sive piae fiant; nihilve ludicrum etiam devotionis causa, in Natali Domini, Sanctorum Innocentium festo, aut in hebdomada maiori, et alio quocumque die misceatur.

§ xiii. In die Parasceves Parochi et suggestu enarrent pie, et devote Passionem Domini Nostri Jesu Christi excitando fideles ad gratiarum actionem, vitiorum fugam, et novam vitam coram aliqua Jesu Christi a Cruce pendentis Imagine. Tollatur tamen consuetudo repraesentandi, aut Crucificionem, aut descensum a cruce. Ecclesia enim Mysteria Nostrae Salutis, non comice in memoriam revocat fidelium, sed Verbi Dei praedicatione, quae omni gladio ancipiti penetratior est, pertingens usque ad divisionem animae, et spiritus.

§ xiv. Denique Provincialis Synodus, Parochis, et Ecclesiarum Rectoribus commendat, ut in ducendis Processionibus, et festivitatibus celebrandis ea omnia praestent, quae fideles ad compunctionem potius, et vitae emendationem inducant, quam ad laetitiam, plausus, et risus excitent. Id vero efficient si in his solemnitatibus gravitatem magis quam opulentiam et modestiam potius quam vanitatem, sectentur.

DECRETUM II
De Veneratione Sanctorum Reliquiarum

§ i. Imagines Sanctorum, quae aut imperitia artificum, aut vetustate, aut alia quavis de causa deformes sunt, aut truncae, quas multas apud se Indos retinere compertum est, a suis dominis auferantur, et sepeliantur. In pingendis, sculpendis, vestiendisque Iconibus modestia servanda est, ne vel muliebri mundo, aut meretricio magis cultu ornentur, tortis crinibus, monilibus, et vanis ornamentis ex usu quam decenter, et pie, ita ut inter aurum, et lapillos, modestiae et gravitatis fulgor eluceat.

§ ii. Aliena supellex nullo praetextu ad vestiendas sacras Imagines admittatur, nisi in perpetuum donetur. Valde enim est indecens gemmas, et monilia, quibus feminae ad vanitatem aut irretiendas fortasse animas utuntur, ad breve tempus Sanctis commodare. Qui ergo scienter postea aliquid ad ornatum Imaginum concesserit, id amittat. Eadem lex circa Altarium tam intra, quam extra Ecclesiam, vel ipsarum Ecclesiarum ornamentum, quomodolibet ad usus sacros spectans, intelligatur.

§ iii. Oporteret, ut Sacrae Imagines a Sacerdotibus vestirentur, sed quum id haud facile obtineri posset, id saltem praecipit Provincialis Synodus ut Sacrae Imagines nullo praetextu, aut consuetudine, etiam immemorali ad laicorum domus deferantur, ut a Camerariis feminis vestiantur aut nudentur, sed id ab ipsis, aut a sacristis in Ecclesia fiat. Ut autem ad domos laicorum deferendi Imagines abusus tollatur, jubet Provinciale Concilium, ut nulla de causa, etiam ad modicum tempus id permittatur.

§ iv. Scapulare Carmelitarum auro non ornetur, illudque ad vanitatem extra domum non adhibeatur. Idem de aureis, et gemmatis Rosariis, quae ad ornatum tantum deserviunt, intelligatur.

§ v. Sanctorum Reliquiae, quae vel authenticam non habent, vel Episcopi approbationem, sepeliantur, praecipue si de earum veritate dubium probabile sit, ne id colatur, quod veneratione dignum non est.

DECRETUM III

De Miraculis, et Eleemosynarum Quaestoribus

§ i. Nulla nova miracula publicentur sine Episcopi approbatione, qui adhibitis in consilium Theologis, et piis viris, ea faciat, quae veritati, et pietati consentanea judicaverit. Quoniam vero ob Indorum credulitatem circa id abusus irrepsit, Episcopi diligenter inquirant de locis, in quibus miracula contigerunt, eorumque auctores gravissimis paenis coerceant.

§ ii. Miraculorum auctrix quaestorum exstitit avaritia, ideoque Provincialis Synodus statuit, et decernit, ut nullus sine Episcopi et Magistratuum licentia questuari permittatur, circa quod Parochorum, et Magistratuum gravat conscientias. Episcopi vero hujusmodi quaestoribus, si quando justa aliqua de causa questuari permiserint, in scriptis id faciant, illis et territorium, et tempus designantes. Extra territorium vero Ecclesiae, cujus de causa questuandum est, numquam, aut rarissime, et tunc quidem, si publica exigat utilitas, questuandi licentiam Episcopi faciant.

§ iii. Parochi invigilent in Quaestorum vitas, et si quos invenerint ebrietati deditos, aut scandali occasionem praebentes, ad Vicarium Foraneum transmittant. Si Paroeciae suae in egestate sint, aut Ecclesias pauperes habeant, Parochi, nulla via questores, quamvis licentiam habeant, in suo territorio questuari permittant. Questores per itinera nullas deferant Imagines.

§ iv. Nosochomio Sancti Joannis de Deo per omnes Provincias sine ulla limitatione, de licentia tamen Episcopi et Magistratus mendicare liceat, quoniam illius Charitas nemini non nota ad omnes extenditur, ejusque zelus communi servit utilitati.

DECRETUM IV
De Jejuniorum Observantia

§ i. Jejunia Ecclesiae caste observentur, ideoque Provincialis Synodus hortatur Parochos, Confessarios, et Concionatores, ut fideles doceant pure, et integre Ecclesiae servare jejunia, quae ad id instituta sunt, ut carne per abstinentiam macerata orationi homines incumberent accuratius, et de ipsius abstinentiae fructibus pauperes Christi alerentur.

§ ii. In sacratioribus hebdomadae Sanctae diebus mos est Manilae in propatulo varia eduliorum genera habere, quod quum illorum dierum sanctitatem maxime dedeceat, omnino tollatur.

§ iii. Doceant Parochi ab omnibus servanda esse jejunia, quos privilegium, labor vel necessitas non excusaverit. Eos vero, qui utriusque Medici habita licentia in diebus jejuniis, carnibus uti permittuntur, annuntient Parochi, Concionatores et Confessarii non posse, carnes, et pisces in eadem mensa adhibere, et teneri ad servandam formam jejunii, nisi speciali licentia hac lege liberentur.

§ iv. Quum in his Insulis immemorialis sit consuetudo utendi butyro loco olei, et edendi lacticinia, etiam in jejuniis quadragesimalibus, Provincialis Synodus ad tollendos scrupulos, qui ob publicationem Bullarum Bend. XIV, et Clement. XIII. quae incipiunt "Universalis Ecclesia" et "Venerabiles fratres," aliquibus nati sunt, declarat supradictas consuetudines legitimas esse et praefatis Bullis nequaquam infringi. Ideoque tuta conscientia, et sine necessitate petendi licentiam, fideles uti posse butyro, seu pinguedine, et lacticiniis in Quadragesima, caeterisque jejuniis.

DECRETUM V
De Piis Legatis et Tutoribus

§ i. Legata pia ab Episcopis, ut dictum est, visitentur, et semel saltem in anno eorum Administratores coram Episcopo, et aliis duobus Ecclesiasticis rationem reddant.

§ ii. Non sine lacrymis Provincialis Synodus multorum tutorum intueri potest temeritatem, et malam fidem, quae suae curae commissa testamenta dilapidant, et de alienis bonis ditescentes, pupillos in summam adducunt egestatem. Ne vero de caetero hujusmodi homines avaritia sua haeredes defraudent, summam circa id vigilantiam Saecularibus Magistratibus commendat Provincialis Synodus.

§ iii. Ne vero piis dispositionibus eadem calamitas obtingat, jubet Provincialis Synodus, ut antequam sepeliatur testator, testamenti executores Episcopo referant legata pia in testamento contenta; intra annum vero eidem testimonium exhibeant de eorum executione, aut si discedendi testamentarios compellat necessitas fidejussorem idoneum relinquant. Qui vero aut legata pia, aut pupillorum haereditatem dilapidaverint, anathemate feriantur.

DECRETUM VI
De Simonia

§ i. Nihil commendatius antiqua, et recentia habent Concilia, quam id quod Scriptura inculcat: "Gratis accepistis, gratis date." Nostra ergo Manilana Synodus praecipit universis Episcopis, et caeteris Ecclesiasticis Viris, ut omnibus viribus simoniacam labem abluere studeant, et a foro Ecclesiastico expellere, hocque vitio infectos canonicis poenis coercere.

§ ii. Declarat Provincialis Synodus Parochos et fori Officiales non posse ulla jura exigere praeter ea quae in taxa continentur, nec aliis titulis quam ibidem contentis. Qui vero aut maiora jura, aut aliis titulis, non contentis in taxa exegerit, aut acceperit, ultra obligationem restituendi in foro conscientiae, tamquam simoniacus habeatur, et restitutione in duplum mulctetur.

§ iii. In commemoratione omnium fidelium defunctorum Sacerdotes non possunt nisi pro prima Missa stipendium accipere, nec majus ultra taxam Dioecesis, vel provinciae, quamvis sponte offeratur. Provincialis autem Synodus pro eo tantum die stipendium Missae unum aureum designat; pro caeteris autem aurei medietatem.

DECRETUM VII
De Confraternitatibus

§ i. Nullae confraternitates sine Episcoporum licentia erigantur; erectae vero, ab ipsis visitentur, et si quas aut inutiles jam, aut relaxatas repererint, aut penitus aboleant, aut pristino restituant decori.

§ ii. Quae vero aut sine licentia contra Canonicas, et Regias leges stabilitae sint, aut praescripta a Clemente VIII. in Bulla; Quaecumque non observant, penitus aboleantur ab Episcopis.

§ iii. In festis Confraternitatum convivia nulla, neque in Ecclesia, neque in domo Praepositi, aut alio loco habeantur; idemque in novis electionibus servetur. Confraternitatis nomine Tertii Ordines intelligantur, salvis tamen Apostolicis privilegiis.

DECRETUM VIII
De Rebus Ecclesiae Alienandis Vel Non

§ i. Nullus fundos, agros, aut bona mobilia, vel stabilia Ecclesiae alienare, vendere, aut commodare audeat sine Episcopi licentia in scriptis obtinenda, quovis praetextu. Ut autem Episcopis constet quae bona unaquaeque habeat Ecclesia, omnes Ecclesiarum Rectores habeant librum rubricis Notarii Provinciae munitum, et cum decreto Vicarii Foranei, in quo describatur inventarium bonorum mobilium, et stabilium Ecclesiae. Ubi vero hujusmodi libri non habentur, intra mensem a notitia hujus decreti, fiant, iisdem rubricis et auctoritate liber accepti et expensi adornetur.

§ ii. Si quis Notarius ad occultandum Parochorum crimen, aut malam fidem in administratione Ecclesiasticorum bonorum alicui libro, aut inventario suas rubricas malitiose adjecerit, excommunicationem maiorem ipso facto incurrat, et restitutione maneat obnoxius.

§ iii. Ne vero Oeconomi Ecclesiarum ex Praelatorum incuria occasionem sumant dilapidandi Ecclesiasticos reditus, quotannis ii ante Episcopum vel ab eo designatum rationem reddent suae administrationis.

§ iv. Nullus ex iis ad quos quomodolibet bonorum Ecclesiasticorum spectat administratio, sive in Cathedralibus sive in Parochialibus. Saecularium vel Regularium, sive in aliis quibusvis Ecclesiis, sine Licentia Episcopi, in scriptis obtinenda, res Ecclesiae quomodolibet alienare, vendere, commodare, alio asportare, etiam ad modicum tempus, in aliam formam mutare audeat, quovis praetextu, sub poenis a jure statutis, et aliis arbitrio Episcopi. Sumptus vero, praeter id, quod ad quotidianum usum vini, olei, tritici, candelarum, et thuris necessarium sit, vel ad reparationem tenuem vestium sacrarum, qui in asportandis, mutandis, aut quomodolibet alienandis rebus Ecclesiae fiant, in computum non admittantur.

§ v. Praecipit Provincialis Synodus omnibus Vicariis Generalibus in Sede vacante ut omnia tum Ecclesiarum, tum habitationis Episcopalis bona in eodem statu conservent successori, in quo acceperunt, nullaque de causa eis liceat aliquid alienare vendere, mutare, de una in aliam Ecclesiam asportare sub poena Excommunicationis maioris ipso facto incurrendae. Episcopi vero statim ac possessionem adierint suae Ecclesiae a Vicario rationem exigent tum bonorum Ecclesiarum tum habitationis Episcopalis, non minus ac de Dioecesis regimine Episcopi in hoc negligentes ad resarciendum damna illata Ecclesiis per Vicarios in sede vacante teneantur.

§ vi. Unaquaeque Ecclesia libros proprios habeat Rituale Romanum, Bibliam Sacram, Auctorem aliquem probatum Theologiae mysticae, Vitas Sanctorum, Catechismum Romanum, summam Moralem P. Concinae, Decreta hujus Synodi, Statuta Synodalia et libros Edictorum Episcopalium, Epistolarum Pastoralium, et casuum conscientiae in Kalendis resolutorum.

DECRETUM IX

De Libris Prohibitis

§ i. Curent Episcopi, ne Haereticorum libri, aut obsceni, quique piis auribus offensioni esse possint grassentur; libros etiam laxae doctrinae ab eorum manibus amoveant, qui discrimen facere vix possunt inter laxas, et probabiles doctrinas, ne incaute ea discant quae populo fideli sint nocumento.

§ ii. In scholis vero, et publicis studiis juxta sanam D. Augustini, et D. Thomae doctrinam Theologiae disciplinae tradentur, et usus Patrum Conciliorum, et Sacrae Scripturae invehatur.

DECRETUM X

De Maleficis, Sortilegis, Calumniatoribus, Maledicis, et Concubinariis

§ i. Malefici, si qui vere inveniantur, ad Vicarium Foraneum mittantur et cuculla in signum ignominiae imposita verberentur, et ad triremes damnentur. Sortilegi autem iisdem poenis afficiantur.

§ ii. Quoniam vero in Bisaiis accedere solet, ut ii qui vel levi rumusculo malefici putantur ab oppidis exturbentur aut occidantur, Provincialis Synodus Parochis illarum partium magnopere commendat, ut si quem noverint injuste molestia affici, eum accito auxilio brachii saecularis defendant.

§ iii. Babaylanes autem, seu publicae divinatrices in illis partibus publice cuculla imposita verberentur. Rogat autem Provincialis Magistratus, ut hanc pestem a Christiana Republica extirpent.

§ iv. Si quis per malitiam calumniator extiterit cujusvis sit status et conditionis, talionem subeat. Quoniam vero Indi ad calumniandum Parochis faciles sunt, Episcopi contra animarum Pastores caute excipiant subditorum accusationes. Si quae vero admittantur, contra accusatum non procedatur, donec, data ei defendendi se copia, reus fuerit convictus.

§ v. Quum autem ex Parochorum severitate et punitionibus multi calumniandi occasionem sumant, jubet Provincialis Synodus, ut nullus Parochus sive Saecularis, sive Regularis verberandi aut puniendi assumat auctoritatem, sed si aliquem verberibus dignum repererit moneat Capitaneum, ejusque id curae relinquat. Contrarias quascumque consuetudines etiam immemoriales tollit Provincialis Synodus.

§ vi. Severa sunt digni poenitentia ii, qui vel propriis relictis uxoribus cum aliis turpe exercent commercium aut matrimonio non juncti concubinas habent. Ideo Provincialis Synodus ad tollendum hoc crimen, in his regionibus satis frequens, pro modo culpae eos, qui hoc vitio irretiti inveniantur, post canonicas et charitativas monitiones ad formam Tridentini Concilii excommunicatione etiam, et ignominia afficiendos declarat.

§ vii. Festina natio Indorum ad maledicentiam, et imprecationem quum sit, horum criminum rei arbitrio Episcopi poenis corporalibus aut aliis affligantur. Si quis autem blasphemasse convincatur, durius cum eo agatur.

DECRETUM XI
De Haereticis

§ i. Quum ad has Insulas haeretici, schismatici et Infideles commercii causa confluere soleant, ne inter Catholicos suos inducant errores, et imperitis fucum faciant, Provincialis Synodus rogat Illmum. Gubernatorem ut hujusmodi sectarios aliquod signum gestare cogat, quo a caeteris secernatur. Episcopi autem curent, ut aliquot pii Sacerdotes Armemorum, Sinensium, haereticorumque conversioni insistant.

§ ii. Episcopi, ubi aliqua Haereticorum, aut Infidelium navis appulerit diligenter rescire contendant, an aliquot in ea Catholici Romani adventent ab illisque exigant litteras commendatitias alicujus Ministri Orthodoxi. Si qui vero Catholicum se asserens litteras commendatitias non habet, anathematizet ab Ecclesia damnatas haereses, et juret se esse Catholicum et sub hac cautione Orthodoxus habeatur donec de veritate constet. Si quis hac in re fraudulenter Religionem simulasse reperiatur, ejus bona regio fisco adjudicentur.

§ iii. Parochi, in quorum territoriis hujusmodi exteri Catholici degunt, diligenter inquirant in eorum vitas, an observent Ecclesiae praecepta et cum aliis haereticis in spiritualibus communicent.

§ iv. Sanctiones prohibent Ecclesiasticae, ne quis Haereticus, Schismaticus, Excommunicatus, aut Infidelis ad sacra mysteria admittatur ideoque Provincialis Synodus Ecclesiarum Rectoribus praecipit ut post Evangelii lectionem ab Ecclesia arceant Armenos, aut alios quoscumque Sacratiori Missae assistere interdictos.

DECRETUM XII
De Sententia Excommunicationis

§ i. Excommunicationis gladio, qui ad aedificationem non ad destructionem datus est, non temere, sed magna circumspectione utendum est, ne si frequenter vibretur, in contemptum veniat.

§ ii. Nullus ergo ob levia delicta communione privetur, sed tantum ob gravia, et atrocia crimina, nec id prius quam, vel scelus sit confessus, vel de eo evidentissime convictus. Vicarii Foranei nullum audeant excommunicare inconsulto Episcopo.

DECRETUM XIII
De Abusibus Laicorum

§ i. Solent feminae discooperto capite Ecclesias aliquando ingredi, quod et si in Indis ob paupertatem possit tolerari in Hispanis ferri non potest. Curent ergo Concionatores, et Confessarii hunc abusum extirpare non minus ac excessus qui Balneorum tempore committuntur.

§ ii. Diligenter in detractorum investigatione versentur

Parochi, et quos cum scandalo hoc vitio laborare repererint, ad Judicem Ecclesiasticum transmittant, ut pro modo culpa puniantur. Auctores vero libellorum famosorum, et earum schedularum, quae paschines dicuntur et satyrarum, excommunicentur.

§ iii. Ab Indis usurpatur stapedarum genus, quae Mitrae Episcopalis inversae figuram praeseferunt; qui mos, quum originem trahat a larva illa, quae Angelopoli in contemptum venerabilis Ioannis Palafoxii exhibita fuit, intra mensem, a publicatione hujus Decreti tollatur, cujus observantiam Magistratibus, et Parochis commendat Provincialis Synodus.

§ iv. Sunt alearum, et chartarum ludo adeo indulgentes, etiam inter feminas, ut brevi magna patrimonia dilapident, quorum extirpationem saecularibus Magistratibus vehementer commendet Provincialis Synodus. Parochi autem in aleatores inquirant, et quos cum excessu, aut scandalo hoc morbo laborare invenerint, ab Ecclesiae ingressu prohibeant, et publice e suggestu Sacramentorum indignos pronuncient, quod si non emendantur certiorem faciant Episcopum, aut Judicem Ecclesiasticum.

§ v. Praecipit Provincialis Synodus, ut nullus laicorum, feminis exceptis, cooperto capite Ecclesiam ingrediatur omnesque hortatur, ut summo honore Sacerdotes Dei proequantur non attendentes personas, sed dignitatem. In templis autem modeste se gerant paventes sanctuarium Dei. Ideoque in Ecclesiis, aut in earum janui, et sacristiis, colloquia, nullus misceat, nullus deambulet, sed a Deo, cujus Domus illa est, suorum criminum exoret indulgentiam.

§ vi. Vehementer hortatur Provincialis Synodus omnes utriusque sexus fideles cujusvis status et conditionis sint, ut si quae habeant mancipia baptizata manumittant et libertate donent. Valde enim dedecet non emancipare quos Christus per baptisma a captivitate Daemonis liberavit. Declarat Provincialis Synodus Indos non posse harum Insularum Infidelibus tanquam mancipiis uti, circa quod Parochorum et Magistratuum gravat conscientias. Indi enim hac de causa Infidelium impediunt conversionem.

§ vii. Plures laici, necnon Ecclesiastici plurimi eo temeritatis devenerunt, ut de Religionis dogmatibus sententiam suam ferant. qui quum saepe illiterati sint et parum pii, multa absurda effutiant non sine pusillorum scandalo. Fit inde, ut de auctoritate Romanae Ecclesiae, aut de Episcopali, et Ecclesiastico statu disputantes, quum sibi sapere videantur aliis fucum faciant, et a veneratione Romani Pontificis, et Ecclesiastici status abducant. Tantam temeritatem detestatur Provincialis Synodus et hujusmodi temerariis laicis et Ecclesiasticis excommunicationem minitatur. Theologis vero, et doctis viris inhibet Provincialis Synodus coram lacis de Religionis dogmatibus disputationes movere; et si quos laicos de his rebus tractantes viderint, ut acriter reprehendant hortatur.

§ viii. Ex nationum commercio in superiore bello ebrietates, et comessationes adauctae sunt inter Hispanos, ideoque eos hortatur Provincialis Synodus, ut sobrie et caste viventes Deo non in comessationibus impudicitiis, et ebrietatibus, sed in pietatis operibus serviant.

§ ix. Mos est Indis post mortem charorum convivium funebre agere et defuncti laudes antiquo ritu cantare. In cantibus, Christianae virtutes non celebrantur, sed fortitudo, et aliae dotes corporales. Curent ergo Parochi hunc morem evellere et fideles doceant pro defunctis orare.

§ x. Nulla modestia in feminis Indis observatur quae sine ullo pudore nudo pectore et toto fere corpore, petulanter per vias etiam publicas incedunt. Parochi ergo assidua Praedicatione in modestiam, et christianum pudorem, amorem instillent. Praecipue ad id puellulas scholares hortentur.

DECRETUM XIV
De Regularibus

§ i. Quum ex vitae communis inobservantia Religiones ab antiquo defecerint splendore, Provincialis Synodus Praelatos Regulares hortatur, ut totis viribus eam perfecte inducere conentur, ad quod gravissime eos teneri Apostolicae edicunt sanctiones.

§ ii. Declarat Provincialis Synodus Indos posse et debere

admitti ad Religiones dummodo canonicis impedimentis non sint irretiti, ut Regia statuunt diplomata.

§ iii. Denique Provincialis Synodus Regulares Praelatos hortatur ut constitutionum observantiam promoveant, subditosque a saecularium familiaritate abducant eosque crebris exhortationibus ad perfectionis apicem excitent. Monet etiam Provincialis Synodus ut in Capitulis modeste se gerant, turbas, et seditiones non moveant, circa quod Praelatorium Regularium gravat conscientias.

DECRETUM XV
De Usuris

§ i. Usuram, magnum malum, et satis frequens ignorare vix possunt homines, qui naturali lumine docentur eadem, quae sibi fieri volunt aliis facere. Sed avaritia omnium vitiorum radix, homines excaecat, ne videant lucem et indurat, ne audiant concionatorum verba.

§ ii. Omnes ergo avaritiae quum studeant, ab eo studio revocari non possunt nisi Deus, in cujus manu hominum sunt voluntates, eos mutet in novos homines. Itaque quum Provincialis Synodus huic morbo medendo impar sit omni ex parte, Deum orat ut Spiritum suum bonum super hoc grege efundat; Confessariis vero, Concionatoribus et Magistratibus commendat, ut huic malo quantum ad se spectet, totis viribus obsistant, et fideles doceant, juxta saniores doctrinas, usuras fugere, et misericordiam exercere.

§ iii. Ut autem Mercatores tuta conscientia negotiationem exerceant, et de faenore, et iniquitate non ditescant, tenentur sapientissimorum Theologorum et Jurisperitorum, quos pietas etiam commendet, consilium exquirere, idque diutino examine, et meditatione, purioribus aequitatis regulis, et auctoribus, qui prae caeteris praedicantur, conformetur.

§ iv. Si vero, qui se ab usurarum labe immunes censeri volunt, admonendi sunt ab iis, quorum consilium exposcitur ut contractum instituendum ante declarent, et conditiones inserendas explicent, et quem fructum ex eadem pecunia postulent quod magnopere confert, et ad valorem contractuum in foro externo, et ad scrupulos evitandos.

§ v. Contractus *sanglang bili,* qui ad emptionem et venditionem, cum pacto retrovendendi reducitur, ab usura immunis est, si pretio justo et stabili, rectoque animo fiat, ad quod expedit ut coram populi scriba cum expressione justi et stabilis pretii et sine imminutione libertatis celebretur et ab emptore, et venditore ad majus robur subscribatur.

§ vi. Usuram certe admittunt qui salva semper sorte, et sine periculo maris, quotaquaque hebdomada, vel mensa, assecurato etiam capitali, octavam sortis partem exigunt, qui contractus inter pauperes obtinuit. Sunt etiam qui verum mutuum nomine usurae pupillaris palliantes quinque ex centum quibusque aureis pro commodata exigant pecunia, contra quos tanquam usurarios procedendum est.

§ vii. Relatum est inter Indos alicubi obtinere, ut debitores, qui solvere non possunt in servitium redigantur a creditoribus, ita tamen ut servitium nihil imminuat debitum, quin potius vestis, et cibus si creditore datur, ejus pretium, debito principali accrescat. Qui mos quum barbariem antiquam sapiat, omnino tollatur a saecularibus Magistratibus.

§ viii. In contractu pignoraticio abusus irrepsit, ut hi, qui pignus acceperunt, eo utantur pro libito; ob usum vero nihil detrahitur, quum sors mutuata redditur. Contra hunc abusum frequenter declament Parochi.

§ ix. Monopolii species qua tacite divites mercatores conspirant emere orizam omnem, et omnes fere merces, ut maiori, quam par est foenore eas vendant, hanc Rempublicam in magnas angustias saepe adduxit. Cui pesti mederi cupiens Provincialis Synodus Magistratus saeculares enixe rogat, ut immanes hos societatis hostes gravissime puniant, in eosque inquirant diligentissime, prohibentes hujusmodi monopolia, donec pauperes saltem sibi necessaria possint comparare.

§ x. Sunt qui sine ulla lucri spe mutuantes mille aureos ad sex menses, iis exactis, si eis sese offerat occasio pecuniam negotiationi dare, ea spe, ut ex centum quibusque quindecim aureos lucrentur, pecuniam a mutuatario exigunt; qui quum saepe solvendo, tunc par non sit, novum contractum inire cogitur, quo quindecim aureos per centum quibusque pecuniae domino solvat, quibus lucrum cessans, sine ullo periculo compensatur. Hic contractus ab omnibus usurarius censeatur.

§ xi. In locationibus animalium ad agrorum culturam accidit, ut locatores a locatariis exigant exacto tempore, non modo pretium locationis sed etiam pretium animalis, quod nulla locatorii culpa, sed furto, vel fulmine periit. Hic contractus usurarius censeatur.

§ xii. Ii qui egestatis tempore orizae (quam vendere statuerant) v. g. sex modios commodant ea lege, ut messis tempore commodatarius solvat duodecim, si ad id cogunt mutuatarium, ablata ei libertate solvendi aequivalens pretium oriza aut argento usurarii censeantur.

§ xiii. Injuste agunt, qui contra leges naves occulte pecunia onerant, quod vulgo *embarcar por alto,* dicunt, et ne Regi cujus sumptu navis construitur, et mittitur, sexdecim pro centum quibusque aureos solvant, cum custodibus conveniunt ad invehendas pecunias eis quinque ex centum quibusque aureis offerentes. Idem de his intelligatur, qui occulte merces inducunt, ne regia solvant jura.

§ xiv. Accidit ut quum aliquis, necessitate compulsus ab alio pecuniam exigit, eam pignorata veste assecuret ea lege, ut singulis mensibus mutuatarius mutuanti solvat octavam sortis partem, eique liberum sit pignore uti, quin hac de causa aliquid mutuatae pecuniae detrahatur. Qui contractus satis frequcns usuraria labe infectus est.

§ xv. Aliqui solent pignorantibus praefinire pretium et tempus ad redimendum pignora a se ipsis praevidentes faciendo satia pares, haud fore qui pignora dederunt. Elapso vero statuto tempore pignoratarii medio, aut infimo pretio a pignorantibus emunt pignora. Hic vero contractus est usurarius.

§ xvi. Commodant aliqui pecuniam ea lege, ut certo mense, et die restituatur, statuentes mutuatario poenam conventionalem si statuto tempore non solvit, quae poena eo magis augetur, quo plus differtur solutio, etiam si mutuantes praevideant, aut certo sciant mutuatarium solvendo parem non fore statuto tempore. Hujusmodi contractus tanquam usurarius habeatur.

§ xvii. Sinensibus olim, nunc vero eorum filiis commodare aliqui pecuniam solent, his legibus, ut eam pignore aliquo assecurent et quarto quoque mense mutuanti decimam aut quintam capitalis partem solvant cum obligatione reddendi sortem statim ac mutuans pignus restituat. Qui contractus apertissime usurarius est.

§ xviii. Non desunt qui mutuum dantes mutuatarios cogant sortem solvere oriza, aut aliis rebus, ex quibus aliquam utilitatem praevident nascituram. Alii ob dilatam solutionem carius justo pretio merces suas vendunt. Alii denique in ea sunt opinione ut putent licitum esse lucrari quantum possunt, non quantum debent, unde usurare innumerae nascuntur. Cum iis ergo omnibus tanquam quum usurariis agendum est.

§ xix. Usurarii publici Ecclesiastica careant sepultura, etiam si testamento restitutionem mandaverint, nisi pro eorum facultatibus re ipsa satisfactum sit iis a quibus usuras exegerunt aut iis absentibus, Episcopo, Vicario vel Parocho, in cujus territorio habitarant, vel Notario publico de restitutione cautum sit pignoribus, aut idonea sponsione facta. Parochus, qui his non servatis usurarium sepelierit scienter, excommunicationem incurrit.

§ xx. Si quae contra aliquem usurarium delatio fiat, si publicum delictum non sit, eum adeat Parochus de veritate prius disquisitione facta, eumque ad restitutionem hortetur sine dilatione; si non emendatur coram duobus, aut tribus testibus illum conveniat, et non restituentem ad Vicarium cum summaria transmittat.

§ xxi. Contractus trinus quamvis ab Ecclesia necdum prohibitus uti minus consonans Sixtinae Constitutioni, maxime periculosus est, quapropter Provincialis Synodus hortatur in Domino omnes harum Insularum fideles, ut propriae saluti consulentes ab ejus celebratione abstineant, Scriptura enim dicit: Qui amat periculum, peribit in illo.

DECRETUM XVI
De Decimis

§ i. Lege divina cautum est, ut sacerdotes ex decimis viverent fidelium quod quum in his Insulis hucusque executioni non sit demandatum, Reges Catholici pro sua pietate Ministros Altaris suis stipendiis aluerunt.

§ ii. Sed quum aequum non sit, post duo saecula harum partium fideles tam sancta, et universali lege liberare, et Regium gravare Patrimonium, jubet Provincialis Synodus ut omnes Parochi, Confessarii, et Concionatores crebro fidelibus explicent obligationem solvendi decimas statim ac ab Ecclesia exigantur paratumque ad id animum habere debere.

§ iii. Magistratus vero saeculares eadem Synodus enixe hortatur ut circa decimarum exactionem invehendam maxime invigilent, Regiamque in hoc voluntatem, quae aperta satis est, non obstantibus quibusvis impedimentorum larvis exequentes. Certe Apostolus gentium difficilioribus temporibus fideli populo significare non dubitavit, dignum esse operarium mercede sua, nullumque suis stipendiis militare.

DECRETUM XVII
De Observantia Dictorum

Frustra conduntur leges si earum observantia negligitur. Quapropter Provincialis Synodus vehementer hortatur Episcopos, caeterosque Praelatos ad quos quomodolibet spectet, horum Decretorum observantiam exigere, ut omnibus viribus provideant Decretorum observantiam promovere poenis statutis, aut aliis, prout expediens judicaverint in transgressores; animadvertendo, et falsa impedimenta quae a carnalibus objicientur, parvipendendo.

ACTIO VIa
DE PROMULGANDIS DECRETIS ET FINIENDO CONCILIO

Habita die XXIV. Novembris — Anni MDCCLXXI

DECRETUM I
De Concilii Promulgatione

§ i. Ne legum multitudo et varietas confusionem pariat, declarat Provincialis Synodus Mexicani Concilii observantiam, quae ex decreto Urbani VIII hactenus viguerat, nullo iam modo fideles harum Insularum obligare, eosque unice teneri definit ad nostrorum Decretorum executionem.

§ ii. Ut autem ad omnium, quorum interest notitiam, decreta nostra perveniant, Provincialis Synodus vehementer commendat Episcopis ut statuta laicos spectantia, hispane reddita, aut vulgari lingua quotannis publicari faciant inter Missarum solemnia, ut omnes sciant quid fugere, quidve facere oporteat.

§ iii. Prae oculis etiam habeant Episcopi juxta Regium Tomum ea omnia quae ad disciplinam attinent et Cleri Regularis subjectionem in officio officiando, sine ulla mora executioni demandare, praestentque ut Parochi, et caeteri Ecclesiastici sibi compareant exemplar authenticum nostrae Synodi, quod facile consequentur, si ad Vicarios Foraneos unum transmittant exemplar, ex quo Parochi sui territorii necessaria scribant exemplaria.

§ iv. Quoniam vero Decretis nostris Episcopus Neo-Cacerensis obsistet pro virili, nisi Deus mitiorem instillet animum, et qui concilium veritus nihil est contemnere, eo finito liberius in Episcopos debacchabitur, Provincialis Synodus huic malo occurrere cupiens Rmum. Metropolitam hortatur, ut Concilii nomine, Cacerensis Episcopi conatus retundat, accito etiam auxilio Illmi. Gubernatoris eo modo quo magis in Domino expedire videatur.

DECRETUM II

De Obedientia Erga Regem

Provincialis Synodus Catholico Regi Carolo, cujus Imperio congregata est perpetuas gratias apprecans omnes hortatur Christi fideles ad veram erga tantum Principem ejusque Magistratus obedientiam, cujus leges quum conscientiam ligent ad peccatum etiamsi poenales sint nemo non videt et tanquam Deo obtemperandum esse. Per me enim, inquit Spiritus Sanctus, Reges regnant et legum conditores justa decernunt.

DECRETUM III

De Subjiciendo Concilio Correctioni Ecclesiae

Placetne vobis ut omnia nostra Decreta Sanctae Romanae Ecclesiae correctioni maneant subjecta? RESPONDERUNT: PLACET.

DECRETUM IV

De Fine Concilii

Placetne vobis ad Dei omnipotentis laudem hujus primae Provincialis Manilanae Synodi declarare finem iam fieri et factum iam esse? RESPONDERUNT: PLACET —

Ego Basilius Archiepiscopus Manilanus definiens subscripsi.
Ego Michael Episcopus Novae Segoviae definiens subscripsi.
Ego Clemens Procurator Episcopi Zebuensis definiens subscripsi. —
In veritatis testimonium nomen meum subscripsi —
Doctor Joachimus Traggia a Sancto Dominico, Secrett:—

Nos Infrascripti Concilii Manilani Notarii fidem facimus Decreta Provincialis Manilanae Synodi in Ecclesia Metropolitana lecta, et publicata fuisse, praesentibus Bachalaureis D. Maximo Ignatio, D. Vincenti Flores, Parochis de Manila. D. Juliano Galang, Parocho oppidi Sancti Jacobi extra urbis menia. Manilae die vigesima quarta Novembris anni millesimi septingentesimi septuagesimi primi:

Bs. Nic. Dorotheus Masangcay et Coronel: Concil. Not.
Bs. Josephus Rodrig. Not. Conc.

CHAPTER IV

COMMENTARY ON *ACTIO II, DE EPISCOPIS* OF THE MANILA PROVINCIAL COUNCIL OF 1771

Certainly great and sublime indeed is the dignity of bishops for they are the leaders in the Church, successors of the Apostles, and vicars of Christ Himself.[1]

The Provincial Council of Manila of 1771[2] considered that if they (the bishops) who are placed over the faithful live consistent with their office and regulate their whole conduct accordingly, the faithful may derive therefrom the example of a holy life, and thus a restoration of the ecclesiastical discipline and a reform of morals will easily be accomplished. For this reason the council treated not only of the person of the bishop, of his duties and obligations, but treated also of his house, his furniture, his table and the household personnel immediately about him. Thus *Actio II* contains four titles: on the bishop's house, on the bishop's ministry, on visitation, and on synods. The first title contains three *Decreta*. *Decretum I* with six paragraphs treats of the *familia inferior* of the bishop; *Decretum II* in two paragraphs, of the household and the table of the bishop; and *Decretum III*, of the *familia superior* of the bishop.

TITULUS PRIMUS
DE DOMO EPISCOPI

DECRETUM I
De Episcopi Familia Inferiori

This *Decretum* contains six paragraphs dealing with the following subjects: first, the limitation of the bishop's

[1] *Acta et Decreta Concilii Provinciae Remensis Anno MDCCCXLIX Celebrati* (Lutetiae, Parisiorum, 1850), tit. XIII, cap. I, pp. 96-97.

[2] *Concilium Provinciale Manilanum Celebratum Anno MDCCLXXI sub Illustrissimo et Reverendissimo Archiepiscopo Manilano Basilio Sancho a Santa Justa et Rufina* (6 *Actiones*, unpublished) (hereafter cited as *Manilanum.*)

familia inferior to the necessary personnel and to persons of blameless reputation; second, the bishop's duty to provide for the material needs of them; third, the conduct and behavior of the *familia inferior;* fourth, the bishop's concern with the daily spiritual acts of piety of his *familia inferior;* fifth, the religious instruction, confession and Holy Communion of the *familia inferior;* and sixth, the appointment of a member of the *familia superior* as immediate supervisor of the *familia inferior.*

§ i. The Fathers of the Provincial Council of Manila of 1771, hereafter cited as "the Manila Council," quoted a Scripture passage that states: "A bishop should rule well his own household . . . for if a man cannot rule his own household, how is he to take care of the church of God?"[3] In relation to this, they spoke at some length and decreed that a bishop should take special care, so that to his *familia inferior* there are admitted only as many as are necessary, and only those who possess the testimony of a good life.

From a comparison with *Decretum III* of this *titulus,* which stated that the *familia superior* of a bishop was to be composed of clerics,[4] it is obvious that here the lay *familia* of the bishop was meant. This follows also from the fact that the *familia inferior* was placed under the supervision of one of the members of the *familia superior* (§ vi). Furthermore, it is obvious that the *familia inferior* referred not to the "family" in the common sense of relatives, but to members of his household, the "lower" group, among whom were those who took care of matters not assigned to clerics of the *familia superior.* In other words, they were the bishop's lay servants.[5] It is of course possible that religious

[3] 2 Timothy III: 4-5.

[4] Cf. *infra,* p. 153.

[5] It was common for bishops in the islands to have some servants who lived with the bishop in his residence, or in apartments or quarters within the premises of the bishop's residence. This clearly can be seen from the letter of Fray Miguel, Bishop and Archbishop-elect of Manila, to King Philip III: ". . . a site was set apart for the episcopal residence. The place was very convenient, as it is close to the

of the class of lay brothers were included in the group for many of the bishops in the Philippine Islands at that time belonged to religious Orders.

The number of the *familia inferior* was not to be excessive. In other words, there were to be only as many persons as were needed for the household duties, which, of course, depended upon the size of the bishop's home and the amount of household work to be done.

The testimony of a good life had to be possessed by these persons, otherwise they were not to be admitted or retained by the bishop in his *familia inferior*. Such testimony was to attest their good name or reputation. Of course, the good name required of them was not the equivalent of the good name required of bishops or other public officials. It sufficed if they were known by others to be uncontentious, not given to wine, not disrespectful, not covetous, not arrogant, not blasphemous, nor lovers of pleasure.[6] Needless to say, above all they needed to be good and practicing Catholics.

§§ ii-v. The *familia inferior* had to be provided by the bishop with what was necessary for a decent living. It was a matter of justice that the bishop, the head of his *familia inferior*, provide them with the necessary support or maintenance. He could not be a good ruler if he failed to practice justice in his household. He had to see to it that his *familia inferior* shunned vice and embraced virtue; that they manifested decorum in their attire, in their behavior, and in all their actions,[7] in such a fashion that they could be recognized by others as "the bishop's family." But the *familia inferior* could not achieve such qualities of life if the needed spiritual means were not afforded them in due measure. For that reason the Manila Council decreed that a bishop had to see to it that his *familia inferior* rose at a fixed time in the

church; but it is very cramped . . . there is not room for the prelate to go out in the plazas for his health and recreation to take a little air . . . and who must have apartments for servants. . . ."—Blair and Robertson, *op. cit.*, XII, 124-125.

[6] Conc. Trident., sess. II, *de modo vivendi, etc.*

[7] Conc. Trident., *loc. cit.*

morning and "gave their heart to resort early to the Lord that made them, and prayed in the sight of the most High"[8] in the domestic oratory. After their meditation they were to take part in the Holy Sacrifice of the Mass.[9] In the evening they were to devote some time to meditation and to the recitation of the rosary. Instruction in Christian doctrine was to be given to them once or twice a week by someone assigned by the bishop.[10] Salutary documents like the pastoral letters[11] had also to be explained to them.[12] It was fitting that they receive the sacraments of Penance and Holy Communion frequently, especially on the occasion of the solemn feasts[13] and first Sundays of the month. A pious instruction was to precede the reception of these sacraments, so that greater spiritual fruit might accrue.[14]

§ vi. One of the members of the bishop's *familia superior*[15] was to be appointed by the bishop to exercise supervision

[8] *Ecclesiasticus*, XXXIX: 6.

[9] "Episcopo Missam celebranti vel audienti frequens familia adsit..." Ratti, *Acta Ecclesiae Mediolanensis ab eius initiis usque ad nostram aetatem*, Vol. II (Mediolani, 1890), (Pars I, *Concilia Provincialia*, Pars II, *Synodi Dioecesanae*), Pars I, p. 427 (hereafter cited as *Act. Eccl. Mediol.*); cf. Mansi, XXXIV, 279.

[10] "... Singulis hebdomadis, bis minimum, qui de familia sua sunt rudiores et christinae fidei Doctrina... ab aliquo instituantur cui id curae Episcopus dederit."—*Act. Eccl. Mediol.*, Pars I, p. 426.

[11] Cf. *infra*, p. 158.

[12] Cf *infra*, p. 158; *Act. Eccl Mediol.*, Pars I, p 416; cf. Mansi, XXIV, 278.

[13] The holy days of obligation in the Philippines at that time were the following: all Sundays, Christmas, Epiphany, Ascension, "Corpus Christi," "Candelaria," Annunciation, Assumption, Nativity of our Lady and the feast of Sts. Peter and Paul. Cf. Alonso de Santa Ana, *Explicacion de la Doctrina Christiana en Lengua Tagala* (Manila, 1672).

[14] "Unusquisque de familia singulis mensibus confessus, Sacram Eucharistiam sumat una cum reliquis qui in familia sunt."—*Act. Eccl. Mediol.*, Pars I, p. 426, c. I; cf. Hardouin, *Acta Conciliorum et Epistolae Decretales ac Constitutiones Summorum Pontificum* (12 vols., Parisiis, 1715), X, 664 (hereafter cited as Hardouin); Mansi, XXXIV, 278.

[15] Cf. *infra*, p. 153.

over his *familia inferior* for the purpose of preventing quarrels, idleness, detraction or any unbecoming conversation among them.[16]

Contemporary provincial councils such as the IV of Mexico (1771) and the VI of Lima (1772) did not incorporate any special sections on the *familia inferior*. Nevertheless, some rules on the personnel of the bishop's household may be found there too.[17]

DECRETUM II

De Supellectili et Mensa Episcopi

This *Decretum,* consisting of two paragraphs, treats of the bishop's furnishings and table respectively.

The Manila Council, in reminding the bishops that they were successors of the materially poor apostles and followers of the crucified Lord, Who lived in poverty here on earth, declared that it was not expedient for them to have precious furnishings. [18] The bishops, therefore, were not to have any gold, silver, or very costly personal or household things. In the Islands, it was common for the people to have chairs, tables, closets, bookcases, beds or other household furnishings that were made out of wood. But if this furniture had been ornamented with carvings or some other special decorations, it would have cost very much, and consequently a bishop's possession of it would have militated against the conciliar provision. Some decorations in the house, namely draperies, table cloths, etc., if they were made with special

[16] "Habeant deinde ecclesiasticam personam spectatam et probatam quae praefacta sit moribus familiae ac de omnium salute sollicita . . ." —*Acta Eccl. Mediol.*, Pars I, p. 62; cf. Mansi, XXXIV, 33.

[17] *IV Mexicano*, Lib. III, tit. I, § v, p. 104; Vargas Ugarte, *Concilios Limenses*, II, 77.

[18] Furnishings *(supellex)* in the bishop's residence denoted whatever was destined for use in the residence. Although the domestic oratory was a part of the bishop's residence, as in most cases in the Philippine Islands, nevertheless the furnishings in said oratory were not inclusively contemplated in this decree. The Manila Council would have employed the term "*sacra supellex*" had it meant to treat of the furnishings of the bishop's domestic oratory.

embroidery, could likewise have infringed on the spirit of this provision, for the special embroidery constituted an especial luxury. Pictures in picture frames used to be very common decorations for homes in the Philippine Islands. If the picture frames were made of gold or silver, or with special carvings, their display in the bishop's residence likewise entailed a violation of the decree. Other customary things which would have been at variance with this *Decretum* if in the Philippines they had been kept in the bishop's residence were such things as costly paintings of an elaborate character or of a multi-colored composition, or also a lavish supply of kitchen utensils or of expensive kitchenware. The maintenance of a stable of horses in excess of the number needed for the discharge of the diocesan visitations similarly implied a violation of this *Decretum.*

The Manila Council prohibited the bishops from having *monilia aurea et argentea.* Presumably, the fathers of the council were referring not to the chain of the bishop's pectoral cross, nor to the bishop's ring. But buttons and cufflinks, buckles on shoes, or also a watch, could all be included under the term *monilia.* The Manila Council by way of exception allowed a bishop to possess for his table the ordinary tools or implements when made of gold or silver, or when gold or silver-plated. Tableware, if made of gold or silver, proved to be very expensive, and consequently did not fall within the exception.[19]

The Manila Council declared also that it was not becoming for bishops to have very costly clothes. Silk robes or clothes, extravagantly embroidered surplices, or such as were made of costly cloth, were not allowed. It was also to be noted that for bishops the use of expensive trappings on their horses and of exquisitely tooled saddles, as was

[19] *Manilanum,* Actio III, tit. II, Decretum I, § v; cf. *supra,* p. 85; cf. Mansi, XXXIV, 32; Hardouin, X, 663; "Episcopus vilem supellectilem . . . habeat . . ."—Antonius Augustinus, *Iuris Veteris Doctoris et Iuris Pontificii Veteris Epitome* (3 vols. in 1, Parisiis, 1641), I, 136.

commonly done in the country, was opposed to the spirit of this decree.[20]

The Manila Council called for the observance of frugality in the setting of the bishop's table. The fare was always to be simple and moderate, minus the luxury of delicacies and rare dishes. It was not consistent with his office and dignity as a bishop to be given to expensive or extravagant foods and drinks. It was unbecoming for a bishop to tender or to attend sumptuous banquets, especially with laymen. The Manila Council further stated that bishops were not to overlook the offering of grace before and after meals, and their meals were to be accompanied with a reading of the Bible, or of the writings of the Fathers of the Church on pastoral duties so that the soul would not be without its nourishment while the body was being fed.[21]

Regarding the frugality of the bishop's table in the Philippine Islands, the Manila Council, with reference to the bishop's table on the occasion of his parochial visitations decreed that not more than five courses of food should be served.[22] Although it is true that the above-mentioned provision refers expressly to the maximum number of courses at the bishop's table on the occasion of his episcopal visitation, the writer sees no reason for its non-applicability to the bishop's table when he ate at his residence. In this connection the mandatory frugality for the bishop's table would have demanded that the number of courses of food should not be more than five.

The provision of the Manila Council regarding the bishop's furnishings and table was a reiteration of the provision of the Council of Trent, which stated that cardinals and prelates of the Church must not only have plain furniture but also must maintain a plain table.[23] The IV Provincial Council of Mexico (1771) and the VI Provincial Council of

[20] Actio III, tit. II, Decretum I, § v—*supra*, p. 85; *Act. Eccl. Mediol.*, Pars I, p. 65; cf. Mansi, XXXIV, 32.

[21] Cf. *Act. Eccl. Mediol.*, Pars I, p. 66; cf. Mansi XXXIII, 277-278.

[22] Cf. *infra*, p. 207.

[23] Sess. XXV, *de ref.*, c. 1.

Lima (1772) likewise provided that a bishop be moderate in his house furnishings and preserve sobriety in his table service.[24]

DECRETUM III

De Superiori Familia

This *Decretum* consists of one paragraph. It deals with the membership and the functions of the bishop's *familia superior*.

Unlike the *familia inferior*, which consisted of lay servants, the *familia superior* of the bishop was made up of clerics.

The term *clerici* was used by the Manila Council in several of its decrees with variations in its meaning. In the second paragraph of *Decretum IV, titulus II, Actio II*, the term *clerici* obviously meant priests: "*Episcopi aegrotorum in valetudinariis jacentium . . . paternam curam gerant, providentes, ut aliquot clerici, diebus saltem festis, illorum confessiones excipiant . . .*" Only clerics who were priests could have been told to hear the confessions. In another decree the term *clerici* is used in the sense of a simple cleric without any major orders.[25] Then in another decree, the term *clerici* is employed in the sense of a subdeacon, or of a deacon at most.[26] Another decree seemed to indicate that the members of the *familia superior* of the bishop should comprise at least one or two priests. According to the decree, the bishop was exhorted to engage himself in meditation in common with his *familia superior*. After the meditation he was either to celebrate or to attend Mass.[27] If no one of the *familia superior* had been a priest, then the bishop would

[24] *IV Mexicano*, Lib. III, tit. I, § 13, p. 106; Vargas Ugarte, *op. cit.*, II, 77.

[25] "Provincialis Synodus . . . jubet ut magistri, antequam Cathedras adeant, et clerici priusquam sacris initientur, juramentum praestant . . ." Actio III, tit. I, Decretum II, § v—*supra*, p. 84.

[26] ". . . Provincialis Synodus edicit ne clericus sacris initiatus . . . procuratoris nomine causas agat . . . Actio III, tit. II, Decretum IV, § i —*supra*, p. 87.

[27] "Provincialis Synodus summopere hortatus omnes Episcopos, ut mane surgentes, per horam saltem, cum superiori familia orationi

have been without the choice of attending Mass. The decree referred to no others as present in the domestic oratory than the bishop and his *familia superior.*

According to Blair and Robertson, whenever the term *clerici* referred to priests it always implied secular priests in contradistinction to the regulars or religious of the monastic Orders.[28] This distinction was consistent with the common canonical usage; it also corresponded to the way the Laws of the Indies employed the terms *Clerigo* and *religioso.*[29] But the fathers of the Manila Council also used the terms *clerici saeculares* and *clerici regulares* expressly in many of the council's decrees.[30]

The I Provincial Council of Milan (1565) (on which the Manila Council based most of its provisions about the bishop's family) strongly exhorted the bishop to have in his family at least two clerics, *sacris initiati,* who would be *quasi testes et imitatores actionum et sanctae conversationis Episcopi.* [31]

vacent in Oratorio Domestico, qua finita, vel sacrificium offerant vel missae intersint . . ." Actio II, tit. II, Decretum VI, § i—*supra,* p. 70.

[28] *The Philippine Islands,* L, p. 319, footnote 158.

[29] "Que ningun clerigo, ni religioso pueda venir a estos Reinos sin las licencias que esta ley declara."—*Recopilacion,* Tomo I, Lib. I, Tit. XII, Ley XVI, p. 62; "Que si los clerigos y religiosos quisieren venirse de las Indias . . ." *Ibidem,* Ley XVII, p. 63.

[30] "Seminarii curam ad clericos saeculares . . . declarat Provincialis Synodus et insuper prohibet ne Seminarii regimen ullo tempore, et ulla de causa ad quasdam transeat Regulares . . . Actio III, tit. I, Decretum II, § ix, *supra,* p. 84; "Nullus est sive saecularis sive Regularis, qui sine titulo paroecias possit obtinere . . ."—Actio IV, titulus Unicus, Decretum XIV, § i, *supra,* p. 106; "Quum Episcopi idem valeant a parochis Regularibus exigere quod a saecularibus . . ."—*ibidem,* § ii, *supra,* p. 106; "Declarat . . . Regulares ex charitate . . . donec Episcopi non habent clericos saeculares . . ."—*ibidem,* § iii, *supra,* p. 106; "Declarat denique Provincialis Synodus Parochos Regulares quantum ad sacramentorum Paroeciarum . . . obligari ad executionem eorum omnium quae in hac Synodo circa saeculares parochos . . ." *ibidem,* § iv, *supra,* p. 106; "Utile admodum esset . . . ut Episcopi quandoque aliquot Missionarios saeculares vel Regulares . . ."—Actio IV, titulus Unicus, Decretum VIII, § ix—*supra,* p. 101.

[31] *Act. Eccl. Mediol.,* Pars I, p. 67.

The writer, however, believes that on account of the delicate functions entrusted to the *familia superior* of the bishop, namely, to be the *custos et testis vitae episcopalis,* this *familia superior* had to comprise elderly priests with a good reputation, a wide experience and a solid learning. Of course clerics, *sacris initiati,* could also be members of the *familia superior.* They could very well supervise the *familia inferior.*[32]

TITULUS SECUNDUS
DE MINISTERIO EPISCOPI

Without doubt the dignity of bishops is great and sublime, and accordingly their responsibilities are manifold and onerous.[33] Principal among the duties are sacred preaching, vigilance, care of the poor and the distressed, the safeguarding of christian doctrine, and devotedness to prayer. The second title of *Actio II* of the Manila Council dealt with all of these, setting down some decrees wherewith to urge a more competent fulfillment of them.

DECRETUM I
De Sacra Praedicatione

There are three paragraphs in this *Decretum.* The first dealt with the personal obligation of the bishop to preach when that was feasible. The second treated on the bishop's Pastoral Letters to the faithful. The third treated of the bishop's Pastoral Letters to the pastors, confessors and preachers.

Among other things that pertain to the salvation of the christian people, the word of God is above all necessary, because as the body is nourished by material food, so is the soul nourished by spiritual food,[34] since "not in bread alone

[32] Cf. *supra,* p. 149.

[33] *Acta et Decreta Concilii Provinciae Remensis Anno MDCCCXLIX Celebrati* (Lutetiae, Parisiorum, 1850), tit. XIII, cap. II, p. 97.

[34] IV Lateran (1215) canon 10. Cf. H. J. Schroeder, *Disciplinary Decrees of the General Council's Text, Translation and Commentary*

doth man live, but in every word that proceedeth from the mouth of God."[35]

The obligation to preach was imposed upon a bishop when, during his episcopal consecration, the following words were addressed to him: "Receive the Holy Gospel, go and preach to the faithful entrusted to you."[36]

Preaching is a principal duty of a bishop.[37] It is a function recognized in the Church from the earliest ages as the personal obligation of bishops.[38]

§ i. The Manila Council when reiterating the declaration of the Council of Trent regarding the bishop's personal and principal duty of preaching the word of God,[39] decreed that bishops should preach personally when it was feasible *(ubi id licuerit)*, especially during Lent, Advent, and on the more solemn feasts. It should here be noted that the Manila Council did not add the clause, *"si legitime impediti fuerint,"* as the Council of Trent had done and as the contemporary provincial councils did regarding this duty of the bishops.[40] It used instead the clause, *"ubi id licuerit"* which differed greatly from the clause, *"si legitime impediti fuerint."*

Regarding the meaning or interpretation of the clause "if they be legitimately hindered," the Provincial Council of

(St. Louis: Herder Book Co., 1937), p. 251 (hereafter cited as *Disciplinary Decrees*).

[35] Matthew, IV: 4.

[36] *Pontificale Romanum Summorum Pontificum iussu editum, a Benedicto XIV et a Leone XIII Pontificibus Maximis recognitum et castigatum* (Mechliniae, 1895), Pars I, p. 109 (hereafter cited as *Pont. Rom.*); Lucius Ferraris, *Bibliotheca Canonica, Juridica, Moralis, Theologica, necnon Ascetica, Polemica, Rubricistica, Historica* (editio novissima, 9 vols., Romae, 1885-1899), s.v. *Praedicare*, n. 1 (hereafter cited as Ferraris).

[37] J. Turrecremata, *Gratiani Decretorum Libri Quinque* (2 vols., Romae, 1726), I, c. XI, p. 111 (hereafter cited as Turrecremata); Ferraris, s.v. *Praedicare*, n. 2.

[38] IV Lateran, c. 10; Wernz, *Ius Decretalium*, III, n. 34; Conc. Trident., sess. V, *de ref.*, c. 2.

[39] Sess. V, *de ref.*, c. 2; sess. XXIV, *de ref.*, c. 4.

[40] Sess. V, *de ref.*, c. 2; sess. XXIV, *de ref.*, c. 4; *IV Mexicano*, Lib. III, tit. I, § 6, p. 105; Vargas Ugarte, *op. cit.*, II, 19-20.

Toledo (1565) had stated that only an urgent necessity with resultant harm, spiritual or corporal, to the public or the private welfare of the bishop could constitute a lawful hindrance.[41] Canon 10 of the IV General Council of the Lateran (1215) had declared that one could be lawfully hindered by his manifold duties, bodily infirmities, hostile invasion, and the like. The Manila Council also declared that by a *legitima causa* was to be understood whatever confined one to bed or necessitated a preoccupation with some important business.[42]

The clause, "when it is feasible," simply means "when it is possible or practicable, or when the matter can be dealt with successfully." A bishop, therefore, might not have been legitimately impeded from preaching personally, but inasmuch as preaching was not possible or practicable he could nevertheless have been excused from it. Thus the Manila Council used the clause, *"ubi id licuerit"*—when it is feasible—for a reason very peculiar to the Philippine Islands. This reason was the diversity of the extant dialects. At that time there was no national language in the Philippines. Among the very many dialects, the principal ones spoken were Tagalog, Visayan, Iloko, Bicol, Pongasinan, Ibanag (Kagayan) and Zambal.[43] The whole Philippine Archipelago, consisting of more than seven thousand islands and islets,[44] formed only one ecclesiastical province at that time.[45] On account of the difficulty of the means of communication, people of one dialect could not be understood by others. Even in one and the same diocese the people using one dialect could not be understood by the people using another. For instance, in the Archdiocese of Manila some

[41] Act. II, 2—Hardouin, X, 1148.

[42] Cf. *infra*, p. 233.

[43] Zaide, *Phil. Pol. Cult. Hist.*, I, 71; Dean Worcester, *The Philippines, Past and Present* (2 vols. in 1, New York, 1921), p. 934.

[44] Eufronio Alip, *Political and Cultural History of the Philippines* (2 vols., Manila, Philippines: Alip and Briones Publication, 1949), I, 5 (hereafter cited as *Pol. Cult. Hist. Phil.*)

[45] Cf. *supra*, p. 33.

of the dialects spoken were Tagalog, Pangasinan, Zambal, Pampango, etc. In the diocese of Nueva Segovia some of the dialects spoken were Iloko, Ibanag, Kagayan, etc., . . . Accordingly, when the audience consisted of people of different dialects, the bishop's preaching even in one of the dialects of the people who attended did not prove feasible. But on the occasion of a parochial visitation, with most of the people speaking the same dialect, the bishop's preaching in the dialect of the people proved readily feasible indeed.

§ ii. On account of the variety and the confusion of the dialects, the bishops could not oftentimes undertake the duty of sacred preaching. In order to meet this difficulty, the Manila Council advised the bishops to issue pastoral letters for the faithful at least three times a year. The doctrine contained in these pastoral letters was to be within the intellectual reach of the people and in response to their actual need. Over and above this, the pastoral letters were to be translated into the native dialect by persons who were well versed in the dialect of the people to whom the pastoral letters had been directed. For the translation of his pastoral letters, the bishop certainly stood in need of experts in the different dialects spoken by the people under his jurisdiction. Through these letters, the bishops were to nourish their flock with wholesome doctrine, teaching them "not in the persuasive words of human wisdom, but in the showing of the Spirit,"[46] how to enter "that narrow way which leads to life."[47]

§ iii. The Council of Trent placed in the hands of bishops the thunderbolt of ecclesiastical censures to be imprecated on those mute priests[48] whom the Spirit of God stigmatizes as "dumb dogs not able to bark."[49] In this connection the Manila Council prescribed that bishops were to issue pastoral letters also for the pastors, confessors and preachers, with the aim of admonishing them to preach the sound doc-

[46] I Cor., II: 4.
[47] Matthew, VII: 14.
[48] Sess. V, *de ref.*, c. 2.
[49] Isaias, LVI: 10.

trine of God to his people, at the same time impressing upon them a passage of the Scripture that states: "How narrow is the gate and strait is the way that leads to life, and few there are who go in thereat."[50]

In passing one should mention that pastors especially, and also confessors, preachers, and missionaries in the Philippines, could feasibly undertake the close study of the dialects for the purpose of sacred preaching, since according to the Laws of the Indies no priest at that time could be given the *"cura animarum"* or be assigned as missionaries and preachers if they did not at least substantially know the dialect of the people under their care.[51]

DECRETUM II

De Vigilantia

This *Decretum* has two paragraphs. The first concerns the exhortation to bishops to watch assiduously the flock entrusted to their care. The second deals with the bishop's registers.

§ i. Referring to a Scripture passage that states, "I am the good shepherd and I know mine and mine know me. . . . I lay down my life for my sheep,"[52] the Manila Council urged the bishops to exercise a close vigilance over their flocks in order that they might know them better, and that in consequence of this better knowledge they might afford them the necessary nourishment and protection, and ultimately bring back to the fold also such members as had gone astray.

The provision of the preceding paragraph seems nothing more than a forceful reminder to bishops regarding their sublime duty of watching dutifully over their faithful. The purpose of the vigilance was simply that the bishops might know their people, protect them from spiritual danger, and

[50] Matthew, VII: 14.

[51] *Recopilacion,* Tomo I, Lib. I, Tit. XV, Ley V, p. 89; Lib. I, Tit. XIII, Ley IV, p. 65.

[52] John, X: 14-15.

bring back again to a good observance those who had lapsed.

§ ii. In order that bishops might know their flock better, the Manila Council prescribed that they keep two registers (memorandum books). In the first register the names of all the ecclesiastics of the diocese were to be recorded, with the corresponding age of each and with notes relative to their family, their academic attainment, their capability, their character, their manners, their office and their title of ordination. In the other register, the names of publicly known sinners were to be kept upon information received from the vicars forane, so that admonition and correction could be given them if necessary.

The first register (memorandum book) obviously was to contain the record of the ecclesiastics of the diocese. The decree expressly stated that among the items to be entered in the register were the names of the ecclesiastics of the diocese and mention of their title of ordination. But the second register, even though it too seemed to refer to the ecclesiastics, nevertheless could be interpreted as applying to both the clerics and also the faithful in general. The reason for this is that, if this second register had really been meant by the Council for the clerics only, then it would have seemed to be concerned with the bishop's vigilance over the clergy alone, and not over the faithful. But this could not be so, for the decree referred to the bishops as the pastors of the flock. The Christian "flock" comprised not only the clergy but also the faithful; the vigilance of the bishop was to extend over the entire flock.

This decree of the Manila Council in its prescription that the bishops keep the two registers (memorandum books) evinces another peculiar requirement. Presumably the fathers of this Council based it upon a certain provision of the III Provincial Council of Mexico (1585) which, similarly had prescribed two registers or books to be kept by the bishops. The first book was to contain a description of all the parochial churches and some annotations about the pastors, records and vicars in the diocese. The second was to contain a record of the visitations personally made by the bishops, and also of those made by visitors whom the bishops had deputed in their place.[53]

The Manila Council prescribed also an additional register of the clergy in which the names of the clerics of the city of Manila were to be recorded. The register was to be kept by the Pastor of *Sta. Cruz,* Manila.[54]

Two separate registers were to be used for the calends clerical meetings. One contained the minutes of the calends, and the other contained the report made by the public witnesses before the vicar forane and a notary.[55] The vicars forane informed their bishops about the result of the calends. The registers recorded the status of the parochial churches, the pastors, the clerics, and the faithful, according to the report of the public witnesses.[56] Vicars forane could thus furnish an accurate report to the bishop. Of course not all that was contained in the registers of the calends was to be copied in the registers kept by the bishop. There was no need of this for it was within the bishop's right to demand the registers for inspection. The register of the bishop was to list the *"nomina peccatorum,"* namely, the persons who had committed very serious and notorious offenses, the contumacious sinners who had been denounced publicly during the calends, and the delinquent priests whose offenses were very grievous and scandalous. The proper person to administer the necessary corrective measures and punishment to these persons was their own Ordinary, and not the vicar forane.[57] Although the vicars forane were to serve as the ordinary source of information regarding the names of sinners to be recorded in the register containing the *"nomina peccatorum"* (§ ii), nevertheless, the bishop could use other sources of information about his clerics and the faithful, v. gr., priests or laymen on the occasion of the

[53] *III Mexicanum,* Lib. III, tit. I, § xiv, p. 147.

[54] Cf. *infra,* p. 235.

[55] Cf. *infra,* p. 233.

[56] Cf. *infra,* pp. 228 ff.

[57] Cf. *infra,* p. 231.

parochial visitation,[58] or also on other occasions. With these registers the bishops were enabled not only to ascertain who had been led astray but also to provide the necessary vigilance over the rest of the faithful entrusted to their care.

DECRETUM III

De Cura Pauperum

This *Decretum* contains four paragraphs and deals with the following items: (1) the bishop's care of the poor; (2) the bishop's care of the beggars through a cleric of the seminary; (3) precautions against feigned beggars, and the spiritual care for true beggars; (4) petition to the Governor of the Islands regarding the establishment of a workhouse for the poor.

§ i. The Manila Council bitterly complained that "covetousness, which is a form of idol-worship,"[59] tyrannized over the faithful of the Philippines in such a manner that even the beggars themselves sought to practice usury with the alms they received. The Council, therefore, strongly reminded the bishops[60] to take care, with the help of the civil authority if necessary, that those who were truly poor[61] should not be commingled with those who pretended to be such.

[58] Cf. *infra*, pp. 192 ff.; 197 ff.

[59] Coloss., III: 5.

[60] In this *Decretum* the term *Metropolitanos* was used. Presumably this was a mistake on the part of the person who made the manuscript, for there was only one Metropolitan at that time, namely, the Archbishop Basilio Sancho de Santa Justa y Rufina. If the Council meant the Metropolitan, it surely would have stated *Metropolitanum* (singular) and not *Metropolitanos* (plural). Apart from this reason, there were other bishops concerned with beggars in their respective dioceses, which beggars were in the same condition as the beggars of the Metropolitan See. Consequently the Council would not have used the term *Metropolitanos* or *Metropolitanum*, but *Episcopos* or *Ordinarios*.

[61] "Pauper est qui de praesenti nihil habet unde vivat, et suis manibus laborare non potest . . ." Reiffenstuel, *Jus Canonicum Universum* (5 vols. in 7, Parisiis, 1864-1870), Appendix ad Lib. IV, § viii, nn. 372 and 379.

Without transgressing the boundaries of charity and respect for the dignity of man, the New Testament demands discretion in the giving of alms and condemns professional begging.[62] The Manila Council was very particular in its demand for the verification of those who were truly poor. For seeking out the truly poor from "professional" beggars (who very well could have found work) the bishops could employ the help of the civil authority. Therefore the provisions for aid to the poor were combined with police measures.

A special abuse received mention in the decree, namely, the usury which the beggars practiced by lending out on interest the alms they had received. At that time usury was common among the natives. They declined to lend succor even in cases of need unless they had some assurance of profit.[63] The natives were cooperative only when they feared punishment.[64] Consequently, in the face of intervention from the civil authorities, the usurers were thoroughly afraid to beg. Those who were just pretending to be beggars readily quit plying their devious trade for fear of the civil punishment that threatened them.

§§ ii-iii. An elderly priest[65] from the seminary who was of good standing had to be assigned by the bishop to supervise the poor and to extend to them the needed spiritual care. No one was to be allowed to beg from door to door without first giving his name to this priest. It was this priest's duty to investigate diligently from what place the poor came and whether they had any permanent residence.

[62] I Thess., IV: 11; I Tim., V: 13 ff.

[63] Pedro Chirino, S.J., *Relacion de las Islas Philipinas* (Roma, 1604), cap. XXXVI, p. 103. For the different kinds of usury practiced in the Islands at that time, cf. *Manilanum*, Actio V, tit. II, Decretum XV, *De Usuris—supra*, pp. 139 ff.

[64] Blair and Robertson, *The Philippine Islands*, XLVIII, 199.

[65] The term *aliquem clericorum*, i.e., *clericum* as used in this decree obviously means a priest, since the final clause of this paragraph, *nisi prius nomen suum designato dederit*, implicitly equates the term *sacerdoti* with the expression *aliquem clericorum*. For a commentary on the term *clerici*, cf. *supra*, pp. 153 ff.

If they were found to be vagabonds, they were not to be allowed to beg. The physical condition of their life had also to be investigated. For if they were physically fit to work, they could not be allowed to beg. But over and above this duty, the priest had to extend spiritual care and help to the poor. He had to see to it that they attended the catechetical instructions conducted by him at a certain hour on holy days of obligation, and that they satisfied their obligation of annual confession and Communion.

§ iv. The Manila Council further prescribed that the Governor of the Islands be requested to have a workhouse (training school) constructed in which the poor could be taught and trained to work according to their capacity. By devoting themselves to work instead of begging the inmates of such an institution could be rendering service to the nation. And once trained and accustomed to work, the poor could learn to avoid laziness, which is the root of many evils. They could certainly be made to be useful citizens in the nation.

The provision of the Manila Council regarding the bishop's fatherly care of the poor was a reiteration of that of the Council of Trent, which made it mandatory for bishops to exercise a paternal care over the poor.[66]

The Councils both of Mexico (1771) and of Lima (1772) decreed provisions similar to that of Manila regarding the bishop's care for and help of the poor.[67]

DECRETUM IV

De Cura Aliorum Miserorum

The two paragraphs contained in this *Decretum* treated of the bishop's care of unfortunate people either in person or through others.

§ i. Other people in whose behalf the bishop's paternal care had to be exercised were such unfortunate persons

[66] Sess. XXIII, *de ref.*, c. 1; sess. VIII, *de ref.*, c. 15.

[67] *IV Mexicano*, Lib. III, tit. I, § iv, p. 104; Vargas Ugarte *op. cit.*, II, 78.

(miserabiles personae) who had nothing to live on.[68] The term *miserabiles personae* generally pointed to persons whose very condition compelled a natural expression of compassion, such as orphans, widows, the sick and other unfortunates.[69]

Among the unfortunate persons expressly mentioned by the Manila Council were widows, the sick, prisoners and orphan girls. It did, however, include all other *personae miserabiles* with the phrase *"aliis personis miseris."* The fathers of the Manila Council in specifying the class of widows contemplated by them used the language of Scripture, *"vere viduae et desolatae."*[70] Accordingly, the bishops were to see to it that help would be extended to those who indeed were widows and bereft of all help. "But if a widow has children or grandchildren, let these first learn to provide for their own household and make some return to their parents, for this is pleasing to God."[71]

Unfortunate widows of honorable character especially when they were burdened with many children and weighed down with heavy obligations, were also to be aided.[72]

The Council further declared in this decree that idle and lazy persons, like cesspools of all evils, were to be subjected to due constraint. Idleness was a common vice among many natives at that time.[73] Indeed, "idleness hath taught many much evil!"[74]

[68] Joannes de Solorzano Pereira, *De Indiarum Iure* (2 vols., Lugduni, 1672) II, p. 272, n. 64; *Concilium Provinciale Toletanum* (1566), ad XIII, Hardouin, X, 1151.

[69] "Per miserabiles personas generatim loquendo intelliguntur illae super quibus natura movetur ad miserandum uti sunt pupilli, viduae, diuturno morbo fatigati, debiles, aliique fortunae injuria miserabiles." Reiffenstuel, *Appendix ad Lib. IV,* § viii, n. 375.

[70] I Tim., V: 5.

[71] Ibidem, 4.

[72] Solorzano, *op. cit.*, II, p. 272, n. 64.

[73] "... They (the natives) are idle, improvident and extravagant; they might be rich if they would labor even moderately ..." Blair and Robertson, *op. cit.*, XLVIII, 21.

[74] Eccles., XXXIII: 29.

The bishop's paternal care over the unfortunate was to be exercised personally. The bishop could of course be preoccupied with other important matters of the diocese. As a result it could become impossible for him to extend this care himself. He then had to see to it that his paternal care went out to the unfortunates through some good and practical Catholic laymen of means or through some Catholic institutions or organizations in form of food and clothes.[75]

§ ii. The bishops had to make provision for priests[76] to attend to the spiritual needs of the sick confined in convalescent homes[77] and of the prisoners, to the hearing of their confessions, and to the imparting of catechetical instruction at least on feast days. To the orphan girls in the *colegios*[78] the bishop's care was likewise to be extended. In this connection the bishop had carefully attended to it that no cleric went unaccompanied to these institutions for girls. Even the bishops were warned by the Council not to go to the *colegios* and *beaterios*[79] of women without the company of a number of clerics.[80]

This provision of the Manila Council should not be cause for any *admiratio populi.* It is a substantial repetition of a decree of the III Council of Carthage (397).[81]

[75] For orphanages and charitable institutions in Manila, cf. *infra,* pp. 214 ff.

[76] The term *clericus* was used here. The Council obviously thought of a priest, for in the same sentence of the decree it was stated that this *clericus* was to hear confessions, etc. For a detailed commentary on the use of the term *clericus,* cf. *supra,* pp. 153 ff.

[77] The Council did not mention the sick in the hospitals. Presumably the reason was that the hospitals in the Philippines had been founded by the religious Orders and thus were duly cared for. Cf. Gregorio Zaide, *Catholicism in the Philippines* (Manila: Sto. Tomas University Press, 1937), p. 104 (hereafter cited as *Cath. in Phil.*).

[78] Cf. *infra,* pp. 215-216.

[79] Cf. *infra,* pp. 214 ff.

[80] Cf. *infra,* pp. 215-216.

[81] C.XXV: V clerici, vel continentes ad viduas vel virgines, nisi jussu vel permissu episcoporum aut presbyterorum non accedant, et hoc non soli faciant, sed cum clericis vel cum iis cum quibus episcopus jusserit vel presbyter, nec ipsi episcopi aut presbyteri soli habeant

In relation to the purpose of the Manila Council regarding the bishop's paternal care over the poor and other unfortunate people, one may fittingly quote the following:

> The object of ecclesiastical provision for the poor is first the removal of their immediate need, then the nullification of the demoralizing effects of poverty, encouragement, the fostering of a desire for work and independence, and thus the exercise of an educative influence on the soul: "the care of souls is the soul of the care of the poor." There is in addition the social object of promoting the public welfare and of procuring for the greatest possible number of persons a share in the goods of material and intellectual civilization. From this object arise the general duties of ecclesiastical relief of the poor: to prevent those able to earn their living from falling into poverty, to assist with alms the sick and the poor, to raise the religious and moral condition of the poor, and to render social life a blessing for needy mankind . . .[82]

DECRETUM V

De Cura Doctrinae

In regard to the teaching of Christian doctrine, the Council of Manila forbade both secular and religious pastors to use any catechism other than those edited or approved by the Council. This prohibition was to bind under pain of a major excommunication imposed by anticipatory sentence *(latae sententiae)* and reserved to bishops, and also under pain of the privation of office and benefice (§ i). The Council advocated the use of two catechisms, an elementary one with a substantial explanation of the truths necessary for salvation, and a more advanced one with a more detailed presentation of the Catholic doctrine (§ ii). It also encouraged the faithful to advance beyond the catechism to a pro-

accessum ad hujusmodi feminas, nisi aut clerici presentes sint aut graves aliqui christiani." Bruns I, 126.

82 "Poor," *The Catholic Encyclopedia* (15 vols., Index and Supplements, New York: Robert Appleton Co., 1907-1922), XII, 236 (hereafter cited as *CE*).

founder knowledge of their religion, provided that this knowledge was sought from approved sources (§ iii).

The Manila Council did not specify in this decree (§ i) whether the catechisms which were to be used in the Islands were to be patterned after or based on the Catechism of the Council of Trent, called the *Catechismus Romanus.*[83] This catechism was not specified in *Decretum IV,* § i, of *Actio IV,* which prescribed the use of a *brevis catechismus a concilio edendus vulgari lingua,* nor in *Decretum V,* § iii, of the same *Actio,* which mentioned a *doctrina christiana hispana et vernacula lingua juxta brevem catechismum a concilio edendum.* Presumably the fathers of the council in using the expression *brevis catechismus* had in mind the abridged catechism conscientiously extracted from the Roman Catechism *(catecismo abreviado escrupolosamente extractado del Catecismo Romano),* as mentioned in the *Real Cedula* or *Tomo Regio* of King Charles III. It had been issued in 1769.[84]

It must be remembered that it was King Charles III of Spain who issued the *Tomo Regio* and ordered the Archbishops of the Indies and of the Philippines to hold a provincial council without delay. It was he who charged the Archbishops to propose, discuss, and decide during the council matters pertaining to discipline, but principally the twenty points he set forth in the *Tomo Regio.* Regarding the proposed abridged Roman Catechism mentioned in point V of the *Tomo Regio,* it was perfectly right and practical for the use of the natives. It was in harmony with the provisions of the Council of Trent and with the various pronouncements of the Holy See.[85] Therefore there could not have

[83] Sess. XXV, de ref. in fine sess. *De Indice Librorum et Catechismi* etc.

[84] "V. *Que se arregle, teniendo presente el catecismo romano, llamado del concilio, un catecismo abreviado, escrupolosamente estractado del romano . . .*" Vargas Ugarte, *op. cit.,* II, 208.

[85] Sess. XXII, *De Sacrificio Missae,* c. 8; sess. XXIV, *de ref.,* c. 7 and 4; sess. XV, *continuatio Sess. De Indice Librorum et catechismi*

been any reason for the fathers of this Council not to decree the use of an abridged Roman catechism for which provision had been made in the king's *Tomo Regio*. Consequently, the term *Brevis Catechismus,* as mentioned in some of the decrees of this Council, referred to the abridged Roman catechism *(abreviado catecismo Romano)*. Presumably, too, the fathers of this Council used the phrase *brevis catechismus* without adding the phrase *extractado del catecismo Romano,* as it was employed in the above-mentioned *Tomo Regio,* so that, in making mention during this Council of the *Catechismus Romanus* itself, they did not have to make any explanation in respect of the original or the non-abridged *Catechismus Romanus.* In fact, the fathers of the Council, in one of the decrees, mentioned the *Catechismus Romanus,*[86] and not the abridged one. Similar to the Manila Council's decree on the catechism, the IV Provincial Council of Mexico (1771) had its own catechism for use in the whole ecclesiastical province of Mexico. This did not mean that the use of the *Catechismus Romanus* was excluded.[87] The VI Provincial Council of Lima (1772) advocated a catechism called *"Catecismo Mayor,"* in the form of questions and answers, which contained the doctrine and order according to the *Catechismus Romanus.* This served for the advanced class. The other catechism of the VI Provincial Council of Lima was the one which was printed in a brief and concise form for the use of the children and the unlettered.[88]

But long before the holding of this council there were several catechisms in use. They were written in various

etc.; Pius V, const. *Ex debito pastoralis officii,* 6 oct. 1571—*Fontes,* n. 141; Clemens VIII, const. *Pastoralis,* 15 iul, 1598—*Coll. Lac.,* I, 401; Benedictus XIV, const. *Etsi minime,* 7 febr. 1742—*Fontes,* n. 324; Clemens XIII, const. *In Dominico agro,* 14 iun. 1761, Cf. *Coll. Lac.,* III, 435 c; 378 c.

86 "Unaquaeque Ecclesia libros proprios habeat... Catechismum Romanum..." Actio V, tit. II, Decretum VIII, § vi—*supra,* p. 134.

87 Cf. *IV Mexicano,* Lib. I, tit. I, § i, p. 3.

88 Cf. Vargas Ugarte, *op. cit.,* II, 19.

native dialects to facilitate a learning of the Christian doctrine by the natives.[89]

In 1593 two catechisms were printed in Manila, one in Spanish and Tagalog,[90] the other in Spanish and Chinese.[91] Bearing the common title *Doctrina Christiana,*[92] these books proved invaluable as aids to the Spanish missionaries. Both were prefaced with a listing of the more common prayers, the Commandments, the Sacraments, the Works of Mercy and the Capital Sins. The catechism proper contained forty questions and answers concerning the fundamentals of the Faith. To this the Chinese version appended an explanation of the Mysteries of the Rosary and a list of the holy days and days of fast and abstinence, along with a small treatise on death.

In addition to these catechisms, several others were printed in the Philippines prior to the Council of Manila. A translation of the catechism of Cardinal Bellarmine was written in the Bisayan dialect by Fr. Cristobal Jimenez, and published in 1610 for the Bisayan-speaking people. The title of the catechism was the *Doctrina Christiana de Belarmino en lengua Bisaya.*[93] In 1621 a translation of Cardinal Bellar-

[89] Sess. XXIV, *de ref.*, c. 7.

[90] The native language of Manila and the middle region of Luzon. It belongs to the Malaya-Polynesian language group. Cf. Frank R. Blake, *A Grammar of the Tagalog Language* (New Haven, 1925) p. 1.

[91] This was printed for the convenience of the Sangleyes, a segment of the Chinese population. A version of the origin of the term Sangley (plural Sangleyes) was that, when the Spaniards asked the Chinese merchants in Manila who they were and what they wanted, they replied, "xang lai" i. e. "we come to trade." The Spaniards, not knowing the Chinese language, mistook the words to mean the name of a country: thus they combined the two words and called all Chinese *Xanglais* or *Sangleyes*. Cf. Zaide, *op. cit.*, I, pp. 270-271.

[92] *Doctrina Christiana. The First Book Printed in the Philippines, Manila, 1593.* A Facsimile of the copy in the Lessing J. Rosenwald Collection, Library of Congress, Washington, with an Introductory Essay by Edwin Wolf 2nd: (Philadelphia, Stern & Co., 1947).

[93] Trinidad Pardo de Tavera, *Biblioteca Filipina* (Washington, 1903), p. 217; Retana, *Origines de la Imprenta Filipina* (Madrid, 1901) p. 87 (as found in Zaide, *op. cit.*, p. 100).

mine's catechism appeared in the Ilocano dialect for the inhabitants of the Ilocos region.[94] For the benefit of the Pampango speaking people, a book entitled "*Catecismo y Doctrina Cristiana en Lengua Pampanga*" was published by Fray Francisco Coronel, in 1621.[95] Another catechism in Tagalog by Fray Alonso de Sta. Ana was written in 1628, entitled *Explicacion de la Doctrina Cristiana en Lengua Tagala.*[96] In 1645 the *Explicacion del Catecismo*, written by Dr. Francisco de San Jose, A. R., was printed in Manila.[97] For the Bikol region there was published the *Explicacion de la Doctrina Christiana* in the Bikol dialect.[98] In 1708, Fray Domingo Martinez wrote the *Doctrina Cristiana en Idioma Bikol.*[99] The *Catecismo del Cardinal Belarmino en Idioma Pampango* was composed by Fray Juan de Medrano in 1717.[100] In 1740 a catechism in Tagalog-Spanish, written by Fr. Tomas Ortiz, was published.[101]

But before the above-mentioned catechisms were published or used, they were certainly subjected to an examination by the bishop as a safeguard against differences and

[94] The translation was made by Fr. Francisco Lopez, O.S.A. Cf. Pardo de Tavera, *op. cit.*, p. 238; Leopoldo Yabes, *A Brief Survey of Iloko Literature* (Manila, 1936), p. 18 (as found in Zaide, *op. cit.*, p. 109).

[95] Encarnacion Alzona, *A History of Education in the Philippines 1565–1930* (Manila, 1932), p. 33 (hereafter cited as *Hist. Edu. in Phil.*).

[96] Alzona, *op. cit.*, p. 39.

[97] Francisco Sadaba, A.R., *Catalogo de los Religiosos Agustinos Recoletos de la Provincia de San Nicolas de Tolentino de Filipinas* (Madrid, 1906), p. 93 (as found in Zaide, *op. cit.*, p. 110).

[98] Written in 1647 by Fr. Andres de San Agustin, O.S.F. Cf. Fr. Marin y Morales Valentin, O.P., *Ensayo de una Sintesis de los Trabajos Realizados por las Corporaciones Religiosas Españolas* (2 vols., Manila, 1901), II, 515 (as found in Zaide, *op. cit.*, p. 110).

[99] Alzona, *op. cit.*, p. 40.

[100] Alzona, *op. cit.*, p. 40.

[101] Jose Toribio Medina, *La Imprenta en Manila* (Santiago de Chile, 1904), pp. 80-81; Catechisms in various dialects as written by different authors during the 18th century are mentioned in this book on pages 12, 21, 49, 53, 61, 63, 83 and 112.

disagreements in the doctrine, for the Laws of the Indies made this provision.[102]

In connection with the authority enjoyed by the bishops to examine books before they were printed, published, or used, according to the Laws of the Indies,[103] bishops could well comply with the provision of the Constitution of Benedict XIV which stated that, if other catechisms were to be used because of some necessity peculiar to certain places, then the bishops were to see to it that such catechisms did not contain anything alien to Catholic truth.[104] Although the bishops as such did not enjoy the prerogative of infallibility in teaching, nevertheless they truly were doctors or masters under the authority of the Roman Pontiff in regard to the faithful entrusted to their care. Evidently the bishops in the Philippine Islands, while enjoying the power of examining books in line with the provision made in the Laws of the Indies, would by no means have allowed any catechism containing any dogmatic error to be printed or used. The bishops would have violated not only the Laws of the Indies[105] but also their sacred duty of vigilance,[106] if they had allowed catechisms containing some erroneous doctrine to be printed or used.

In passing one may note that the Tagalog translation of the *Doctrina Christiana* written perhaps by Father Juan de Placencia[107] was approved as the standard Tagalog text in

[102] *Recopilacion*, Tomo I, Lib. I, Tit. XXIV, Ley III, p. 143; *Doctrina Christiana*, pp. 14-15.

[103] *Recopilacion*, Tomo I, Lib. I, Tit. XXIV, Ley III, p. 143.

[104] Const. *Etsi minime*—7 febr. 1742—*Fontes*, n. 324.

[105] *Recopilacion*, Tomo I, Lib. I, Tit. XXIV, Ley III, p. 143.

[106] *Concilium Manilanum*, Actio II, Tit. II, Decretum II, § i. Cf. *supra*, p. 68.

[107] The Franciscans maintained that the *Doctrina Christiana* in Spanish-Tagalog version was written by Fr. Placencia; the Augustinians claimed that it was written by Fr. Agustin Alburqueque; the Dominicans contended that it was written either by Fr. Francisco Blancas de San Jose or by Fr. Domingo de Nieva. But the discovery of a copy of the Spanish-Tagalog *Doctrina Christiana* in the Vatican Archives with the name of Fr. Domingo de Nieva in it apparently vindicated him as its real author. Cf. Zaide, *op. cit.*, p. 97.

the synod convoked by Domingo de Salazar, first bishop of Manila and the Philippines, in 1582.[108]

Therefore there is no room for doubt that the catechisms drawn up in the various dialects of the natives were issued with the authorization of the competent authority, namely, the bishop, in virtue also of the Laws of the Indies,[109] all of which was in accordance with the provision of the III Provincial Council of Mexico (1585), then the binding conciliar legislation in what later became the Ecclesiastical Province of Manila.[110]

Regarding the penalty mentioned in § i, the Council used the term *excommunicatio major*[111] to distinguish it from the *excommunicatio minor*.[112] The "*excommunicatio major*" pronounced by the Manila Council was of a "*latae sententiae*" character[113] and in addition was reserved to the bishops for its remission.[114] In addition to the above-mentioned excommunication, there followed also automatically the privation of office and benefice.

DECRETUM VI
De Orationis Studio

The fathers of this Council, presumably having in mind

[108] Juan de la Concepcion, *Historia General de Philipinas* (14 vols., Manila, 1788-92), II, 45-46.

[109] *Recopilacion*, Tomo I, Lib. I, Tit. XXIV, Ley III, p. 143.

[110] "... Non tamen propterea exclusum volumus catechismum Summi Pontificis auctoritate confectum, aut ab aliis inferioribus auctoritatem habentibus, in posterum conficiendum."—*III Mexicanum*, Lib. I, tit. I, § i, p. 7.

[111] Excommunicatio major est censura ecclesiastica qua christianus separatur a communione fidelium absolute et simpliciter, sive privatur omnibus bonis communibus, scilicet sacramentis ecclesiae tam quoad administrationem, quam susceptionem, publicis suffragiis, et convictu seu societate civili."—Ferraris, s. v. *Excommunicatio*, n. 12.

[112] "Excommunicatio minor est censura ecclesiastica qua christianus privatur solum passiva preceptione sacramentorum."—Ferraris, s. v. *Excommunicatio*, n. 13.

[113] "Excommunicatio latae sententiae est ea quae ipso facto incurritur, sive criminis perpetratione sive sententia judicis."—Ferraris, s. v. *Excommunicatio*, n. 16.

[114] Benedictus XIV, *De Synodo Dioecesana*, Lib. V, cap. 4, n. 3.

that which our Lord Jesus Christ said: "Without me you can do nothing,"[115] strongly exhorted the bishops to spend in their oratories each morning at least one hour in meditation, to celebrate the Holy Sacrifice of the Mass or to assist at it, to pray the divine office attentively and devoutly, and to devote the rest of the day to spiritual reading and other useful occupations. They were to shun all useless visits. At night, before going to bed, they were to examine their conscience well, considering what good they had done or omitted in the interests of their flocks. They were to pray for them and to implore God's mercy upon them. They were to look to the example of Job, who day by day offered sacrifice to God for the sins of his children (§ i).

This decree wisely reminded the bishops of the already existing spiritual obligations pertaining to themselves, i. e., to their spiritual life. It was in full harmony with the spirit of the various decrees of the Council of Trent. In Session VI, on Reform, in Chapter 1, it was decreed: "The Holy Council of Trent... wishing to restore a very much collapsed ecclesiastical discipline and to reform the depraved morals of the clergy and the Christian people, has deemed it proper to begin with those who preside over the major churches, for unblemished character in those who govern is the salvation of those governed."[116] The twenty-second session of the Council of Trent declared that there was nothing that led others to piety and to the service of God more than the life and example of those who had dedicated themselves to the divine ministry. For as they were observed to be raised from the things of this world to a higher position, others fixed their eyes upon them as upon a mirror and derived from them what they were to imitate.[117] The Council of Trent emphasized: "For it is not to be doubted that the rest of the faithful will be more easily roused to religion and innocence, if they see those who are placed over them con-

[115] John, XV:5.

[116] Translation by H. J. Schroeder, *Canons and Decrees of the Council of Trent*, pp. 46-47.

[117] Sess. XXII, *de ref*. c. 1—translation by Schroeder, *op. cit.*, p. 152.

centrate their thoughts not on the things of this world but on the salvation of souls and on their heavenly country."[118]

The spiritual acts and pious exercises mentioned in this decree of the Manila Council, namely, meditation, the celebration of or assistance at Mass, the attentive and devout praying of the divine office, engagement in useful things, examination of conscience, regular assistance at Divine services at the Cathedral, particularly in Lent, Advent, and on solemn feasts of the year, and the confession mentioned in the following decree of this council, were means intended to sanctify the bishops. If clerics were bound to a higher degree of sanctity in their interior and exterior life than were the laity, to whom they were to furnish an example of superior virtue and right conduct,[119] how much more were bishops bound? For the Council of Trent declared: "For the state and order of the entire household of the Lord will totter if what is required in the body be not found in the head."[120] This decree of the Manila Council substantially agrees with the provisions of the III Provincial Council of Mexico (1585) and the IV (1771) regarding prayers, meditation, Mass, examination of conscience, and confession.[121]

The Manila Council in this decree exhorted the bishops to engage in the meditation and the other acts of piety in common with their *familia superior* (§ i). Certainly the fathers of the Manila Council, in exhorting the bishops to make their meditation, etc., together with the *familia superior*, seemed to have in mind the following words of Holy Scrip-

[118] Sess. XXV, *de ref.* c. 1—translation by Schroeder, *op. cit.*, p. 232.

[119] C. 3, D. LXI; c. 14, X, *de officio iudicis ordinarii,* I, 31; Conc. Trident., sess. XIV, *de ref., Proemium;* sess. XII, *de ref.*, c. 1; sess. XIII, *de ref.*, cc. 11, 13; Leo X (in Conc. Lateranen. V), const. *Supernae dispositionis,* 5 maii, 1514, § xvi—*Fontes,* n. 65; Benedictus XIII, const. *In supremo,* 23 sept. 1724, § vi, 28—*Fontes,* n. 283; Benedictus XIV, ep. encycl. *Apostolicum ministerium,* 30, maii 1753—*Fontes,* n. 425.

[120] Sess. XXIV, *de ref.*, c. 1—translation by Schroeder, *op. cit.*, p. 190.

[121] Cf. *III Mexicanum,* Lib. III, tit. I, §§ iii and iv, pp. 137-138; *IV Mexicano,* Lib. III, tit. I, §§ ii and iii, p. 104.

ture: "For where two or three are gathered together for my sake, there am I in the midst of them."[122]

It must be noted that the Manila Council simply used the expression *vacent orationi* in § i. The fathers of this Council certainly thought not only about the vocal prayers but also about the meditation, which ordinarily is attended to before the celebration of Holy Mass by bishops and priests. The III Provincial Council of Mexico (1585) employed the phrase *Orationi impendere,* but from the clause immediately following it, namely, *in quo alta mentis contemplatione perpendant,* it becomes apparent that mental prayer or meditation was referred to.[123] The IV Provincial Council of Mexico (1771) used the clause, *dediquense todos los dias a la oracion en la hora señalada.* Like the Manila Council, it did not distinguish vocal prayer from meditation. But it differed from the Manila Council in that it provided that the one hour to be devoted to the *oracion* could either be continuous or divided.[124] The IV Provincial Council of Milan (1576), however, had mentioned expressly both the *oratio* and the *meditatio* to which bishops must devote a certain hour every day.[125]

The bishops were to assist at the divine office in the cathedral church,[126] particularly in Lent, Advent, and on the

[122] Matthew, XVIII: 20.

[123] *III Mexicanum,* Lib. III, tit. I, § iii, p. 138.

[124] *IV Mexicano,* Lib. III, tit. I, § ii, p. 104.

[125] "In oratione, sanctisque meditationibus cum eos frequentes esse oporteat; certam sibi horam quotidie sumant, quam in contemplationum divinarum studio exercitationeque attentissimis religiosae mentis cogitationibus ponant."—*Act. Eccl. Mediol.,* Pars I, p. 422.

[126] It may be of interest to mention that the cathedral church of Manila at the time of the Council (1771) was the third cathedral constructed since the creation of Manila as a diocese (1579). The first parish (church) was converted into a cathedral dedicated to the Immaculate Conception in a Papal Bull of Gregory XIII. But it was terribly damaged by the typhoon of 1583. The second cathedral was rebuilt in 1592. In 1600 it suffered volcanic disturbances that damaged the uncompleted cathedral; then it was rebuilt again in 1614. It was again completely ruined by earthquake on Nov. 30, 1645; its rebuilding was inaugurated in 1671. After almost exactly a century

solemn feasts of the year. If the bishops did not do so, then clerics might all too readily follow their example of non-attendance at these services (§ ii). Indeed it was the duty of bishops to inform their clerics by means of pastoral letters that their assistance at the divine functions, especially on holy days of obligation, was to be a part of their obligation in their vocation to the sacred priesthood, and that it could merit recognition for their promotion. Negligence, therefore, on the part of the bishop to assist at the divine offices in their cathedral churches could induce a similar negligence in clerics with reference to their obligation to assist at the sacred functions in their parishes.[127] The Manila Council did not state any excusing cause for which bishops could absent themselves from the diocesan functions. The Council of Trent, however, declared that episcopal duties such as confirmation, visitation, etc., could call bishops from their cathedral during the above-mentioned periods.[128]

In passing, one may point out that it seems a little bit surprising that the fathers of this Council did not make specific mention of the bishops' daily recitation of the Rosary of the Blessed Mother. Even the children recited the holy Rosary in the church on all feast days, in order to progress in their love of and devotion to our Blessed Mother, Queen of the Rosary.[129] One of the first two catechism books printed in Manila (1593), entitled "*Doctrina Christiana,*" contained in Spanish-Chinese version an explanation of the mysteries of the holy Rosary.[130]

DECRETUM VII

De Consultoribus et Confessario

This *Decretum*, consisting of two paragraphs, deals with

(1771) the Manila Provincial Council was held. Cf. Zaide, *op. cit.*, p. 151.

[127] Vargas Ugarte, *op. cit.*, II, p. 209, n. IX.

[128] Sess. XXII, *de ref.* c. 1.

[129] Actio IV, Tit. Unicus, Decretum IV, § ii. Cf. *supra*, p. 95.

[130] Cf. *supra*, p. 170.

the bishop's consultors and confessor together with their respective qualifications.

In reliance upon the Scriptural word, "lean not upon thy own prudence,"[131] the Manila Council declared that it was expedient for a bishop to have consultors. The consultors here mentioned were not the diocesan consultors, otherwise the decree would have had a wording like *De Consultoribus Dioecesanis.* Apart from this reason, there was no need of diocesan consultors in the Philippines at that time, for even then there already existed cathedral chapters, as mentioned in many of the decrees of this Council.[132] Long before the Manila Council was held, the Spanish King had sent to the archbishops and the bishops of the Indies and the Philippine Islands *Cedulas Reales,* in which directions were given regarding the appointment of visitators as made by the bishops or by the cathedral or ecclesiastical chapters in the event of the vacancy of the see.[133]

Furthermore, these consultors could not be identified with the parish priest consultors, since the juridic institute of parish priest consultors goes back only to St. Pius X.[134] Therefore, it must be maintained that these consultors were mere private or personal advisers whom the bishops could consult in case of need.

The responsibilities of a bishop are certainly weighted with difficulties and dangers. Consequently, he needs some consultors or advisers.[135]

The Manila Council did not determine the maximum number of private consultors the bishops might have. But there could not be fewer than two, inasmuch as the decree spoke in

[131] Prov. III: 5.

[132] Actio II, tit. IV, Decretum III, §§ xix-xxi; cf. *supra*, pp. 80-81.

[133] Cf. *Recopilacion*, Tomo, I, Lib. I, Tit. VII, Leyes XXIV-XXV, p. 41.

[134] S. C. Consist. decr. *Maxima cura*, 20 Aug. 1910—*AAS* II (1910), 636 ff.; *Fontes*, n. 2074.

[135] J. Migne, *S. Bernardi Opera Omnia* (editio nova, 6 Vols. in 4, Lutetiae Parisiorum, 1854-1855), I, c. I, p. 810.

the plural, *De Consultoribus*. Concerning their qualifications, the Council explicitly mentioned that they had to be upright men, gifted with frankness *(libertas evangelica)*. The bishops, having manifold and delicate tasks, certainly needed upright, capable, sincere and prudent men, whose advice and service could be of help to them. The Council was silent on whether these consultors were to be priests or laymen. It depended upon the bishops' discretion and upon the nature of their consultation, whether priests or laymen were to be the private consultors.

The provision that the bishops have private or personal consultors seems a singular and peculiar rule. In order to appreciate this provision of the Manila Council, one must understand the times and conditions of the bishops in the Philippines. The 300 years of Spanish rule in the Islands were marked by bitter struggles between the authorities of the Church and those of the State,[136] and by complicated controversies betwen bishops and friar *curas (Religiosi habentes curam animarum)*, namely, the visitation and secularization controversies.[137]

§ ii. In the first place, the bishops were necessarily to have the best and most prudent confessors, who could be of service in directing them, especially when they were burdened by the magnitude of their responsibilities and obligations. The Manila Council pointed out another sterling quality that the bishop's confessor had to possess. It was the virtue of courage, like that of John the Baptist, who said to Herod the Tetrarch: "It is not lawful for thee to have her."[138]

The greater one's dignity is, the stronger also is one's

[136] Zaide, *op. cit.*, I, 207 ff.; Donald Parker, *The Church and State in the Philippines, 1896–1906* (Chicago, 1936), p. 354.

[137] T. H. Pardo de Tavera, *Reseña Historica de Filipinas desde su Descubrimiento hasta 1903* (Manila, 1906), pp. 36-41; Fr. Serapio Tamayo, O.P., *Sobre una Reseña Historica de Filipinas* (Manila, 1906), pp. 20 ff.; See also *Manilanum*, Actio IV, Titulus Unicus, Decretum XIV, §§ ii-iv. Cf. *supra*, p. 106.

[138] Matthew XIV: 4.

temptation to egotism or pride. It was for this reason that a bishop had to have confessors with the above-mentioned qualities, who could enlighten him and call his attention prudently to any and every needed personal reform. Needless to say, the confessor served primarily for receiving the sacramental confession of the bishop.

The Manila Council apparently advocated certain persons as consultors for the bishop, and a distinct person as his confessor. Other provincial councils, however, did not have any section dealing with the bishop's personal or private consultors. But they expressly mentioned the bishop's confessor.[139] The IV Provincial Council of Milan (1576) had not made mention of the bishop's consultors as the Manila Council later did, but it seemed to indicate that the bishop could at times utilize the counsel and recommendation of the confessor, especially when the bishop's important business and problems were to be considered.[140]

The bishops who had their consultors and a confessor, as was advocated by the Manila Council, could by that fact more than by mere word edify and encourage the priests and the faithful of the dioceses to have recourse to some qualified men for consultation whenever necessary, and to a prudent confessor for spiritual advice, for, as the saying goes, *verba movent, exempla trahunt.* Finally, the bishop who had to see to it that his priests made use of the sacrament of penance frequently did well indeed if by his own personal example he reflected the fulfillment of this noble ideal.

TITULUS TERTIUS

De Visitatione

The third title, "On Visitation," consists of five *Decreta. Decretum I* treats of the annual visitation. *Decretum II,*

[139] *III Mexicanum,* Lib. III, tit. I, § iv, p. 135; *IV Mexicano,* Lib. III, tit. I, § iii, p. 104.

[140] "Confessarium saecularem vel regularem deligant adhibeantve ... cujus etiam studio, et consilio, et praecationis spiritu, in rerum graviorum deliberationibus aliquando uti possint."—*Act. Eccl. Mediol.,* Pars I, p. 423.

with five paragraphs, and *Decretum III*, with six paragraphs, deal respectively with the rules and the preparation for the visitation. *Decretum IV*, with four paragraphs, insists on lightening the burdens of pastors during the course of the visitation. *Decretum V*, with six paragraphs, treats of the visitation of schools or institutions for girls.

Visitation is the act of inquiring into the current observance of obligations according to the circumstances of every place and person, with a view to maintaining that observance at a high level, to correcting existing abuses and excesses, to punishing the guilty, and to restoring the called for observance wherever neglects and defaults had occurred.[141]

The Council of Trent stated that the chief purpose of visitation was, after the extirpation of heresies, the restoration of sound and orthodox doctrine, the guarding of good and the correcting of evil morals, the animating of the people with religious exhortations and admonitions, the promoting of peace and innocence, and the regulating of discipline for the benefit of the faithful, in the light of the visitor's prudence and in line with the demands that the time, the place, the occasion and the situation might suggest.[142] On the other hand, the Laws of the Indies charged the bishops of the Indies to institute a personal visitation of their dioceses, in order to learn about the state or the condition of the *doctrinas* (parishes of the natives), to ensure the preaching of the Holy Gospel, to encourage and aid the conversion of the people, and to carry out administration of the sacrament of confirmation.[143] The Manila Council, therefore, considering the importance of the above-mentioned provisions of both the Council of Trent and the Laws of the Indies, legislated some measures regarding visitation.

[141] Bouix, *Tractatus de Episcopo ubi et de Synodo Dioecesana* (2. ed., 2 vols. in 1, Parisiis—Insulis, 1873), II (hereafter cited as *Tract. de Episc.*); Barbosa, *De officio et Potestate Episcopi* (Lugduni, 1656), Pars III, Alleg. 73, n. 1.

[142] Sess. XXIV, *de ref.* c. 3.

[143] *Recopilacion*, Tomo I, Lib. I, Tit. VII, Ley XXIV, p. 41.

DECRETUM I

De Visitatione Annua

This *Decretum* contained six paragraphs which treated of the following: first, the employment of vicars forane in the visitation of those parts of the diocese in which the bishop could not conduct a personal visitation during the year because of the large extent of the diocese; second, the setting of the period of visitation during the two weeks preceding Lent, with one day only to be spent in each parish; third and fourth, the powers and modified restrictions for vicars forane with reference to the churches and pastors visited by them; fifth, the freedom of the bishop to designate another visitor in place of the vicar forane as long as the deputy was not a member of the chapter; sixth, the freedom of the bishop to postpone the second vicarial visitation.

§ i. In consideration of the vast extent of the dioceses in the Philippine Islands, plus the fact that parochial churches were far apart, roads were poor, and means of transportation were difficult, the bishop himself could not complete personally the visitation of all his parishes within a year or two. It was for these reasons that the Council of Manila decreed that it sufficed for the fulfillment of the visitation if the bishop visited personally some parts of the diocese during the year, and the rest through his vicars forane. This decree was in harmony with the provision of the Council of Trent concerning the employing of other persons for the visitation of some parts of the diocese if the bishop alone could not effect the visitation in his own person.[144]

If in view of the large extent of his diocese a bishop was unable to make a complete visitation of the diocese annually, then the Council of Trent allowed him either in person or through his deputy visitors to cover the greater part of the diocese, so that in two years the task of the visitation would be completed.[145]

The Manila Council specifically designated the vicars

[144] Sess. XXIV, *de ref.* c. 3.

[145] Sess. XXIV, *de ref.* c. 3.

forane as the bishop's deputy visitors (§ i), although in *Decretum II*, § i, there occurs the phrase *per visitatorem Generalem*, in *Decretum III*, § i, the phrase *Visitaturi episcopi aut eorum nomine alii* (which could be anyone appointed as a visitor by the bishop), and in *Decretum IV*, § i, simply the word *visitatori* apart from any closer specification (which could be anyone designated as visitor, as in *Decretum III*, § i). And in § v it is expressly mentioned that the bishops can freely appoint another person instead of the vicar forane as visitor, except anyone who is a member of the chapter. The reason for this exception was given by the Manila Council: neither in the case of a see's vacancy nor during the occupancy of a see, were canons to be made or appointed visitors (§ v). Of course amid the occupancy of a diocese *(sede plena)* the cathedral chapter could have acquired the right of visitation through prescription or by way of privilege. Such a right the Council of Trent duly acknowledged.[146] Consequently, if a bishop desired that instead of the vicar forane a canon should make the visitation, the proper mode of procedure was to let the selection of the canon visitor rest with the cathedral chapter, which itself held the vested right. For the bishop it simply remained to furnish approval for the one who was duly selected by the chapter.[147]

During the vacancy of a diocese *(sede vacante)* certainly a canon was not to be appointed as visitor, since the right and the obligation to make the visitation devolved upon the elected vicar capitular. But if the cathedral chapter had not the right, either by prescription or privilege, to make visitations, then the writer sees no canonical reason why the Manila Council precluded the appointment of members of the chapter as visitors. If covisitors could be chosen from the cathedral chapter irrespective of any privilege or custom to the contrary,[148] why should there have been precluded the bishop's appointment of capitular members as visitors? Pre-

[146] Sess. XXIV, *de ref.*, c. 3.

[147] Conc. Trident., *loc. cit.*

[148] S.C.C., *Angnina*, 27 maii, 1713—*Fontes*, n. 3120.

sumably the reason which the fathers of the Manila Council had for declaring that members of the chapter could not be appointed as visitors was based on the *Real Cedula* of the Spanish king, issued at Madrid on April 4, 1627.[149] Immediately upon the vacancy of the see, which could result from the bishop's death or for some other reasons, the government of the diocese was vested with the cathedral chapter.[150] But once the vicar capitular was elected, the bishop's ordinary jurisdiction in spiritual and temporal matters was transferred to him. Consequently the right and the obligation to make the visitation devolved upon him.

Regarding the appointment of visitors in the event that the bishop became legitimately impeded from personally visiting his diocese, the Laws of the Indies distinguished between laymen and ecclesiastics, the favored position yielding to the latter. The learned, God-fearing and exemplary ecclesiastics were to be appointed visitors by the bishop. Laymen were distinctly barred from such an appointment.[151]

Regarding the time limit for the completion of the visitation of the whole diocese, the Council of Trent had left room for a period of two years.[152] In the Philippines bishops were allowed by the Manila Council to permit some parts of the diocese to be visited by vicars forane appointed for that purpose. A bishop, therefore, could distribute the territories and have each of them visited by one vicar forane. In this way the complete visitation of the entire diocese could be effected at least once a year.

The cause expressly mentioned by the Manila Council for employing another person for the act of visitation was the geographical largeness of the diocese and the inaccessibility of the churches. It did not use the clause *si fuerint legitime*

[149] "... y porque se ha entendido que los procedimientos de algunos no han sido cuales conviene ..."—*Recopilacion,* Tomo I, Lib. I, Tit. VII, Ley XXV, p. 41.

[150] S.C. Ep. & Reg., *Aquilan.,* 4 aug. 1578—*Fontes,* n. 1336—*Lycien,* 22 dec. 1628—*Fontes,* n. 1735.

[151] *Recopilacion,* Tomo I, Lib. I, Tit. VII, Ley XXIV, p. 41.

[152] Sess. XXIV, *de ref.* c. 3.

impediti, as the Council of Trent had done,[153] and as other contemporary provincial councils did, like the IV Provincial Council of Mexico (1771)[154] and the IV Provincial Council of Lima (1772).[155] Even the Laws of the Indies used the phrase *legitimamente impedido* with reference to the prelate's visitation of the diocese.[156] The Manila Council, however, in one of its decrees declared what was understood by a *legitima causa.* It was one which confined a person to bed or necessitated his preoccupation with some serious business.[157] This definition one could apply for judging whether the bishop was legitimately impeded from making the visitation. The Spanish Provincial Council of Toledo (1565) interpreted the clause *"si legitime fuerint impediti"* as referring to any cause that would be seriously detrimental to the bishop's personal, spiritual and corporal welfare, or to the public's welfare.[158]

§ ii. The vicars forane were annually to make the visitation of the parishes within their own territory during the two weeks preceding Lent. Before the visitation they were to consult with the bishop for any advice or message he wanted them to convey to the people.[159] Presumably the reason why the fathers of the Council designated the two weeks before Lent as the visitation period was that this time of the year was not within the rainy season in the Philippines. A visitation during the rainy season would have proved very inconvenient both for the visitor and the visited.

[153] Sess. XXIV *de ref.* c. 3.

[154] *IV Mexicano,* Lib. III, tit. I, § xii, p. 106.

[155] Vargas Ugarte, *op. cit.,* II, 46.

[156] *Recopilacion,* Tomo I, Lib. I, Tit. VII, Ley XXIV, p. 41.

[157] Actio II, Tit. IV, Decr. III, § xxiii; "Declarat Provincialis Synodus causae legitimae nomine eam tantum intelligi qua quis vel lecto aegrotus decumbit vel aliqua gravi occupatione, Episcopo significanda detinetur impeditus." Cf. also *infra,* p. 233.

[158] Act. II, 2: "... ut nisi maximo cum detrimento vel publicae vel propriae salutis spiritualis vel corporalis, per seipsos eam visitationem exsequi non valeant."—Hardouin, X, 1148.

[159] The last part of this paragraph will be considered under *Decretum IV* of this Title. Cf. *infra,* pp. 212 ff.

During rainy seasons, the rainfall was heavy and continuous for days. The roads and the whole area became muddy, or at times even completely submerged under water for a long period. For this reason great difficulties would have attended the act of visitation.[160] Another probable reason for relegating the visitation to this time of the year was the desire to prepare the faithful and to give them an opportunity to receive the sacraments of penance and the Holy Eucharist any day during the season appointed for the fulfillment of their Easter duties, i.e., from *Septuagesima* Sunday to the second Sunday after Pentecost.[161]

§§ iii & iv. The Manila Council granted no faculties to the vicars forane to introduce any innovation, or to punish delinquent pastors, on the occasion of the visitation. What they were empowered to do was to determine whether the statutes of the synods were observed. They were to investigate also the life of the pastors. After the visitation it was the bishop's duty to admonish, reprimand, and correct the delinquent pastors, in order to have them observe the statutes of the diocese. Such admonition, reprimand, and correction was to be based upon the information furnished by the vicars forane. The bishop had to proceed with justice, charity, and prudence.[162] If the vicars forane in the course of the visitation found out that the church needed repairs, they were empowered to indicate to the pastor a time limit within which to undertake making these repairs. If the pastor failed to have the repairs made within the prescribed

[160] The dry season in the Philippines runs from March to June. The rainy season runs from July to October. The intervening period (November to February) is neither notably dry nor notably wet. Cf. Zaide, *op. cit.*, I, 6.

[161] *Manilanum*, Actio V, Tit. I, Decretum III, § xii—*supra*, p. 111; cf. *III Mexicanum*, Lib. III, tit. II, § i, p. 155.

[162] "... Monentur praedicti omnes et singuli patriarchae, primates, metropolitani et episcopi ad quos visitatio spectat, ut paterna charitate chrisitanoque zelo omnes amplectantur...."—Conc. Trident., sess. XXIV, *de ref.*, c. 4; Bouix, *Tractatus de Judiciis Ecclesiasticis* (3. ed., 2 vols., Parisiis, 1884), II, 60, 61; Reiffenstuel, Lib. V, tit. I, nn. 150-152.

time, the vicars forane had also the power to order the execution of the repairs, payment being made out of the income of the pastor. According to the Council no reason on the part of the pastor for the delay in making the repairs was admissible. Nevertheless, if the delay was due to a legitimate cause, such as sickness on the part of the pastor, or the lack of available workers, or the extreme poverty of the church, it could have become both imprudent and unjust to take the cost of the repairs out of the income of the pastor. Accordingly, the provision of the Council in assessing the pastor for the repairs which he had neglected to make were to be understood as applying only to ordinary circumstances, i. e., when the church had the money and the workers were available, but the pastor nevertheless held off making the needed repairs. With reference to the amount of the expenses for the repairs of the church, the vicars forane ordinarily had the faculty of giving the pastors the permission to spend no more than *decem argenti uncias*[163] out of the parish funds even for necessary repairs.

With the bishop's advice or permission even a great sum could be spent for the repairs of the church.[164] The Council was silent regarding the specific duration of time in which the pastor needed to effect the repairs. Much certainly depended on the part of the church needing repairs. The more important and necessary a part of the church was, the shorter was the period of time in which the repairs were to be completed. Thus for the repair of the main altar, the vicars forane could limit the pastor to a shorter period than the one granted for the repair of a side altar; or for the repair of the roof over the church's nave, a shorter period than for the repair of the roof over the belfry.

§ v. On the occasion of the visitation the customary things

[163] The natives at that time used pulverized gold or silver instead of coinage. For every six ounces of pulverized silver from the Spaniards, the natives gave one ounce of pulverized gold. Cf. Montero y Vidal, *Historia General de Filipinas*, I, 64-65.

[164] *Manilanum,* Actio IV, Tit. unicus, Decretum VI, § iv—*supra,* p. 99.

were to be examined. In general, they were: (1) places, such as churches, other ecclesiastical edifices, cemeteries, etc.; (2) things, such as sacred furnishings, sacred vessels, relics, images, statues of the saints, pious bequests, hospitals, schools, seminaries, temporal goods of the church, etc.; (3) sacred functions, such as the preaching of the word of God, the administration of the sacraments, etc.; and (4) persons, such as clerics, male and female religious, confraternities, school-teachers, the faithful, and all other things instituted in the diocese pertaining to the worship of God, the salvation of souls, and the support of the poor.[165]

Places: The Manila Council admonished the vicars forane to have the utmost care in examining the various physical considerations in reference to the churches—whether the churches were in an unbecoming state in consequence of the poverty or perhaps the negligence of the pastor; whether the materials with which the churches were built were bamboo, straw, nipa palm, or some other kind of material, common in the Islands and easily subject to combustion; whether the church, the altar, the roof, the floor or the walls needed repairs, etc.[166] Churches of the regulars were likewise subject to visitation.[167] In an attempt to regulate the desire of the natives to erect unneeded *visitas* (small churches of the natives, or chapels) the Council demanded a close examination of whether permission had duly been granted for the erection of them.[168]

The following points were to be investigated in regard to private oratories: on what days or how many times were

[165] Wernz, *Ius Decretalium,* II, 554; Conc. Trident., sess. VII, *de ref.*, cc. 7 & 8; sess. XXI, *de ref.*, c. 8; sess. XXV, *de regularibus*, c. 11; *III Mexicanum,* Lib. III, tit. I, §§ iii-iv, pp. 280-284; Gregorius XV, const. *Inscrutabili,* 5 febr. 1622—*Fontes,* n. 199; S.R.C., *Ariminen.,* 16 jun. 1663—*Fontes,* n. 5539; Benedictus XIV, const. *Firmandis,* 6 nov. 1744—*Fontes,* n. 349; *Recopilacion,* Tomo I, Lib. I, tit. XV, Ley XXVIII, p. 93.

[166] Actio IV, Tit. unicus, Decretum VI, §§ i-iv—*supra,* pp. 98-99.

[167] Actio IV, Tit. unicus, Decretum XIV, § iv—*supra,* p. 106.

[168] Actio IV, Tit. unicus, Decretum I, § v—*supra,* p. 91.

Masses celebrated; in what numbers did the faithful attend and what was the condition of the sacred furnishings in these oratories.[169] The cemetery likewise was to be inspected —whether it had fences around it, or perhaps was open and accessible to all animal life; whether it was overgrown with trees; whether it was defaced with litter and rubbish, with the result of presenting an appearance of untidiness, etc.[170]

Things: The vicars forane were to investigate the custody and care of the holy oils in order to determine if they were kept in a safe place, v. gr., in an ambry or a repository in the wall of the sacristy or baptistry, under lock and key and whether the key was kept by the pastor.[171] The materials, the forms and the patterns of the sacred vestments also were to be examined.[172]

Inquiries were to be made in ascertainment of whether the church bells perhaps were rung at times other than the prescribed times.[173] Parish vaults were to be inspected— whether the three prescribed keys were faithfully kept by the three designated persons.[174] The inventory of the movable and fixed properties of the church was to be inspected. The books, too, which this Council demanded to be kept in the parish house or church were to be inspected.[175]

Confessionals, likewise, were to be inspected—whether they were constructed with double grills with a four-inch distance between them and whether the perforations or openings were kept small enough to prevent the insertion of even the little finger.[176] The visitors carefully had to investigate whether the images or statues of the saints were crude representations or sculptures, whether there was ex-

[169] Actio V, Tit. I, Decretum IV, § xix—*supra*, p. 118.

[170] Actio IV, Tit. unicus, Decretum VI, § iv—*supra*, p. 99.

[171] Actio V, Tit. I, Decretum II, § ii, and Decretum V, § iv—*supra*, pp. 109 & 119 respectively.

[172] Actio V, Tit. I, Decretum IV, § xvii—*supra*, p. 118.

[173] Actio V, Tit. II, Decretum I, § x—*supra*, p. 127.

[174] Actio IV, Tit. unicus, Decretum VI, § iii—cf. *supra*, p. 99.

[175] Actio V, Tit. II, Decretum VIII, §§ i & vi—*supra*, pp. 132 & 134.

[176] Actio V, Tit. I, Decretum III, § ix—*supra*, p. 111.

travagant ornamentation or ridiculous costuming, etc., etc., whether the relics were authentic, etc.[177]

Hospitals also were to be visited. If they had been founded by Royal Patronage, then a person appointed by the king or the governor of the place was to accompany the ecclesiastical visitor of the hospital in the course of the visitation.[178] The visitors moreover had to investigate whether the pious wills and bequests had been faithfully complied with and executed.[179] Institutions or houses which were under the Royal Patronage and its immediate protection were to be visited in respect of all spiritual matters.[180] Schools and colleges were to be inspected—the doctrine, the books, and the deportment of the teachers.[181] The *colegios* and *beaterios* that strove for the girls' education were to be inquired into —their building, rules, statutes, life of the students and inmates.[182] The visitors were to inspect the seminaries, and were also to determine whether they were established in the buildings vacated by the Jesuits, whether the doctrine was imparted to the seminarians within the pattern of thought followed by St. Augustine and St. Thomas, and whether other things pertaining to the government of the seminaries, spiritual and material alike, were duly executed.[183] They were to investigate the temporal goods and properties of the church—its administration, etc.[184]

Sacred functions: On the occasion of the visitation, the visitors were to inquire about sacred preaching—the doc-

[177] Actio V, Tit. II, Decretum II, §§ i, ii & v—*supra*, pp. 128-129.

[178] Actio II, Tit. III, Decretum V, § v; Actio V, Tit. II, Decretum III, § iv—*supra*, pp. 76 & 130 respectively.

[179] Actio V, Tit. II, Decretum V, §§ i-iii—*supra*, p. 131.

[180] Actio II, Tit. III, Decretum V, § iv—*supra*, p. 75.

[181] Actio IV, Tit. unicus, Decretum V; Actio V, Tit. II, Decretum IX, § ii—*supra*, pp. 96 ff. & 134 respectively.

[182] Actio II, Tit. III, Decretum V, §§ i-iii—*supra*, p. 75.

[183] Actio III, Tit. I, Decretum II, §§ i, ii, iv, v, ix—*supra*, pp. 83-84.

[184] Actio V, Tit. II, Decretum VIII, §§ i, ii, iii, iv, & v—*supra*, pp. 132-133.

trine preached, the manner and method employed, etc.[185] They were also to investigate the teaching of Christian doctrine in the parish—the teachers, the language used, the method employed, etc.[186]

An investigation also regarding the administration of the sacraments was to be made during the visitation:—regarding the baptism: whether the tagalog form was used, whether premature foetuses were baptized, whether the rite of baptism was repeated, as some natives were in the custom of doing, what kind of water was used, whether the sponsors had the required qualities, whether there was any abuse regarding the number of sponsors employed, whether baptism was conferred within nine days after the child's birth, etc., etc.[187]

Regarding the sacrament of penance: whether the confessors led a holy life and had a sufficient knowledge of the required doctrine, and whether young priests were hearing the confessions of persons of the other sex; also to be inquired into was the number of penitents a confessor heard in a day, the giving of conditional absolution, the absolving of the sick continuously, the absolution of habitual sinners and recidivists, the place for the hearing of women's confessions.[188]

Regarding the Holy Eucharist: whether the Sacred Host was given due care and custody against all risk and danger of profanation, where Paschal Communion was being received, within what length of time the priest ordinarily completed the celebration of Mass; how thoroughly were his preparation for and thanksgiving after Mass, what altar furnishings were needed for the celebration of Mass, and what were the conditions of the vestments and sacred vessels used by the priest.[189]

[185] Actio IV, Tit. unicus, Decretum III, *supra,* pp. 93-95.

[186] Actio IV, Tit. unicus, Decretum IV, supra, pp. 95 ff.

[187] Actio V, Tit. I, Decretum I, *supra,* pp. 107 ff.

[188] Actio V, Tit. I, Decretum III, §§ i-ix, xv—*supra,* pp. 109-111; 111-112.

[189] Actio V, Tit. I, Decretum IV—*supra,* pp. 114 ff.

Regarding extreme unction: whether the priests wore surplice and stole in their administering of this sacrament, and whether the sacrament was administered to boys who were capable of making their confession, even though they had not yet received their first Holy Communion.[190]

Regarding matrimony: the visitors were to determine whether certain native customs were still prevailing, such as a man's personal or domestic service with residence in the home of the girl for a long time before he contracts marriage with her, or the bestowal of dowries, which the natives called *pasusu* and *bigay caya.* The visitors were likewise to determine whether the contracting parties had a sufficient knowledge of Christian doctrine and of other things necessary to know for a proper safeguarding of the sanctity of the sacrament.[191]

Persons: The visitation was to include an examination of the life, conduct, and knowledge of the clerics, as well as their wearing of the ecclesiastical garb.[192] Visitors were to conduct a careful inquiry and investigation into the pastor's life, activities, and administration of the parish;[193] they were to ascertain whether he was complying with the law of residence.[194] They were also to examine his relations with the civil authorities,[195] his relations with his parishioners,[196] his care for the poor, and his performance of other works of mercy.[197]

Confraternities existing in the parishes were subject to investigation on whether they were established with the needed permission from competent authority, and on whether they perhaps had become inactive and useless organizations.[198] Chaplaincies and benefices were to be inquired

[190] Actio V, Tit. I, Decretum V, §§ i-iii—*supra*, p. 119.

[191] Actio V, Tit. I, Decretum VIII—*supra*, pp. 121 ff.

[192] Actio III, Tit. II, Decretum I, §§ i-v—*supra*, p. 85.

[193] Actio IV, Tit. unicus, Decreta II & XIII, *supra*, pp. 91 ff.; 105 ff.

[194] Actio IV, Tit. unicus, Decretum IX, *supra*, p. 102.

[195] Actio IV, Tit. unicus, Decretum X—*supra*, pp. 102 ff.

[196] Actio IV, Tit. unicus, Decretum XI, *supra*, pp. 103 ff.

[197] Actio IV, Tit. unicus, Decreta XI & XII—*supra*, pp. 103-105.

[198] Actio V, Tit. II, Decretum VII, §§ i & ii—*supra*, p. 132.

into.[199] Other particular individuals who were to be investigated in the course of the visitation were the school teachers,[200] the *pater familias*,[201] the *zelatores*,[202] and the public witnesses.[203] Pastors, though they were members of a religious Order, were to be included in this visitation.[204]

Finally, the laity in general had also to be taken into consideration by the visitors. They were to inquire into the state of their religion and their morality. They were to ask about the laity's performance of the Sunday duties,[205] of fast and abstinence,[206] of the Easter duties,[207] and of whatever mandatory practices existed among the natives. They were further to inquire if there existed any practices contrary to the true faith and religion, as well as other sinful abuses, such as simony,[208] heresy,[209] usury,[210] divination, concubinage, calumny, cursing,[211] sacrileges, profanations, superstitions, and other evil practices.[212]

The bishop or his deputy visitor was to make a diligent inquiry in this regard so that he could give the advice and indicate the measures necessary for the extirpation of all

199 Actio V, Tit. I, Decretum VI, §§ iv-vii—*supra*, p. 120.

200 Actio IV, Tit. unicus, Decretum V, §§ ii, iv, vi, viii—*supra*, pp. 97 ff.

201 Actio IV, Tit. unicus, Decretum III, § vii—*supra*, p. 94.

202 Actio II, Tit. IV, Decretum IV, § ii; Actio IV, Tit. unicus, Decretum VIII, § ii—*supra*, pp. 81 & 100 respectively.

203 Actio II, Tit. IV, Decretum IV, §§ i, ii—*supra*, p. 81.

204 Actio IV, Tit. unicus, Decretum XIV—*supra*, p. 106.

205 Actio V, Tit. II, Decretum I, § ii—*supra*, p. 125.

206 Actio V, Tit. II, Decretum IV—*supra*, p. 130 ff.

207 Actio V, Tit. I, Decretum IV, §§ ix-xi—*supra*, pp. 116 ff.

208 Actio V, Tit. II, Decretum VI—*supra*, pp. 131 ff.

209 Actio V, Tit. II, Decretum XI, § i—*supra*, pp. 135 ff.

210 Actio V, Tit. II, Decretum XV, §§ vi-xviii—*supra*, pp. 140-142.

211 Actio V, Tit. II, Decretum X, §§ ii, iii, iv, vi, vii—*supra*, pp. 134-135.

212 Actio IV, Tit. unicus, Decretum I, § i; Decretum VIII, §§ iii, iv, v, vi, viii; Actio V, Tit. I, Decretum I, §§ i, iv, vi, ix, xii, xiii; Decretum II, § ii; Decretum III, § x; Decretum IV, §§ i, iii, xiv; Decretum VII, § ii & iv; Tit. II, Decretum XIII, § iii, iv, ix, x—*supra*, pp. 90; 100 ff.; 107 ff.; 109; 111; 115 ff.; 122 ff.; & 137 ff., respectively.

such evils for the restoration of the sound and orthodox doctrine, for the maintenance of good morals, and for the promotion of peace and innocence among the natives of the Islands.

§ v. The bishops were free to appoint another person in place of a vicar forane as a visitor, as long as he forewent the selection of any member of the chapter . . .[213]

§ vi. A second visitation of the vicariates (deaneries) was to be performed or omitted according to the prudent judgment of the bishop. In the event that it was to be performed, the visitation had to be completed before the rainy season. . . . In order to inform himself of the state of the matters entrusted to his supervision, the vicar forane had to visit the parishes of his district at the times specified by the bishop.[214] The fathers of this Council referred to this as a second visitation. The first visitation referred to that visitation which was performed by the vicar forane as visitor when appointed or delegated by the bishop.[215]

If a vicar forane instead of the bishop was to perform the episcopal visitation of the parishes in his district, the bishop could cancel the second visitation, since it could only be superfluous to have the same vicar forane visit the same parishes twice in the same year. The reason for advocating the performance of the visitation before the rainy season was obvious. During the rainy season in the Islands the rainfall was very heavy in all parts of the Philippines except in Cebu and Zamboanga. In some places it could amount to as much as 250 inches yearly.[216]

DECRETUM II

De Praeparatione Visitationis

There are five paragraphs in this *Decretum*. The first concerns the notification of the forthcoming visitation to be

[213] Cf. *supra*, p. 72.

[214] S.C. Ep. et Reg., *Lamacen*, 17 apr. 1613 (used as the footnote to canon 447, § 2, in the Code)—*Fontes*, n. 1656.

[215] Actio II, Tit. III, Decretum I, § i—*supra*, p. 71.

[216] Zaide, *Philippine Political and Cultural History*, I, 6.

sent to the affected parishes, the pastoral letter treating the scope of the visitation, and the announcement of confirmation if it is to be administered. The second concerns the conducting of the *Forty Hours* devotion in the cathedral church. This devotion was also to be held in the parish to be visited, for the success of the visitation. The third refers to the retreat or mission to be conducted by a missionary. The fourth deals with the instruction to be given by a priest on the eve of the visitation with reference to certain incidental matters. The fifth outlines the reception that should be accorded the visiting bishop or his delegate.

The episcopal visitation of a parish embraced so many things[217] that preparations had to be made beforehand in order that the visitation could be diligently, briefly and rightly conducted.[218] Consequently, it was necessary that the church which was to be visited be notified beforehand.[219]

§ i. The written notification *(edictum)*,[220] and the pastoral letter on the scope of the visitation and on the administration of the sacrament of confirmation on the occasion of the visitation (in case the bishop himself conducted the visitation) were to be sent to the pastor of the affected parish prior to the visitation. The pastor was to announce to the people the forthcoming visitation. He was to read and explain the pastoral letter, so that all those things that needed to be known and done by the people might be accomplished. The administration of the sacrament had also to be announced beforehand, so that children could be made ready for it. The Manila Council did not specify the time when the pastor was to make all these announcements and offer accompanying explanations. But all this was to be expedited during the High Mass on at least the two Sundays preceding the day of the visitation. In this manner there would be sufficient time for the whole parish, even for those who were living at a distance, to know about the forthcoming

[217] Cf. *supra*, pp. 71 ff.
[218] *Act. Eccl. Mediol.*, Pars I, p. 433.
[219] Bouix, *Tract. de Episc.*, II, 40.
[220] Bouix, *ibidem*, p. 41.

visitation and to make ready for it. Thus, indeed, the visitation could reach its desired successful issue.

The following is a copy of the edict sent to the parish of Dilao, Manila, by Archbishop Diego Garcia Serrano. He ordered it to be published from the pulpit during High Mass, before his visitations in the parish were to begin:

> We, Don Fray Diego Garcia Serrano, by the grace of God and the holy apostolic see, archbishop of the Philippines, member of his Majesty's council, etc.: To you, the faithful Christians, citizens, dwellers, residents, and inhabitants of the village of Dilao, which is administered by the Order of St. Francis, of whatever state, rank, and pre-eminence you may be, greeting in our Lord Jesus Christ. We cause you to know that the holy fathers, inspired personally by the Holy Spirit in their sacred councils, piously and rightly ordered and commanded that all the prelates and pastors of the universal Church be obliged, in person or through their visitators, to make annually a general visit and investigation of their subordinates and clergy, both seculars and regulars, who have in their charge the administration of souls. This shall include the offices that they hold, in curacies and in churches, hermitages, hospitals, and confraternities, all of which should be directed to the spiritual welfare of souls—which consists in being, through the grace of God, our Lord, separated from sins, especially public and disgraceful sins, which offend His (Divine) Majesty so greatly. In order to fulfill this our obligation, we admonish and order that those of you who shall know or who shall have heard anything said concerning the father *cura,* your minister, who has charge of you in the matter of the administration of sacraments, or of any other person, which cannot or ought not to be tolerated by the citizens and inhabitants of this said village of Dilao, of whatever nation and rank he be, shall tell and declare it to us; especially if he shall have committed what will be mentioned and related to you later in this edict, in whole or in part, or any other thing similar to it. You shall declare and manifest the same before us within the three days first following

after this our letter and edict shall be declared and read to you.

First, if you know or have heard said whether the said father *cura* N., your minister, has been remiss and negligent in the administration of the holy sacraments of baptism, penance, the eucharist, extreme unction, and matrimony.

Item: Whether anyone has died without holy baptism through his neglect and carelessness, or without confession, communion, or extreme unction.

Item: If you know whether the said your minister has not said mass for you on every Sunday or feast that is observed; or whether he has made any signal omission in this; and whether he preaches and teaches the Christian doctrine to you, as he is obliged.

Item: Whether the administration of the holy sacraments takes place with the reverence and propriety that is fitting; whether he has married anyone before daybreak, or without the admonitions ordered by the holy council, or without the notification of our vicars, and their permission having preceded, in the cases in which it ought to be made and asked for; and whether the baptisms that have taken place have been in the baptismal font of the church, with all respect and reverence.

Item: If you know whether the said your minister keeps the tariff of the fees—both those which pertain to him and those that pertain to singers, fiscals, and sacristans—written and placed openly where all may read it, so that they may know what they have to pay; or whether he has forced the natives to give more alms than they owe or are willing to give for marriages, baptisms, or burials, whether in money or in other things.

Item: Whether the said your minister is careful to execute the pious foundations and the wills of his parishioners; or whether these have failed to be observed through his fault.

Item: Whether the said your minister is careful to register his parishioners, both natives and those of other nations, at the time of Lent; and whether he has confessed them during that time, or tried to confess them; and whether he has, after Lent, made any effort to ascertain whether they fulfilled their duties to the church according to their obligation.

Item: If you know whether the said your minister has concealed any public or notorious sin of his parishioners, that has come to his notice, and has not endeavored to have it remedied by the persons who can remedy it.

Item: If you know whether the said your minister has not looked after the property of the church, the silver, and ornaments, and everything belonging to it; and whether any property has been lost by his carelessness and negligence.

Item: If you know whether the said minister, in the public sins that have come to his notice and that he has punished, has condemned the sinners to pecuniary fines, or something of value, such as wax, cloth, or other things; and whether he has failed to apply the said fines to those to whom they belong, in accordance with his Holiness's brief and his Majesty's decrees.

Item: If you know whether the fiscals have performed their duty poorly; or whether they live in sin, or are dishonest, or they conceal sins or concubinage; or whether they receive bribes; or whether with their authority as fiscal they have annoyed the Indians, or have taken rice, fowls, or other things at a less price; or whether they have imposed any tax under pretext of alms for the church, by their authority that they possess as minister of it; or whether they have taken more fees than belong to them by our tariffs.

Item: If you know whether the choristers and sacristans have likewise taken larger fees than are assigned them by our said tariffs, for burials, funeral honors, and other things that belong to them; and whether, when any poor man has died who has not the wherewithal to pay the fees, they have refused to bury him unless they are paid, or unless they receive pledges that they demand before burying him.

Item: If you know whether there are any apostates of our holy Catholic faith, or who practice any evil worship, or who possess or read books of it.

Item: Whether there are any who are living in public concubinage, or as whoremongers; or who keep in their houses slave women, or other women or men of evil life, in order to commit sins.

Item: Whether there are any who have not confessed, or fulfilled the precept of the church, according to their obligation; or whether there are any who have eaten meat unnecessarily during Lent on the fast of Friday or the four ember days.

Item: If you know whether there are any usurers who loan money at usury and interest; or who sell on credit at a dearer price than the things are worth when cash is paid; or who buy at a less price in order to give the money advanced with the imposition of fraud and usury.

Item: If you know whether there are any, either of you natives, or of any other nation, either men or women, who are sorcerers, or witches, or magicians; or those who pray to the devil, or who cast any kind of lots, whether to discover theft, or to ascertain other things by enchantments and witchcraft.

And inasmuch as the above evil is a very great offense and disservice to God our Lord; and as it is advisable to remedy that herein contained that has been committed; we order, exhort, and admonish all the citizens of Dilao (to make known these things), within the said term of three days—under penalty that, if they know it and do not declare it, they shall, if it be proved, be punished most severely.

Given in this village of Dilao, June twenty-four, one thousand six hundred and twenty-two.

FRAY MIGUEL, archbishop

By order of the bishop, my master:

Licentiate Alonso Ramirez[221]

§ ii. The holding of the Forty Hours' Devotion, both in the cathedral church and, for the success of the visitation, was indeed a salutary act that could effectively convince the

[221] Blair and Robertson, *The Philippine Islands*, XI, 57-61.

faithful that the visitation was really a solemn and important event in the life of the parish. Regardless of the number of the parishes the bishop was to visit, the Forty Hours' Devotion was to be held only once in the cathedral church, i. e., before the beginning of his annual visitation tour among the parishes. But it was to be held in every parish scheduled to be visited, and indeed all parishes were to be visited every year. Although its purpose was the success of the visitation, at the same time it could serve to fulfill the obligation of holding this Devotion in every parish annually.[222]

§ iii. The Spiritual retreat or mission conducted by a missionary some days before the visitation was indeed a very highly commended act in the preparing of the faithful for the visitation. In this way, too, the people could no doubt be prepared for the reception of the sacraments of penance and the Holy Eucharist, and thus become properly disposed for gaining the plenary indulgence.[223] The faithful in this matter traditionally cooperated with their pastor and bishop for the success of the visitation.[224] The decree of the Manila Council regarding this matter imposed only a conditional obligation *(si fieri potest)*.

§ iv. In order that the duration of the visitation of a parish be not unduly extended, the bishop was to send an ecclesiastic to the affected parish on the eve of the visitation, or shortly before the arrival of the bishop. This ecclesiastic, chosen by the bishop, could be the vicar forane or any other priest. He was to announce and explain various incidental matters pertaining to the visitation, according to the instruction given him by the bishop.[225] The Manila Council left it to the discretion of the bishop whether or not to send such an ecclesiastic.

[222] Cf. Clemens XI, "Instructio Clementina," 21 ian. 1705—S.R.C., *Decreta Authentica*, IV, 3-138 (as found in Abbo-Hannan, *The Sacred Canons* [2 vols., St. Louis: B. Herder Book Co., 1952], II, 528, footnote 46).

[223] Bouix, *op. cit.*, II, 41.

[224] Cf. *Act. Eccl. Mediol.*, Pars I, p. 433.

[225] Cf. *Act. Eccl. Mediol.*, Pars I, p. 433.

§ v. On the evening before the day assigned for the visitation the bells of the church were to be rung to enkindle the devotion of the faithful. This, certainly, was not the only purpose of the ringing of the bells; it could also serve as a reminder to the people to come and to greet their bishop, and to receive his paternal blessing.[226] On the very day of the visitation, the pastor and the faithful of his parish were to meet the bishop at a certain place within the parish and to accompany him in procession to the parochial church, in the meantime singing hymns and other religious songs.[227] The staging of dances and games during the visitation was prohibited. The Manila Council, however, did not determine the kind of dances and games it prohibited. Neither did it specify the places to which the prohibition was to extend. Regarding dances, it certainly prohibited not only such as were indecent, but also the dances which some fanatic women sometimes performed during the procession.[228]

As to the games, the fathers of the Council certainly referred to the games which in the native dialect were called *beto-beto, dais, sa pula o sa puti* and also to other games of chance in which even the children could for a short time take part with their few petty coins.[229] Presumably it was the purpose of this prohibition to stress the seriousness and, to some extent, the sacredness of the visitation,[230] not only when the people were in the church but even when they

[226] Cf. III Council of Ravenna (1314), c. 6—Mansi, XXV, 539; The ringing of the church bells on the occasion of the bishop's arrival for the pastoral visitation is still a practice prevalent in the Islands; Cf. *Act. Eccl. Mediol.*, Pars I, p. 434.

[227] Cf. *Act. Eccl. Mediol.*, Pars I, p. 433.

[228] A custom of this kind was prevalent in many places. At present within the observation of the writer, it is prevalent in only a few remote places on the Islands.

[229] Addiction to popular amusements in connection with holy days and feast days in general is an old and widespread custom in the Islands. The writer has observed this repeatedly in widely separated localities.

[230] The natives called the visitation *la santa visitacion*, thus reflecting their notion regarding its sacredness.

went to their respective homes. Dances and games such as the ones mentioned above could certainly distract the people. This prohibition was to be imposed upon the faithful by the pastor. A pastor who allowed dances and games in the parish on the occasion of the visitation was subjected to the payment of *decem argenti unciae,*[231] applicable for the seminary.

DECRETUM III

De Regulis Visitationis

This *Decretum,* consisting of six paragraphs, concerns the rules of visitation and covers the following items: (1) Only the bishop or his delegate and such other persons that were necessary for or useful to the visitation were to be part of the bishop's retinue. (2) Good example, but especially charity towards the unfortunates, needed to be exercised throughout the visitation. (3) The meals were to be taken under the accompaniment of spiritual reading, and discussion on theology, dogmatic, moral, pastoral and ascetical, and on the sacred liturgy were to be engaged in with the clergy of the parish. (4) The bishop was to offer advice or administer reproof as necessity demanded. (5) The bishop was to preside in meetings held by him with the school teachers, the *zelatores* of the pastors, the public witnesses, etc., in attendance.

§ i. The Council of Manila did not designate any precise number for the bishop's entourage. It simply provided that only those persons who could serve a necessary or a useful purpose for the fulfillment of the visitation were to form part of the bishop's entourage. It would, of course, have been impractical to set a standard for the bishop's entourage, since particular circumstances might allow a bishop to increase the number, e.g., an aged bishop who could increase his retinue according to his discreet judgment.[232]

[231] Cf. *supra,* p. 187.

[232] . . . Episcopus vero pro suo arbitrio et conscientia augere potest numerum familiarium in actu visitationis quoties in senectute versetur."—*in Potentina Procurationis,* die 10 et 24 Januarii 1705 (as

This provision of the Manila Council was in accordance with the Council of Trent, which admonished the bishop to be content with a modest train of horses and servants.[233] It was also in accordance with the provision of the Sacred Congregation of Council.[234] It was consonant also with the Laws of the Indies, which provided that bishops' entourage be moderate.[235]

The fathers of this Council were certainly mindful of the decree of the III Provincial Council of Mexico (1585) in connection with the bishop's visitation of parishes. Its decree was contained under the following heading: *"Modestia in Visitatione Servanda."*[236]

There were, however, some particular provincial councils which decreed a fixed number in the bishop's entourage for the visitation. The I Provincial Council of Milan (1565) provided that the bishop's entourage be composed of at most fifteen men and twelve horses. If the visitor was of a subordinate status, his entourage was not to exceed eight men and six horses.[237] The IV Provincial Council of Milan (1576) decreed that not more than ten men and six horses were to compose the bishop's entourage.[238]

§ ii. The provision of the paragraph is in line with admonitions given since the early middle ages. Thus the Council

found in Pallottini, *Collectio Omnium Conclusionum et Resolutionum quae in Causis Propositis apud Sacrum Congregationem Cardinalium S. Concilii Tridentini Interpretum Prodierunt, ob anno 1564–1860* [18 vols. Romae 1868-1893], s.v. *Episcopus Quoad Procurationem*, § XV, n. 218) (hereafter cited as Pallottini).

[233] Sess. XXIV, *de ref.* c. 3.

[234] ... Quin imo Episcopus modesto esse debet contentus famulatu; quandoquidem Sacra Congregatio declaravit Episcopum modesto equitatu et famulatu oportere esse contentum, praecise autem numerum famulorum concilium non statuisse, sed Episcopi judicio et modestiae relinquendum.—*in Forosempronien.*, mense nov. 1587 (as found in Pallottini, s.v. *Episcopus Quoad Procurationem*, § XV, n. 317).

[235] "... y hagan estas visitas con moderadas familias ..."—*Recopilacion*, Tomo I, Lib. I, tit. VII, Ley XXIV, p. 41.

[236] *III Mexicanum*, Lib. III, tit. I, § ii, pp. 141-142.

[237] C. XXX, Hardouin, X, 675.

[238] C. III, Hardouin, X, 900.

of Aix-la-Chapelle (813), convoked by Charlemagne, decreed that bishops were to make the visitation once a year, and that the care of the people, especially of the poor, was their particular concern.[239]

A more direct antecedent can be found in the Council of Trent, which declared that the bishops in the visitation were to take cognizance of the support of the poor, regardless of contrary custom, privilege or status.[240]

§ iii. The Manila Council decreed that during the meals of the bishops there was to be public spiritual reading. The content of this reading was to be borrowed from Holy Scripture, from the works of the Fathers of the Church, and from treatises on pastoral duties.[241] The reading at table was mandatory not only in the bishop's house but also in any pastor's house. Good example could thus be given to everybody present.[242]

During the visitation the bishop was also required to spend some time with the clergy of the parish, questioning them on moral theology, on preaching, on the administration of the sacraments, on the liturgy, and on ascetics.[243]

For a proper appreciation of this regulation of the Manila Council, one must at least basically understand the times and the conditions of the clergy. At that time the Filipino secular priests were assigned to parishes even after they had received only a little formal training in the ecclesiastical sciences. Consequently, many of the priests proved unsuited if not also unfit for their noble calling. It was said that many had been recruited from the uneducated classes, especially from the Manila waterfront.[244]

[239] C. XVII—*Monumenta Germaniae Historica, Legum Sectio III, Concilia* (2 vols. in 4, ed. F. Maassen, A. Werminghoff, H. Bastgen, Hannoverae et Lipsiae, 1893-1924), II, Pars I, 252 (hereafter cited as *MGH*); Mansi, XV, 61; Hardouin, IV, 1005.

[240] Sess. XXII, *de ref.* c. 8.

[241] Cf. *supra*, p. 152.

[242] Cf. *Act. Eccl. Mediol.*, Pars I, p. 424.

[243] Wernz, *Ius Decretalium*, II, 554.

[244] Montero y Vidal, *Historia General de Filipinas*, II, 133-134; Zaide, *Catholicism in the Philippines*, p. 177.

Since the clergy were responsible for the training and education of their people, it was imperative that the same clergy be well grounded in theology, dogmatic, moral, and ascetical. It was therefore timely for the Manila Council to pronounce such a decree. It would certainly oblige those priests to pursue more studies, primarily in order to be equipped with the required knowledge and learning priests had to possess, and secondarily to be prepared for the visitation.

§ iv. The provision of this paragraph was a consequence of the preceding paragraph. The bishops, naturally, were to encourage those who were already good to become even better. If they found some priests deficient or negligent in their priestly life, especially in consequence of laziness, the bishops were to strongly reprimand them, but always with a due consideration for human weakness. The admonition or reprimand given by the bishops to their priests or to the laity was to come in a paternal way, and not in a judicial one.[245]

The bishops had to meet and give exhortations to the people, especially to the public sinners, in order that they might change their evil lives. Those who had committed sins reserved to the bishop were to be absolved either by him or by others delegated for this purpose, provided, of course, that they confessed contritely and asked for pardon.[246] If necessary, the bishops were to inflict public penances upon the public sinners for the purpose of deterring others from acting similarly.[247] Sometimes they were sent to the city

[245] "Modus quo visitatio episcopalis ex mente Ecclesiae perfici debet, est potius paternus, non iudicialis."—Wernz, *op. cit.*, II, 554; "Ut iuxta illius supremi post Christum pastoris edictum pastor forma factus gregis ex animo dignoscitur, non dominandi libidine, sed amore recte regendi debet illum salubriter visitare, sic excessus delinquentium quantum potest corripiens, ne revelet, sic increpans, ne confundat: quia, quum iuxta sapientis edictum secreto sit arguendus amicus, amicitiae legem violare videtur, si econtra palam arguat exprobrando . . ."—C. 17, X, *de officio iudicis ordinarii*, I, 31.

[246] Cf. *Act. Eccl. Mediol.*, Pars I, p. 81.

[247] Knowing that most of the natives at that time were still quite

during the celebration of the Calends to undergo the public penance with more solemnity.[248]

§ vi. Finally, the bishops had to ask about the school teachers,[249] the *zelatores,*[250] and the public witnesses.[251]

DECRETUM IV

De Non Gravandis Parochis

This *Decretum* consists of four paragraphs, dealing first with a prohibition against serving sumptuous banquets and against having uncalled-for persons at the banquets; second, with a prohibition against musicians and singers staying in the parish rectory; third, with a prohibition against the accepting of even voluntary offerings from those who were visited by the bishop or his entourage, a penalty being specified in the event of a violation; fourth, with a prohibition against unnecessary delay, again a penalty being specified for any direct violation.

It was in fact a matter of justice that the visited church provide the necessary means for the bishop or his delegates and their retinue for the duration of the visitation. In fact,

barbarous, as well as fickle and narrow-minded, the Fathers of the Council decided that, instead of excommunication, or censures, or other spiritual penalties, exterior and corporeal punishment be inflicted in order to preserve their obedience and respect due to the laws of God and of the church. Some of the public penances were the public whipping, and the balding of the heads of the delinquents. Cf. Vargas Ugarte, *Concilios Limenses, 1551–1772,* I, 365.

The *Barangays* Chiefs in the Philippines were fined or beaten if they were absent form the church on Sundays and certain feast days; other men were given the penalty of twenty lashes in the public highway, and two months labor in the Royal Rope Walk in a certain town called Taal, or in the Galleys of Çavite (a province in the Philippines); if the delinquents were women, the chastisement was one month of public penance in the church. Cf. John Foreman, *The Philippine Islands* (2. ed., London, 1899), pp. 204-205.

[248] Cf. *infra,* p. 231.

[249] Cf. *Manilanum,* Actio IV, Tit. Unicus, Decretum V, §§ ii, iv-viii —*supra,* pp. 97 & 98.

[250] Cf. *infra,* p. 239.

[251] Cf. *infra,* pp. 237 ff.

the bishops were authorized to claim from the visited churches (except from those that were notoriously poor) the *procuratio canonica,* i. e., the sustenance necessary for themselves and their attendants or retinue in the course of the visitation.[252] What was prohibited was the demand for more than a moderate procuration. In this connection the Council of Trent decreed that bishops or their delegates should exercise care not to be troublesome or make themselves a burden to anyone by useless expenses in the course of the visitation.[253]

§ i. The Manila Council, however, decreed that not more than a specific number of courses of food be served to the bishop and his retinue during the visitation, i.e., not more than five courses. It could therefore be less than five but not more, even if the pastor did not have to pay for the extra courses. This decree concerning the limitation on the courses seemed to indicate that the obligation rested only upon the pastor. But it was to be understood that the obligation rested also upon the bishop or his delegate, i.e., not to demand more than five courses of food.[254]

This decree made no distinction between parishes; it was to bind the rich and poor parishes alike. The parishes at that time were clasified as first, second and third class parishes.[255] Therefore, irrespective of the class of the parish, the number of courses of food to be served at the bishop's table was not to exceed five. Certainly the preparation of more than five courses of food would not have been as burdensome to the pastor of a big and rich parish as to the pastor of a poorer parish. But the fathers of this Coun-

[252] C. 3, III, 20 in VI; Conc. Trident., sess. XXIV, *de ref.,* c. 3. Cf. F. Schmalzgrueber, *Ius Ecclesiasticum Universum* (5 vols. in 12, Romae, 1843-1845), Lib. III, tit. XXXIX, n. 100; Ferraris, s. v. *Procuratio,* nn. 1 & 2; Reiffenstuel, *Jus Canonicum Universum,* Lib. III, tit. XXXIX, n. 49.

[253] Sess. XXIV, *de ref.,* c. 3.

[254] "Debet tantum moderata (procuratio) peti et dari."—Reiffenstuel, *op. cit.,* Lib. III, tit. XXXIX, n. 57.

[255] *Manilanum,* Actio IV, Titulus Unicus, Decretum II, § ii—*supra,* p. 91.

cil abstracted from all such consideration. The decree was for all. In this connection the purpose of the decree was not only one of not burdening the pastors, but also one of complying with the *Decretum II*, § ii, of Title I of this *Actio* (emphasizing the frugality of the bishop's table) and with the decree enacted by the Council of Trent.[256]

The Manila Council was not the only one which decreed a specific maximum number of courses of food to be served on the occasion of a parish visitation. The Spanish Provincial Council of Toledo (1565-1566) had declared that three courses of food could be served, or at most four, depending upon the status of the guests. The serving of vegetables and fruits without dressing was not to be counted as one of the three or four courses in question.[257] The I Provincial Council of Milan (1565) allowed only two courses of food to be served on the occasion of the visitation.[258] St. Charles Borromeo was content with one course of food served at his table during the visitation.[259]

To be sure that the preparation of the food would not be a burden for the pastor, the Manila Council decreed also that the food to be prepared for the bishop and his retinue was to be of such a kind that it could be obtained without difficulty in the town. This was a very practical consideration, because if the food that was to be prepared had to be bought from another place the burden would indeed have been great. The difficult means for transportation and the vast distance between the towns in the Philippine Islands had surely to be taken into account.

To prepare a sumptuous table or to serve even more than five courses of food to a handful of persons would not have entailed any serious burden, least of all to the pastor of a rich parish. But the large number of the bishop's entourage or retinue could certainly have rendered the burden an

256 Sess. XXV, *de ref.*, c. 1.

257 Tejada, *Collecion de Canones*, V, 230-231.

258 Cf. Hardouin, X. 675.

259 S. C. Ep. et Reg., *in Caerinen*, 26 aug. 1575 (as found in Ferraris, s. v. *Procuratio*, n. 27).

onerous one, even to a rich pastor. For this reason the Manila Council decreed that only those persons who were necessary or useful for the fulfillment of the visitation should be included in the bishop's entourage.[260] The Laws of the Indies provided that the bishops make the visitation of their parishes with a moderate number in their retinue, for the visitation, if it did not occasion any burden for anyone, would surely be edifying to all the observing faithful.[261]

The table service, therefore, was limited in such a way that only the bishops and his entourage were to share in it. All other persons, including the nobles *(primores)*[262] and the elders *(seniores)* of the community, i.e., the respected citizens of the community and those parishioners who had volunteered to serve the bishop, were not to be admitted, nor served even at the second table. The precaution of not admitting or serving the above-mentioned people was indeed very practical also in its intent of not burdening the pastor. It was a current custom in the Islands for neighbors, friends and relatives, though uninvited, to go to the house of the person holding the party. Their intention was to help the host or hostess in any possible way, v. gr., by cleaning the house, preparing the food, washing the dishes, serving the table, etc.

Naturally, because of such services, the host was obliged to give them food, especially if it was time to eat. It happened at times that the number of such helpers exceeded the number of the guests. Without doubt, to give food to all of them would have constituted another burden on the part of

260 Cf. *supra*, p. 202.

261 "... y hagan estas visitas, con moderadas familias, porque sin molestia de los naturales, sean de ejemplo y edificacion ..."—*Recopilacion*, Tomo I, Lib. I, tit. VII, Ley XXIV, p. 41; Ley XXVI, p. 41.

262 The nobles, called *maharlika* by the Tagalogs, *babaknang* by the Ilokanos, and *malahalon* by the Bisayans, occupied the highest place in society. They included the *datus* (chiefs or kings) and their wives and children. They enjoyed great political and social rights in the *barangays* (kingdom)—cf. Zaide, *op. cit.*, I, 52; Alip, *op. cit.*, I, 54; George Malcom, *The Commonwealth of the Philippines*, (New York, London: D. Appleton-Century Company Inc., 1939), p. 25.

the host, namely, the pastor in the case of the visitation. There was another custom in connection with the occasion of the visitation, namely, that those nobles and elders of the parish who had come to meet the bishop and to witness the visitation in the church then stayed as long as they could with the bishop. For them it was an honor. It was not unlikely for them to stay even up to the time of the meal. The pastor thus felt obliged to serve them something to quench their thirst and to satisfy their hunger.[263]

The provision of this *Decretum,* as expressed in this paragraph, bound the pastor under pain of paying a fine of ten ounces of pulverized gold, applicable to the public witnesses, in the event of an unquestioned violation.[264]

§ ii. No pastor was to allow musicians, singers or choristers to be in the parish house during the visitation, even if they were not to be paid. . . . Ages before the advent of the Spaniards, the Filipinos had already their own musical instruments and songs.[265] During the Spanish regime, the Archbishop of Manila founded a music academy in 1742 for the purpose of training choristers for the cathedral in Manila. The plan of study was similar to that followed in the Conservatory of Madrid. Singing, piano, violin and organ playing were taught in the school. The instruction was of a high quality and the graduates of the Academy gained distinction in their respective lines.[266] For these reasons there was in almost every town or parish a band of musicians and singers.

The natives were so fond of musicians and singers that there could be no celebrations, such as *fiestas* (feasts), processions, or big gatherings, without the playing of musicians or without singing. The parochial visitation was a

[263] These customs no longer exist on the part of the educated people. The writer has observed that in some parts of the Islands, in remote places where people are not well educated, some traces of these customs are still to be found.

[264] Cf. *infra,* p. 233.

[265] Zaide, *op. cit.,* I, p. 70.

[266] Alzona, *A History of Education in the Philippines, 1565–1930,* p. 157.

big affair, for it was the bishop who was coming. For the musicians and the singers, it was a great honor to entertain the bishop and to make the occasion a happy one with their music. But again it was the pastor upon whom fell the additional burden of feeding them when the time of meal came around. It was for these considerations that the Manila Council prohibited the pastor from having musicians and singers in the parish house during the visitation, even if they did not charge the pastor anything for their service.[267]

§ iii. The bishop, his delegate, or any member of his retinue was prohibited, *intuitu procurationis,* to accept even a voluntary offering in the form of money or of a gift from the persons in whose behalf the visitation had been made.[268] This prohibition included the accepting of gifts given even at the time of the bishop's departure after the completion of the visitation.[269] The Laws of the Indies, in harmony with the Council of Trent, provided that bishops or visitors were not to demand any visitorial fees, and that they were to show the greatest care and vigilance in not receiving anything, in whatsoever form, from the ones visited. It further provided that a bishop was not to give consent to anyone of his retinue or family for receiving any offering or gift in connection with the visitation.[270] In accordance with the terms of a Royal decree dated April 22, 1705, it was ordered that the expenses incurred by the prelates on their episcopal visitations were to be met by the royal treasury.[271]

[267] Even at the present time in many parts of the country musicians of the town are still a part of the multitude of people who meet the bishop on the occasion of the visitation. The musicians play from the time when the bishop is met until they arrive at the church. This has been observed by the writer on repeated occasions under divers circumstances.

[268] Conc. Trident., sess. XXIV, *de ref.*, c. 3; Ferraris, s. v. *Procuratio,* n. 26; Fagnanus, Lib. III, *de censibus*, cap. 23, n. 24.

[269] Barbosa, *De Officio et Potestate Episcopi,* Alleg. 73, n. 55.

[270] *Recopilacion,* Tomo I, Lib. I, tit. VII, Ley XXII, p. 40.

[271] Blair and Robertson, *The Philippine Islands,* XVII, 246 & 248; XXXVI, 182.

The Manila Council decreed this prohibition under the penalty of restoring within a month double the amount received. This provision of the Manila Council was a repetition in part of a similar decree of the Council of Trent, which further declared that in addition to the above-mentioned enforced restitution other penalties should be imposed, namely, the ones listed in the acts of the II General Council of Lyons (1274) in its twenty-fourth canon, as well as others at the discretion of the provincial synod.[272] But the penalties specified in the caput *Exigit*[273] were revoked in the Constitution *Sedis Apostolicae,* on October 12, 1869, by Pope Pius IX.[274]

§ iv. Regarding the duration of the visitation of the parish, the Manila Council decreed that it was to be completed in one day if the town was small, but in at least three days if the town was large, unless the delay was caused by the pastor's negligence. In the Philippine Islands the extent of a parish was the extent of a town, i.e., a town was a parish. Even at the present time there are still in the Islands many parishes whose boundaries are the boundaries of the town. In fact, many parishes are known better by the civil name of the town than by the titular name of the parish itself.[275]

The greater the extent of the parish and the number of its parishioners the longer the visitation could reasonably continue in view of the mandatory administering of the sacrament of confirmation. It was a law of the Indies that, whenever the bishop was to make the visitation, he was also to administer the sacrament of confirmation.[276] Consequently, a one-day visitation was not suited for every parish. A

[272] Sess. XXIV, *de ref.*, c. 3. The penal legislation of the II Council of Lyons on this point was incorporated as c. 2, *de censibus, exactionibus, et procurationibus*, III, 20, in VI, in the *Corpus Iuris Canonici.* It was frequently designated as the caput *Exigit.*

[273] Cf. Mansi, XXIV, 97; H. J. Schroeder, *Disciplinary Decrees,* p. 353.

[274] *Fontes,* n. 552.

[275] Cf. Catholic Directory of the Philippines (Manila: Catholic Trade School, 1956).

[276] *Recopilacion,* Tomo I, Lib. I, tit. VII, Ley XXIV, p. 41.

continued visitation for a three-day period in a large parish afforded the bishop the added opportunity of visiting additional churches. There was a time when the Bishop of the diocese of Cebu spent six months in visiting only some parts of his diocese. When he visited the Island of Romblon and the three provinces of the Island of Panay, he confirmed 102,636 persons; on the Islands of Negros and half of Cebu, he confirmed 23,800 persons.[277]

It was the purpose of this provision to prevent the pastor from contracting a debt in consequence of the long stay of the bishop and his retinue in the parish house. If the specified duration of the visitation was violated, either the pastor or the bishop, in accordance with who was the one at fault, had to defray the expenses of maintenance during those extra days. The pastor had to shoulder these expenses if the completion of the visitation was delayed because of his negligence, v. gr., when the parochial records were so disorderly that the bishop needed longer time to examine them. But if the cause of the delayed completion of the visitation centered in the great number of persons to be confirmed, the added expenses were to be taken from the bishop's income; likewise, if the bishop gave himself over to a period of recreation that extended his stay at the parish where the visitation had been conducted.

This provision (§ iv) regarding the time limit of the visitation in a parish was a modification of § ii of *Decretum I* of this Title, which provided that the visitor should stay only one day in every church.

While the Council of Trent was very clear in advising the bishops to strive to complete the visitation as speedily as possible with all due attention,[278] the Manila Council decreed a specific duration for the visitation in every parish (§ iv). The Laws of the Indies, however, emphasized that the visitation should not be unduly prolonged.[279] The III Provincial Council of Mexico (1585) had briefly but concisely decreed:

[277] Blair and Robertson, *op. cit.*, XXVIII, 277 ff.

[278] Sess. XXIV, *de ref.*, c. 3.

[279] *Recopilacion*, Tomo I, Lib. I, tit. VII, Ley XXVI, p. 41.

"Modestia in Visitatione servanda est," in order to prevent the visitation from becoming a burden to the ones visited by the canonical visitor.[280]

Although the title of this *Decretum* seemed to indicate its concern simply for not burdening the pastors, nevertheless it also aimed to nullify every attempt that sought to defeat the purpose of the visitation by means of currying episcopal favor through the setting of sumptuous meals for them (§ i), through the rendering of personal service from outstanding people in the parish (§ i), through the furnishing of entertainment by singers and musicians (§ ii), and through the bestowal of generous gifts (§ iii).

DECRETUM V

De Visitandis Conservatoriis Puellarum

This *Decretum* consists of six paragraphs which deal with the following: first, the visitation of the *colegios* and the *beaterios;* second, the inquiry about these institutions, their rules and their statutes; third, a second visitation of these institutions within the same year for the purpose of finding out if the statutes of the previous visitation were obeyed; fourth, the visitation of houses which were under the Royal Patronage and its immediate protection; fifth, the visitation of hospitals built under the Royal Patronage; sixth, the visitation of all those things commanded by the Council of Trent in Sess. XXII, *de ref.*, c. 8.

To begin with, a *conservatorium* was a place or a house established for the safeguarding of virginal lives. It was also a place or a house which in the course of time served the purpose of reclaiming for a better life such girls or women whose virginity had been stained in the past.[281] The Manila Council used the term *conservatorium puellarum* in reference especially to the girls' *colegios*[282] and *beaterios.*[283]

[280] *III Mexicanum,* Lib. III, tit. I, § ii, pp. 141-142.

[281] Con. Prov. Avenionense (1725), Tit. XLII *Coll. Lac.*, I, 569 d.

[282] *Colegios* were real schools, where academic as well as vocational training was given. Cf. Alip, *Pol. Cult. Hist. Phil.*, I, 224-225.

[283] *Beaterios* were orphanages or special houses that cared for girls

§ i. The Manila Council forcefully commended the care and visitation of the *colegios* and the *beaterios* of women located within Manila and its suburbs to their respective bishop, to whom the duty of visitation belonged. The *colegios* for the education of girls existing in Manila and its suburbs at the time of the Council were the following: *Santa Potenciana* (1589), *Santa Isabel* (1596), *Santa Catalina* (1696) and *Santa Rosa* (1750). The first three were originally *beaterios*, but were converted later into *colegios*. The *beaterios* were *San Ignacio* (1699), *Santa Rosa* (1719), and *San Sebastian* (1740).[284] All these *colegios* and *beaterios* were Catholic institutions. Naturally the bishop of the diocese wherein they were located had the right of visitation.[285]

§ ii. The bishop in his visitation was to examine the documents of foundation of these *colegios* and *beaterios*, their rules and their statutes, revising them as needed, and inquiring into their observance to assure the fulfillment of the purpose of the institution. Likewise he was to investigate the individual records of the inmates, and prescribe for them the schedule of the daily exercises of piety. He was to provide them with a good confessor, and as far as possible an elderly one, who could teach them the Catholic religion and the life of perfection.[286]

§ iii. Aside from this annual visitation, the bishop was to visit the *colegios* and *beaterios* several times during the year. The purpose was to find out if the statutes given in

or women who wanted to live in seclusion. Cf. Alip, *op cit.*, I, p. 225. They were houses for women who preferred to live in seclusion, and who professed a special devotion to a particular saint. A school for young girls was usually to be found in these houses.—Alzona, *Hist. of Educ. in Phil.*, p. 33.

[284] Alzona, *op. cit.*, pp. 31-35; Zaide, *Catholicism in the Philippines*, pp. 92-93, 106; Blair and Robertson, *op. cit.*, XLV, 256 ff. Authors dispute the date of the foundation of Santa Potenciana.

[285] Conc. Trident., sess. XXII, *de ref.*, c. 8; Benedictus XIV, const. *Ad militantis*, 30 mart. 1742—*Fontes*, n. 326.

[286] Cf. *III Mexicanum*, Lib. V, tit. I, § vii, p. 283; Con. Prov. Avenionense (1725), tit. XLII, *Coll. Lac.*, I, p. 569 d.

the previous visitation were obeyed. The bishop had to be accompanied by clerics in making such a visitation. The bishop could visit the *colegios* and *beaterios* as many times during the year as he deemed it prudent, especially if there existed a founded doubt or suspicion that the statutes or rules were not being fulfilled. The provision of this paragraph was in harmony with that of § ii, *Decretum IV,* of Tit. II, which provided that priests should see to it that without a companion they would not approach the girls of these *colegios.*

§ iv. The houses which were under the Royal Patronage and its immediate protection, were to be visited also by the bishops, but only *quoad spiritualia,* and *salvis omnibus juribus Regis.* A house was said to be under the Royal Patronage and its immediate protection when it was established and maintained through a royal grant. Over such a house the bishop of the place had the right of visitation regarding all spiritual matters and such things which in their very purpose served the worship of God and the salvation of souls.[287] In Manila, orphanages and asylums for orphans and destitute children, such as *Santa Potenciana* (1591) and *Santa Isabel* (1596), were established and supported by Royal Grant.[288] Regarding the visitation of these institutions, the rights of the King were to be held and honored intact, such as the internal regulations of *Santa Potenciana* provided by the royal ordinance of June 11, 1594.[289] The right to appoint the administration staff belonged to the king. *Santa Isabel* and *Sta. Rosa* were placed under the Sisters of Charity with the grant of Royal Patronage.[290]

[287] Conc. Trident., sess. XXII, *de ref.*, c. 8.

[288] Zaide, *op. cit.*, p. 106; Blair and Robertson, *op. cit.*, VII, 141 ff. *Santa Potenciana* received from the government annually 700 pesos, 690 gantas of unpolished rice, 25 quintals of wood, and 17 gantas of coconut oil for lighting purposes. See Alzona, *op. cit.*, p. 32.

[289] Alzona, *op. cit.*, p. 32.

[290] Alip, *op. cit.*, I, 227. Other examples of the right of the King regarding the houses under the Royal Patronage and its immediate protection were contained in the Laws of the Indies such as Leyes

§ v. Hospitals which were established under the Royal Patronage were to be visited by the bishops accompanied by a Royal Assistant. This Assistant was not a mere companion of the bishop; he was ordinarily the governor, or auditor of the Royal *Audiencia,* or one delegated by them.[291] According to the Laws of the Indies the visitation of the hospitals that were immediately under the Royal Patronage either because they were established through its total or partial grant, or through the alms and contributions of the cities or towns, was to be undertaken annually by the governor or by his delegate.[292] Ordinarily the governor or his delegate arranged the time of his visitation of the hospitals in such a way that it would coincide with the bishop's visitation. In this case the first act that was to be done in the visiting of such hospitals was to announce that the visitation was being made with the special commission of the King.

As regards hospitals over which the bishops had the right of visitation by royal commission, the bishops were to make investigation not only concerning those things that pertained to the divine worship and the salvation of souls, but also concerning the material condition of the hospital, such as the income through temporal or perpetual donations or alms, the kinds of sickness treated and cured, its specification or service for men or for women, the divisions of its various rooms, etc., etc.[293]

There were many hospitals in Manila and the provinces at the time of the Manila Council. The hospitals in Manila were: *San Lazaro,* founded in 1578; *San Juan de Dios* (1596), *Hospital Real* (1612), *San Gabriel* hospital (1588),

II, VI, VIII, IX, X, XI, XII, XIII, XIV, XV of Lib. I, Tit. XXII. Cf. *Recopilacion,* Tomo I, 128-131.

[291] *Recopilacion,* Tomo I, Lib. I, Tit. IV, Ley V, n. 21, p. 18; Ley XX, p. 22.

[292] *Recopilacion,* Tomo I, Lib. I, Tit. IV, Ley V, n. 21, Ley XX, pp. 18 & 22 respectively; *III Mexicanum,* Lib. V, tit. I, § vii, p. 283; *IV Mexicano,* Lib. V, tit. I, § viii, p. 181.

[293] *Recopilacion,* Tomo II, Lib. III, Tit. XIV, Ley XXV, p. 70.

Hospital of *Bagumbayan* for convalescing patients (1645); and hospitals located outside Manila were: *Hospital de San Jose* in Cavite (1641), *Hospital de Aguas Santas de Mainit* at Los Banos, Laguna (1602).[294]

§ vi. The Manila Council admonished the bishops to see to it that all those things which the Council of Trent prescribed to be inquired into by them be diligently done. Such things aside from those already mentioned in the preceding paragraphs were: confraternities, eleemosynary institutions known as loan foundations, all pious wills and places by whatever name designated, even though the care of the aforesaid institutions be in the hands of laymen and the said pious places be protected by the privilege of exemption. Bishops were to take cognizance of and execute in accordance with the ordinances of the sacred canons all things that had been instituted for the worship of God or for the salvation of souls or for the support of the poor, any custom, even though immemorial, and any privileges or statutes whatsoever to the contrary notwithstanding.[295]

Since the early years of the Spanish regime, religious confraternities were established for charitable purposes. The first of these confraternities was the famous *Hermandad de la Misericordia,* which was founded in 1594 for the purpose of practicing merciful works by means of funds contributed by the members. Prior to the celebration of the Manila Council, other confraternities already in existence were: the *Cofradia de Nuestra la Señora de la Soledad* (1651), the *Venerable Congregacion de San Pedro de Apostol* (1698), the *Venerable Orden Tercersi de Sto. Domingo* (1699), the *Cofradía de la Nuestra Señora de la Correa* (1712), and the *Venerable Orden Tercera de San Francisco* (1729).[296] The bishops were to investigate the documents

[294] Alip, *op. cit.*, I, p. 168; Zaide, *op. cit.*, pp. 104-105; *Recopilacion,* Tomo I, Lib. I, Tit. IV, Leyes I and II, p. 16.

[295] Sess. XXII, *de ref.*, c. 8.

[296] Buzeta-Bravo, *Diccionario Geografico, Estadistico, Historico de las Islas Filipinas* (2 vols., Manila, 1850), I, 166-168 (hereafter cited as *Dic. Geog. Est. Hist. Fil.*); Zaide, *Catholicism in the Philippines,* p. 106.

of erection of the above-mentioned confraternities. They were to abolish those which were found to have been established without the proper permission of the ordinary, and those which were found to be lax or useless.[297] Inquiries were to be made into the faithful fulfillment of pious bequests and last wills.[298] The principal concern of the bishop in his visitation of the hospitals or pious places was to see to it that the constitutions and foundations were being fulfilled and that the founded Masses were being celebrated and other obligations duly executed.[299]

TITULUS QUARTUS
DE SYNODIS

The fourth title contains four *Decreta. Decretum I* deals with the provincial council; *Decretum II,* in five paragraphs, with diocesan synods; *Decretum III,* in twenty-four paragraphs, with the calends; and *Decretum IV,* in five paragraphs, with public witnesses.

DECRETUM I
De Concilio Provinciali

The provision of this council regarding the holding of the provincial councial was conditional *(si qua detur occasio celebrandi provincialem synodum).* It likewise did not determine the frequency for the holding of provincial councils *(eis tamen certum tempus non praefinit).* This provision was not consonant with the provision of the Council of Trent, which specified the obligation of holding the provincial council every three years.[300] It was not even in harmony with the various Apostolic Indults granted to the Indies regarding the requisite frequency for the holding of the provincial council.

297 *Manilanum,* Actio V, Tit. II, Decretum VII, §§ i and ii—*supra,* p. 132.

298 *Manilanum,* Actio V, Tit. II, Decretum VII, §§ i-iii—*supra,* p. 131. Cf. *III Mexicanum,* Lib. V, tit. I, § vii, p. 283.

299 *IV Mexicano,* Lib. V, tit. I, § viii, p. 181.

300 Sess. XXIV, *de ref.,* c. 2.

On April 15, 1583, Gregory XIII granted the Indies the indult of holding the provincial councils every six or seven years. Then, in the Bull of Pope Paul V on December 7, 1610, in response to a petition of the Spanish King, permission was granted for the holding of the provincial council every twelve years, unless some other disposition was made by the Holy See, or unless the archbishops and bishops would subsequently consider a more frequent celebration necessary.[301] This provision was also not in accordance with the directive of the Laws of the Indies, which provided that provincial councils were to be celebrated in conformity with the Apostolic Indult given by Pope Paul V, which had granted the permission to hold provincial councils in the Indies every twelve years.[302] The provision of the Manila Council regarding the holding of provincial councils, apart from being conditional, was only exhortatory *(hortatur Illmos. et Rmos. Metropolitas)*. It could never have the binding force of a law, even if this Council of Manila of 1771 had received recognition form the Holy See.

The purpose of holding provincial councils as stated in this *Decretum*, was the service and utility it could afford to the Church in the Islands *(in commodum et utilitatem hujus ecclesiae)*. Thus the purpose was expressed in a more general form than in the Council of Trent, which had declared that provincial councils should be held for the regulation of morals, the correcting of abuses, the settling of contro-

[301] Morelli, *Fasti Novi Orbis et Ordinationum Apostolicarum*, Ordinatio CLXIII, p. 85 and pp. 263-264; Gomez Zamora, *Regio Patronato Espanol e Indiano*, p. 401; Levillier, 104-106; Solorzano, II, Lib. III, Cap. VII, n. 40; According to Frasso, there was a Royal Patent on June 21, 1570, granting the Indies the permission to hold a provincial council every fifth year; on April 15, 1583, Gregory XIII granted that the provincial council could be held every seventh year. Then Paul V, on Dec. 7, 1610, gave permission for the holding of the provincial council every twelve years; and on Feb. 9, 1621, there was issued another Royal Patent which granted only a six years' interval between provincial councils.—Frasso, *De Regio Patronatu Indiarum*, II, 325, n. 39; Morelli, *op. cit.*, Ordinatio CCXXIII, Anno 1610, 7 Dec.

[302] *Recopilacion*, Tomo I, Lib. I, Tit. VIII, Ley 1, p. 49.

versies, and for other purposes permitted by the sacred canons;[303] indeed, the Council of Manila itself was held for this specified purpose: the protection of the discipline of the Christian religion, the regulation of morality, the correction of abuses, and the settlement of the controversies existing in the Ecclesiastical Province of Manila.[304]

According to the *Real Cedula* (1769) of Charles III, one of the specific purposes in his ordering that provincial councils were to be held without delay in the Indies was the restoration of the monastic discipline, which had fallen into decadence, in regard to both its interior and its exterior observance of the monastic rules.[305] Other considerations which the Spanish King charged the archbishops of the Indies Ecclesiastical Province and of the Philippine Islands to propose, discuss, and decide in this provincial council were the twenty points he set forth in the same *Real Cedula*.[306]

DECRETUM II

De Synodis Dioecesanis

A diocesan synod is a legitimate assembly which the bishop holds in his diocese with his clergy for the purpose of treating of those things which pertain to his pastoral care of the diocese.[307]

This *Decretum*, consisting of five paragraphs, deals with: first, the holding of the diocesan synod every year with the pastors of the whole diocese called to it; second, the number of pastors needed and sufficient for the holding of the

303 Sess. XXII, *de ref.*, c. 2; cc. 2-7, 9-14, D. XVIII; c. 25, X, *de accusationibus, inquisitionibus, et denunciationibus*, V, 1.

304 *Manilanum*, Actio I, Decretum I—Cf. *supra*, p. 60; Actio V, Tit. II, Decreta I-XVII—Cf. *supra*, pp. 125 ff. *passim*.

305 Vargas Ugarte, *op. cit.*, II, 207.

306 Vargas Ugarte, *op. cit.*, II, 207-211.

307 "Synodus dioecesana est legitima congregatio ab Episcopo coacta ex presbyteris et clericis suae dioecesis, aliisve qui ad eam accedere tenentur, in quo de his quae curae pastorali incumbant, agendum et deliberandum est"—Benedictus XIV, *De Synodo Dioecesana*, Lib. I, c. I, n. 4; Bouix, *Tract. de Episc.*, II, 348.

synod; third, the alternate members and the number sufficient for the holding of the synod in case no pastor could attend; fourth, the holding of a diocesan synod six months after the celebration of this provincial council, and the penalty for not holding it; and fifth, the place where the diocesan synod is to be held.

§ i. The Manila Council decreed that bishops convoke annually a diocesan synod. . . . This provision is a reiteration of that of the Council of Trent, which stated that a diocesan synod was to be held annually,[308] which was practically the same legislation as had been binding since the thirteenth century.[309] The Laws of the Indies repeated also that the Council of Trent, charging archbishops and bishops to hold annually a diocesan synod in their respective dioceses, in conformity with the provision of the Council of Trent. And to make this provision effective, civil officials were charged to remind the archbishops and bishops of this obligation every year.[310]

Unlike the frequency prescribed for the celebrating of provincial councils in the Indies ecclesiastical provinces, that of the diocesan synod was not changed by any indult or privilege.[311] There was once an indult that allowed the holding of a diocesan synod every second year, but that was personal, given to Archbishop Sto. Toribio of Lima.[312]

The diocesan synod was to be convoked by the bishops.[313] The bishop alone had this power, and he could exercise it even without the consent of the chapter, unless it could be

[308] Sess. XXIV, *de ref.*, c. 2.

[309] IV Laternen. (1215), cap. 6; c. 25, X, *de accusationibus, inquisitionibus, et denunciationibus*, V. I.

[310] *Recopilacion*, Tomo I, Lib. I, Tit. VII, Ley III, p. 49.

[311] Morelli, *op. cit.*, Ordinatio CLXIII, p. 285 and pp. 263-264.

[312] Haraldus, *Lima Limata*, p. 274 (as found in Rafael Gomez Hoyos, *Leyes de Indias y el Derecho Ecclesiastico en la America Española e Islas Filipinas* [Medellin-Colombia: Ediciones Universidad Catolica Boliviana, 1945], p. 228, footnote 4); Frasso was mistaken in believing that it was a general indult. Cf. Frasso, *op. cit.*, II, c. 93, n. 40; Morelli, *op. cit.*, Ord. CXXXVIII.

[313] Conc. Trident., sess. XXIV, *de ref.*, c. 2.

proved that the necessity of its consent was a legitimate custom still reasonably in force and operation.[314] Not even the vicar general, without special mandate, could convoke the diocesan synod.[315] But if the bishop as the result of some legitimate cause[316] could not hold the diocesan synod, he was to do it through another person delegated by him, v. gr., the vicar general with his bishop's special mandate.[317]

Regarding the persons to be called to the synod, the Manila Council made mention of only two classes of persons, namely, the pastors and the public witnesses (§§ i-iii). This was rather not consonant with the provision of the Council of Trent, which declared that not only must those be called who have charge of parochial or other secular churches, but also all the exempt who would otherwise by reason of the cessation of that exemption be bound to be present at the synod.[318]

§ ii. The *Provincia* mentioned in this paragraph was not the ecclesiastical province. It was the civil province. At that time every diocese in the Philippines was made up of several civil provinces. Each civil province was divided into towns. During those times a town was ordinarily a parish. The fathers of the Manila Council knew very well that there was a tremendous scarcity of priests in the Islands. It was quite impossible that all of them attend the synod, for otherwise people would be left without even one priest in a province.

For this reason the Council declared that one or two pastors from the remote provinces would be sufficient for the holding of a synod. But this pastor or these pastors were to come well instructed or informed about the state of the

314 S.C.C., *Virodunen.*, dec. 1585—*Fontes*, n. 2149; S.C.C., *Calaritana*, 16 iul. 1599—*Fontes*, n. 2327; S.C.C., *Oriolen*, 27 maii 1632, ad 14—*Fontes*, n. 2543; S.C.C., *Fulignaten.*, 26 febr. 1639—*Fontes*, n. 2602.

315 S.C.C., *Nullius*, 4 dec. 1655—*Fontes*, n. 2745.

316 Cf. *infra*, p. 233; Bouix, *op. cit.*, II, 362.

317 S.C.C., *Nullius*, 4 dec. 1655—*Fontes*, n. 2745; Bouix, *op. cit.*, II, 355; Ferraris, s. v. *Synodus Dioecesana*, n. 13.

318 Sess. XXIV, *de ref.*, c. 2.

province. In this manner they could well report to the bishop during the synod what things in the province or provinces needed reform.

The Council accorded a further concession: if on account of a definite cause (which cause had to be manifested to the bishop) no pastor could attend, then the public witnesses[319] of that province (whose pastors could not attend) were to be sent to attend the synod. They were to be equipped with a letter informing the bishop what things needed reform in the province. The Council did not specify what reason would excuse a pastor from attending the synod. But it certainly had to be a legitimate reason.[320] The Council did not specify the number of public witnesses who were to be sent to the synod in case no pastor from a province could be present. Presumably at least two public witnesses were required, for each civil province had at least two public witnesses.[321]

Long before the celebration of the Manila Council (1771) a diocesan synod had been convoked by Bishop Domingo de Salazar of Manila in 1582. The bishop presided over the synod. The most learned persons were present—the Dominican Father Salvatierra, the most outstanding scholars among the Augustinians and Franciscans, the Jesuit Fathers Sedeno and Sanchez, and the Licentiate Don Diego Vasquez de Mercado, as dean of the new cathedral. At this diocesan synod it was discussed whether the natives were to be ministered to in their own language, or whether they were to be obliged to learn the Spanish, and it was decided to instruct them in their own tongue. The divine office, the *Doctrina Christiana,* which Fr. Juan de Placencia had translated into the Tagalog language, was approved. His work, the *Arte y Vocabulario Tagalo,* was judged most useful because of the ease with which it permitted an understanding and thorough knowledge of so foreign a lan-

[319] Cf. *infra*, pp. 237 ff.

[320] Cf. *infra*, p. 233; Benedictus XIV, *op. cit.*, Lib. III, Cap. XII, n. 3; Bouix, *op. cit.*, II, 362.

[321] Cf. *infra*, p. 237.

guage.[322] It was not indicated whether public witnesses attended this diocesan synod, nor was it stated whether those learned religious priests who attended were pastors.

§ iv. The Manila Council pronounced that within six months after the completion of this Council each bishop was to hold a diocesan synod for the purpose of making known to the people the decrees of this Council. The bishop could select the most convenient time for the celebration of the synod. Ordinarily the most expedient time was the occasion of the parochial visitation, when many priests were gathered (§ v). In this regard the Tridentine Law, prescribing the annual celebration of a synod,[323] had not pronounced any definite interval between the provincial council and the first synod. It simply prescribed the annual celebration of a synod. In this respect, therefore, the Manila Council had a stricter provision than the Council of Trent. Presumably the fathers of the Manila Council repeated substantially the decree of the IV Provincial Council of Milan (1576), which had enacted that within six months after the celebrating of the provincial council, a diocesan synod was to be held.[324] This provision of the Manila Council was to bind under penalty of a two months suspension from office, and even to the extent of a pecuniary fine for any bishop who proved indifferent or negligent in holding the synod. Benedict XIV reproved and held as inexcusable any bishop who through carelessness failed to celebrate the synod, and he reminded bishops that for their disobedience they became liable for suspension from office.[325] In this connection the Council of Trent decreed that if bishops proved negligent they were to incur the penalties prescribed by the sacred

[322] Juan de la Concepcion, *Hist. Gen. Phil.*, II, 45-46; Francisco de Santa Ines, *Cronica de la Provincia de San Gregorio Magno de Religiosos Descalzos de N. P. San Francisco en Islas Philipinas, China, Japon, etc. Escrita en 1676* (Manila, 1892), p. 212.

[323] Sess. XXIV, *de ref.*, c. 2.

[324] "Episcopus ad Tridentini Concilii praescriptum singulis annis, ac item semper sex post Provinciale Concilium mensibus, Dioecesanam Synodum habeat . . ."—*Act. Eccl. Mediol.*, Pars I, p. 449.

[325] *De Synodo Dioecesana*, Lib. I, Cap. VI, n. 5.

canons.[326] The pecuniary fine added by the Manila Council was peculiar to it alone.

§ v. Regarding the seat or place of the synod, the Manila Council declared that it could be held outside the city.[327] Without doubt, a bishop could hold the diocesan synod in any part of his diocese. But it was expedient to hold it in the city or the place where his cathedral church was erected.[328] In a case of necessity, such as persecution, expulsion, pestilence, etc., a bishop could hold his synod even outside his diocese as long as the ordinary of the place gave his permission.[329] The church, and if possible the cathedral church, was to be the seat or place of the synod since the *Pontificale Romanum*[330] and the *Caeremoniale Episcoporum*[331] suppose that as the place for the synod. The Manila Council clearly declared that the synod was to be held in a church, even if it had to be held outside the episcopal see.

As in many parts of the world, the Tridentine Law on the diocesan synod was not observed in the Philippines. Some obvious reasons for the non-holding of diocesan synods were the scarcity of priests, the larger territorial sweep of the dioceses,[332] the bitter struggles which embroiled the authorities of the Church and of the State, and the controversies between the bishops and the friar *curas*.[333]

[326] Sess. XXIV, *de ref.*, c. 2.

[327] By the word "city" the fathers of this Council presumably meant the seat of the Episcopal See. At that time not all episcopal sees were located in cities.

[328] Indubitandum est, Episcopum, non solum in civitate, verum etiam in qualibet suae dioecesis parte posse Synodum cogere . . . Expedit tamen, cum nullum obstat impedimentum, ut illam cogat in civitate, quemadmodum declaravit Sacra Congregatio Concilii (*in Acernensi*, die 17 Maii 1636, lib. 15 *Decretorum*, p. 335, a tergo, his verbis: Posse Episcopum etiam in dicto oppido dioecesanam Synodum congregare, sed satius esse ut illam apud suam Cathedralem celebret).—Benedictus XIV, *op. cit.*, Lib. I, Cap V, nn. 2-3; Bouix, *op. cit.*, II, 355-356.

[329] Ferraris, s.v. *Synodus Dioecesana*, n. 77.

[330] III, 5—*Ordo ad Synodum;* cf. Bouix, *op. cit.*, II, 355.

[331] Lib. I, C. XXXI, n. 1; cf. Bouix, *op. cit.*, II, 355.

[332] Cf. *supra*, p. 182.

[333] Cf. *supra*, p. 179.

DECRETUM III

De Kalendis seu Coetibus

This *Decretum* is entitled *De Kalendis* presumably because the reunion or meeting was usually held on the calends of every month, i.e., the first day. *Kalendae* was one of the names by which the chapter or general congregation of the pastors was called in ancient times, especially in France, England, and Germany. Such chapters or *kalendae* were held once or twice a year, or every single month, with the archdeacon or vicar forane presiding over them. Aside from the term *Kalendae*, the chapters or general congregations of pastors were called *consistoria, synodi, sessiones vel collationes.*[334]

This *Decretum* contains twenty-five paragraphs dealing with (1) the day, place, and some ceremonial specifications regarding the calends; (2) the inquiry conducted secretly by the vicar forane from the public witnesses into the life and proper decorum of the pastors; (3) the questionnaire; (4) the inquiry from the same public witnesses about public sinners and other delinquent people; (5) the correction given to the delinquent according to the fraternal way of correcting one's neighbors; (6) the consultation of pastors amongst themselves about the affairs of their respective churches; (7) the clerical conference on moral subjects; (8) the procedure or method of the conference; (9) the minutes and some concluding business before its adjournment; (10) the subscription of the minutes and the letter to the bishop; (11) the penalty for absentees, noise-makers and those who neglected to solve the cases; (12) the solution of the moral cases despite the non-celebration of the calends; (13) the legitimate reason for not attending the calends; (14) the suitable place for the meeting and the table's frugality; (15) the penalty for omitting the con-

[334] Pallottini, s.v. *Parochus,* § viii, n. 99; Thomassinus, *Vetus et Nova Ecclesiae Disciplina circa Beneficia et Beneficiarios* (3 parts in 10 vols., ed. postrema, cum Parisieni accuratissime collata, Magontiaci, 1787), Pars II, Lib. III, cap. 74, n. 10 (hereafter cited as *Vet. et Nov. Eccl. Discip.*).

vocation of the calends or for not solving the moral cases; (16) the publication of the solution of the moral cases; (17) the membership; the division of the vicariates (deaneries) if necessary; (18) the designation of the parish house of *Santa Cruz* as a place of meeting and conference for the clergy of Manila; date and time for the holding of the meeting and the conference; (19) the date and place of the conference on moral subjects for the clerical personnel of the cathedral church; (20) the penalty for absence without a legitimate reason; (21) the application of the money derived from fines; (22) the register or book of conferences; (23) the definition of *legitima causa;* (24) the bishop's unannounced assistance at the meeting and the conference; and (25) the prohibition of card games and of banquets on the occasion of the calends.

§ i. On the first day of every month (unless it was a holy day of obligation) the pastors of every vicariate (deanery) were to assemble in the parish house of their vicar forane. Usually, the vicarial meetings or the calends[335] were to commence with the sacramental confession of the pastors followed by the singing of the Mass for the deceased pastors, during which a sermon on the greatness of the pastoral duty and the way of perfection was to be preached. After the Mass, a procession in honor of the dead was to be held near the cemetery.[336]

§§ ii and iii. The pastors, still vested with surplice, were to join this procession, after which they were to assemble in the sacristy or in any other convenient place. In the meantime the vicar forane was to examine the public witnesses[337] about the life and conduct of the pastors. This investigation was to be made privately before the notary or anybody in his stead. The vicar forane was to ask the

[335] Hereafter the word "calends" alone will be used with a view to avoiding the frequent repetition of the longer phrase "vicarial meetings or Calends."

[336] *I Con. Prov. Mediol.*, C. XXIX; Mansi, XXXIV, 42; Hardouin, X, 672.

[337] Cf. *infra*, p. 237 ff.

public witnesses a set of questions, for instance: (1) whether and how the pastors preached on Sundays and holy days of obligation;[338] (2) whether the pastors performed the Sunday services, such as the Rosary, the Solemn Mass, the sermon, and the catechetical instruction in the morning; the solemn *Salve Regina,* another Rosary, and solemn vespers in the afternoon;[339] (3) whether the pastors gave personally or through others the necessary spiritual help to the dying parishioners;[340] (4) whether through the pastor's negligence and carelessness some one had died without baptism, confession, holy Communion, or extreme unction;[341] (5) whether the pastors celebrated the Holy Sacrifice of the Mass frequently; (6) whether the sick were brought to the church for the reception of the last sacraments as ordered by the pastors; [342] (7) whether the pastors assisted at the funeral rites of the poor; [343] (8) whether the pastors cherished unduly intimate relationships *(familiaritas)* with any woman;[344] (9) whether the pastors demanded excessive stole fees or other taxes in any form, or obliged the parishioner to give him service, etc., etc.;[345] (10) whether the pastors wore the clerical garb;[346] (11) whether the pastors were addicted to the drinking of wine, the playing of card games, and the like;[347] (12) whether the pastors fulfilled the law of resi-

[338] Actio IV, Tit. unicus, Decretum III, § i—*supra,* p. 93; Blair and Robertson, *The Philippine Islands,* XXI, 58.

[339] Actio IV, Tit. unicus, Decretum VII, §§ i & ii—*supra,* p. 99; Actio III, Tit. II, Decretum III, §§ i & iii— *supra,* p. 87.

[340] Actio V, Tit. I, Decretum V, §§ i & iii—*supra,* p. 119; Decretum IV, § vii—*supra,* p. 116; Actio IV, Tit. unicus, Decretum XII, § iii—*supra,* p. 104.

[341] Blair and Robertson, *op. cit.,* XXI, 58; cf. *supra,* p. 197.

[342] Blair and Robertson, *op. cit.,* L, 234; Actio V, Tit. I, Decretum IV, § iv—*supra,* p. 115.

[343] Actio IV, Tit. unicus, Decretum XII, § ii—*supra,* pp. 104-105.

[344] Actio III, Tit. II, Decretum II, §§ i, ii, & iv—*supra,* p. 86.

[345] Actio IV, Tit. unicus, Decretum XI, §§ i, ii & iii—*supra,* pp. 103-104. Blair and Robertson, *op. cit.,* L, 152-153; XXI, 59.

[346] Actio III, Tit. II, Decretum I, § iv—*supra,* p. 85.

[347] Actio III, Tit. II, Decretum IV, § xii; § v—*supra,* pp. 89 & 88 respectively.

dence and lived so as not to furnish reason for any complaint; whether they had gone out of the parish house without any reasonable cause after one o'clock in the morning;[348] (13) whether the pastors kept the church, the altars, etc., clean.[349]

§ iv. After the private inquiry into the pastor's life, the public witnesses were to assemble before all the pastors. The vicar forane was to conduct publicly an investigation regarding the public sinners,[350] drunkards,[351] men in concubinage,[352] sorcerers,[353] the superstitious,[354] the vagabonds,[355] the instigators,[356] and other types of sinners.[357]

Immediately after rendering an account, the public sinners were to be segregated, and the pastors were to consult among one another regarding what action was to be taken.[358]

This inquiry into the life of pastors and of the laity was an exercise of the full judicial power which the bishop possessed, both over his clergy and over his laity. It was the bishop's right to set up his tribunal anywhere within his territory. During the Calends he had his tribunal set up, with the vicars forane presiding. The clergy and the laity were to be obedient to the authority set over them.[359]

[348] Actio IV, Tit. unicus, Decretum IX, §§ i, ii, iv—*supra*, p. 102.

[349] Actio IV, Tit. unicus, Decretum VI, §§ i, iv—*supra*, pp. 98-99.

[350] "... si quis peccator publicus homicidii ut puta, vel adulterii vel perjurii reus ..."—Thomassinus, *Vet. et Nov. Eccl. Discip.*, Pars II, Lib. III, cap. 74, n. 11; "... vitia publica veluti ludos illicitos, concubinatus, blasphemios, usuras et hujusmodi alia ..."—*III Mexicanum*, Lib. I, tit. VIII, § viii, pp. 49-50; *I & II Mexico*, Cap. VI, p. 47.

[351] Actio V, Tit. II, Decretum XIII, § viii—*supra*, p. 138.

[352] *Ibidem*, Decretum X, § vi—*supra*, p. 135.

[353] *Ibidem*, §§ i & ii—*supra*, p. 134.

[354] Actio IV, Tit. unicus, Decretum VIII, §§ iii-vi—*supra*, pp. 100 ff.

[355] *Ibidem*, Decretum I, §§ i & ii—*supra*, p. 90.

[356] Actio V, Tit. II, Decretum XVII—*supra*, p. 143; Decretum XIV, § iii—*supra*, p. 139.

[357] Blair and Robertson, *op. cit.*, XXI, 60-61.

[358] Thomassinus, *op. cit.*, Pars II, Lib. III, cap. 74, n. 10.

[359] Baronius, *Annales Ecclesiastici*, XVII (1067), n. 8, p. 281 (as found in Andrew Leonard Slafkosy, *The Canonical Visitation of the*

§ v. Except for a serious and notorious offense, the punishment was to be imposed in the following order: first, the proper pastor was to punish the sinner; second, if the sinner did not amend, he was to be punished publicly during the following calends; third, if, in spite of this public punishment, the sinner showed no amendment, the bishop was to be informed, in order that he might provide a necessary corrective measure.

This order of correction was also to be observed by the vicar forane regarding the delinquent pastors, unless the gravity of the crime or the resulting scandal demanded otherwise. This manner of correction resembled the manner of correction for the laity and clerics alike during the celebration of the Calends in ancient times in France, England, and Germany.[360]

§ vi. The next act after the correction was to be the consultation or meeting of the pastors among themselves. They were to treat of the affairs of their respective churches, or of matters pertaining to the utility of their respective parishes. There was no doubt that pastors could enlighten each other by their own experience.[361] But they were allowed to ask the counsel of the nobles, if necessary. The nobles, occupying the highest place in the society, enjoyed great po-

Diocese, The Catiholic University of America Canon Law Studies, n. 142 (Washington, D.C.: The Catholic University of America Press, 1941), p. 43.

[360] "... Experimento didicimus, non minus bonam collationem quam lectionem prodesse. Unde statuimus a praesenti ut per singulas plebes singulis Kalendis omnes presbyteri, seu clerici simul conveniant ... Et si forte aliquis inter eos negligens aut reprehensibilis invenitur, a caeteris corrigitur. Quod si corrigi omnino non studierit, mox suo nuncient episcopo, ut hoc acrius emendare quantocius studeat."—Thomassinus, *op. cit.*, Pars II, Lib. III, cap. 74, n. 10; Pallottini s.v. *Parochus*, § viii, n. 99.

[361] "... Deinde presbyteri cujuscumque conditionis, curam animarum habentes, conferant inter se quae ad boni pastoris officium et ad curam animarum, recte gerendam pertinent; consulant de difficultatibus et incommodis suae parochiae, quorum explicatio vel remedium, aliorum consilium et operam requirat ..." *Act. Eccl. Mediol.*, Pars I, p. 80; *I Con. Mediol.*, C. XXIX, Mansi, XXXIV, 42.

litical and social rights. Over and above this, they were considered the wise people in the community. The pastors, therefore, could seek their opinion or advice regarding the material management of the church, e.g., in cases of church repair or construction the pastors could consult the nobles regarding the materials, the workers, the means to enlist the co-operation of the people in contributing to the church construction, etc. They could also consult the nobles about things concerning the good of the people, e.g., how to make the still barbarous natives group together *(reductio)*[362] with a view to facilitating their conversion and administering to their spiritual needs.

§ vii. The presentation of four moral cases *(casus conscientiae)* in Latin[363] was to follow. The solution of these cases was to be based upon the principles of moral theology in the manner in which they were edited by the Council. The solution therefore was in accordance with the doctrines of St. Augustine and St. Thomas.[364] In the presentation of the moral cases, the vicar forane was to abstain from subtle and speculative questions. The cases were to be of a practical character and doubts encountered in the administration of the sacraments were to be clarified. The cases were occasionally also to deal with mystical theology and the liturgy.

§ viii. The presentation of the cases having been made, one who on the spur of the occasion was to be designated by the vicar forane was then for one-half hour to lead a discussion on two points, one of which was to be in line with the *status quaestionis* of the *casus*. After this the vicar was to ask each and every one if any further doubt remained, with a view to finding a solution for the doubt from the rest of the assembly.

§ ix. Then, upon the reading of certain provisions of the

[362] *Manilanum,* Actio IV, Tit. unicus, Decretum I, *supra,* pp. 90 ff.

[363] "... Iidem autem vicarii libellum de casibus conscientiae ... reliquis sacerdotibus legent ..." *I Con. Mediol.* c. XXIX, Mansi, XXXIV, 42; Pallottini, s.v. *Parochus,* § viii, n. 99; Hardouin, X, 672.

[364] Actio III, Tit. I, Decretum II, § iv—*supra,* p. 83.

Provincial Council[365] about pastors,[366] confessors,[367] preachers,[368] or clerics,[369] and upon an announcement of the cases for the following Calends, the Calends were to be adjourned. The acts or minutes of the Calends were to be written in a record book by the notary, or by his substitute. This record was to indicate the place, the day, the month, and the year, with a listing of the members who were present or absent. Denouncements made against pastors were to be recorded in another book.

§ x. The members present were to sign their names in the minutes before leaving; they were also to sign a letter to the bishop, or during the vacancy of the see, to the cathedral chapter. The letter was to contain a report regarding the Calends and the solution of the moral cases.

§§ xi-xiii. A fine of *una argenti uncia*,[370] applicable to the public witnesses,[371] was to be imposed upon those who without any legitimate cause did not attend the Calends. Paragraph twenty-three of this *Decretum* defined a legitimate cause as whatever confined one to bed or necessitated a preoccupation with some important business.[372] Pestilence or heavy rainfall were to be considered also as legitimate causes for non-attendance (§ xii). Any dangerous sailing across the sea was also to be held as a legitimate cause for non-attendance at the Calends (§ xiii). The same penalty attached to those who with any unnecessary noise brought annoyance or disturbance to the Calends, or who neglected to solve the moral cases.

365 "...et aliquot capita tum harum constitutionum, tum earum quae in synodo dioecesana decernentur... vicarii explicabunt..." *I Con. Mediol.* cap. XXIX, Mansi, XXXIV, 42.

366 Actio IV, Tit. unicus, Decreta I-XIV, *supra*, pp. 90 ff.

367 Actio V, Tit. I, Decretum III, §§ iii-ix, xi-xvii, xiv, xxii-xxv—*supra*, pp. 109 ff.

368 Actio IV, Tit. unicus, Decretum III, §§ i-v, viii-x—*supra*, pp. 93 ff.

369 Actio III, Tit. II, Decreta I-IV—*supra*, pp. 85 ff.

370 Cf. *supra*, p. 187.

371 Cf. *infra*, pp. 237 ff.

372 Cf. *infra*, p. 236.

§ xiv. The Calends, being vicarial meetings, were supposed to be held in the parish house of the vicar forane (§ i). But if this house was located inconveniently for the members, some other house, more centrally located in the province, was to be chosen. If on account of the poverty of the parish the expenses for the Calends could not be shouldered by the pastor, then all the pastors and clerics in attendance were *pro rata* to make a contribution for covering these expenses. At any rate, even if the pastor of the place was a man of rich means, not more than three courses of food and fruit could be served at the table. The Manila Council (1771) therefore was intent on the observance of frugality not only at the bishop's table[373] but also at the table of the priests and the clerics.

Though the Manila Council allowed three courses of food to be served at table on the occasion of the Calends, the I Provincial Council of Milan (1565) had allowed only one course of food.[374]

§ xv. The vicar forane was to convoke and preside over the Calends. The penalty for non-compliance with this duty was the payment of a fine of *decem argenti unciae,*[375] five of which were applicable to the seminary,[376] and five to the public witnesses. The same penalty was to bind the vicar forane if, without any legitimate cause, he omitted the presentation of any moral cases. And if in this he was proved negligent, he was to be deprived of his office. Whatever might have been the cause for which the vicar forane did not convoke the Calends or did not present the moral cases, he was to manifest it to the bishop.

§ xvi. The solution of the cases was to be published every month in a book form for every pastor to have in his parish library.[377] But before its publication the text was to be cor-

[373] Cf. *supra,* p. 207; Actio II, Tit. III, Decretum IV, § i—*supra,* p. 74.

[374] Cap. XXIX—Mansi, XXXIV, 42.

[375] Cf. *supra,* p. 187.

[376] Actio III, Tit. I, Decretum II, § xii—*supra,* p. 85.

[377] Actio V, Tit. II, Decretum VIII, § vi—*supra,* p. 134.

rected and approved by a professor of moral theology in the seminary, or by one appointed by the bishop in the event that the diocese was without a seminary. In its order it was to be like a treatise in moral theology.[378]

§ xvii. Pastors, curates, and all other clerics living within a vicariate (deanery) were to attend the Calends and present the solution of the *casus conscientiae.* If geographically or territorially the vicarial district was so extensive that it proved seriously difficult for them to attend, or that it occasioned an absence away from their respective parishes for a rather long time, the bishops were to see to it that such districts were divided into smaller ones.[379]

§ xviii. The Manila Council designated the parish house of Sta. Cruz[380] as the place for the Calends of the numerous pastors and clerics of the vicariate or city of Manila. It was also to be the place for the clerical conference on moral theology that was to be held every first and fifteenth days of the month at five o'clock in the afternoon. The conference, which was to last for one hour, was to be attended by all the pastors and clerics living outside the seminary. The Pastor of Sta. Cruz Parish was to keep a register in which the names of these pastors and clerics were duly inscribed. If the conference could not be held on the designated day, it was to be held the following day.

§ xix. A conference on moral theology was also to take place in the morning, on every first and fifteenth days of the month, in the sacristy of the cathedral church. It was to be

[378] Cf. *supra*, p. 41.

[379] *I Con. Mediol.*, cap. XXIX—Mansi, XXXIV, 42; "Divus Carolus Borromeus primus fuit in Italia qui praecepit ut singuli Episcopi suas Dioecesos in varias partirentur Regiunculas, et unicuique eorum Archidiaconum vel Archipresbyterum seu Praepositum ruralem sub qualitate Vicarii Foranei praeficient. . . ." Pallottini, s.v. *Parochus*, § viii, n. 99.

[380] Sta. Cruz parish is one of the oldest parishes in the city of Manila. Its earliest temple was erected in the seventeenth century by the Jesuits. It was made of stone and wood. Cf. Raymundo Banas, *Brief Historical Sketches of the Philippine Catholic Churches*, (Manila, 1936) p. 79.

attended by the canons, the chaplains, the pastor, the curates and the other clerics stationed at the cathedral church. The conference was to consist in the discussion of two practical cases, and it too was to last for one hour. The *Canonicus Magistralis* was to preside until a Canon Penitentiary could be appointed. In case either of these two was legitimately hindered from fulfilling his duty of presiding, then the *Canonicus Doctoralis* was to preside.

§ xx-xxi. For an unwaranted absence from the clerical conference, a canon, a pastor, or a cleric[381] was to pay a fine of one-half *argenti uncia*[382] for the first absence, and one *argenti uncia* for the second, but upon a third unwarranted absence a pastor or a cleric was to be detained in the seminary for ten days, and a canon was to be detained in the capitular room, also for ten days. The fine imposed upon canons and pastors was to be applied to their respective churches, whereas the fine imposed upon the other clerics was to be applied to the seminary.

§ xxii. A register or memorandum book was to be kept by one presiding over the clerical conferences. In it were to be recorded the subject matter of the conferences, and the names of the absentees as well as of the presentees. He was to see to it that the payment of the fines was made. In case a pastor or a cleric was to be detained in the seminary, the presiding officer was to inform the bishop about it.

§ xxiii. The Manila Provincial Council declared that the *legitima causa*[383] was to be manifested to the bishop. This Council bound the *praeses* in conscience not easily to accept excuses from the negligent, for the Calends and the conferences of this kind, if properly held, proved of great utility to the Church.

§ xxiv. The Manila Council admonished the bishops to attend occasionally the conferences and the Calends without any previous notification of this attendance or to send someone to observe diligently what was being done. It was the

[381] Cf. *supra*, p. 153.
[382] Cf. *supra*, p. 187.
[383] Cf. *supra*, §§ xi-xiii, p. 233.

purpose of this admonition to remove the occasion for laziness on the part of those who presided over the Calends and the conferences. Under the stimulation of such a policy not only the one presiding but also everybody present would prepare himself and would actively participate in the discussion and solution of the *"casus conscientiae."*

§ xxv. In order to make the Calends serve their intended useful purpose for the Church, the Manila Council severely commanded that card games or games of chance, e. g., the *panguingui, monte llampo,*[384] as well as other types of merriment be not associated with the celebration of the Calends. Bishops and vicars forane were to feel bound in conscience not to tolerate such things.

DECRETUM IV
De Testibus Publicis

This *Decretum* consists of five paragraphs, which deal with the following topics: first, the designation during the diocesan synod of two or more public witnesses from each parish as proposed by the pastor, and their qualifications and duties; second, the designation from this group of two or more public witnesses, under whom there shall function the *zelatores majores* and *minores,* and also the duties of the *zelatores;* third, the designation of the private or secret *zelatores* and their duties. Fourth, the penalties for the public witnesses in certain cases of a betrayal of their duties; fifth, the designation of public witnesses during the Calends in case the synod could not be held.

§ i. The pastors were during the diocesan synod to propose two men from each parish. These men were to be upright, of good name, of exemplary life, and of great influence over the natives. They had to be men of at least ordinary wealth, for otherwise, if they were financially poor, they were too readily subject to corruption by bribery. Two or more of these men were to be elected or designated public

[384] Buzeta-Bravo, *Dic. Geog. Est. Hist. Fil.*, I, 252.

witnesses during the synod, or during the Calends[385] in case the diocesan synod could not be celebrated. For every civil province also[386] two or more public witnesses were to be designated. Their duty it was to investigate even hidden vices and to inquire into the life of the pastors.[387]

Before entering upon their office, they were to take an oath of fidelity. These public witnesses, as called for by the Manila Council, were similar to the *testes synodales* or the "questmen" in each and every diocese of the whole kingdom of England during the middle ages. Five or six parishioners, called *testes synodales* or *questmen,* were sworn to furnish, besides their report on the condition of the church and its furniture, a true answer to certain questions about their clergy, viz., the rector or the vicar, the chaplains, and the clerks.[388]

The *testes synodales* as required by the IV Provincial Council of Milan (1576) were to be ecclesiastics. Their principal function was that of inquiring into the pastor's life. They were also to take an oath of fidelity before assuming their office.[389]

The *testes synodales* as required by the III Provincial Council of Lima (1583) were to be upright and blameless persons designated at the Provincial Council or the Diocesan Synod of Lima. It was their primary function to render an account regarding the observance of the decrees of the Provincial Council and Diocesan Synod of Lima. This Council of Lima had not specified whether the *testes synodales* were to be ecclesiastics or laymen.[390]

§ ii. The Manila Council also decreed that two of the public witnesses were to be designated, during the synod,

[385] Cf. *supra,* p. 227.

[386] Cf. *supra,* p. 223.

[387] Cf. *supra,* pp. 228 ff.

[388] Cutts, *Parish Priests in the Middle Ages in England* (London, 1898), chapter XVIII, p. 280.

[389] *Act. Eccl. Mediol.,* Pars I, p. 450.

[390] Cf. Vargas Ugarte, *op. cit.,* I, 308.

to be in charge of instructing the *zelatores*[391] *majores et minores*[392] concerning their inquiry into vices,[393] or about public sinners,[394] drunkards,[395] men in concubinage,[396] negligent fathers of families,[397] inefficient schoolmasters,[398] and the like. They were to denounce during the synod the evil they had detected, even through orders, to the spurning of human respect and the total disregard of all personal preferences.[399]

§§ iii & iv. Two *zelatores ocultissimi* were to be designated by the vicar forane. Their duty it was to exercise vigilance over the life of the public witnesses, and to offer instruction to these for the accurate performance of their office. The aim of this provision was the avoidance of all occasions for the concealing of the truth, and for the allurement of giving way to calumny. Any public witness, if

[391] A *zelator* was a person appointed by the proper authority to practice vigilance. He was a surveillant, an overseer, or an inspector. Cf. *Espasa Enciclopedia Universal Ilustrada Europea-Americana* (70 vols., Barcelona, 1907-1930), XII, s.v. *celador.* At present it is common in many parishes in the Philippines to have zelatores (*celadores* as they are called in Spanish) among the members of certain associations, v.gr., the *Apostolado de la Oracion.*

[392] Presumably this distinction between the *majores* and *minores zelatores* referred to the age of the parishioners over whom they were to practice vigilance, v.gr., the *zelatores majores,* over the elderly parishioners, and the *zelatores minores,* over the younger ones.

[393] Cf. *supra,* p. 230, footnote 357.

[394] Cf. *supra,* p. 230, footnote 350.

[395] Cf. *supra,* p. 230, footnote 351.

[396] Cf. *supra,* p. 230, footnote 352.

[397] *Manilanum,* Actio IV, Tit. unicus, Decretum III, § vii, *supra,* p. 94; *ibid.,* Decretum V, § i—*supra,* p. 96.

[398] *Ibidem,* § ii—*supra,* p. 97.

[399] "... Primo igitur testes synodales, quibus juratis id muneris committetur, ut illud recte praestent, hoc plane perpetuo meminerint; se non amore, non odio, non invidia, non spe, non metu, non poena, non praemio, non cognatione, non ulla denique re commoveri, aut impediri debere, quominus stato tempore Archiepiscopo denuncient ac significent, quaecumque corrigi, emendari, aut reformari utile sit vel necessarium."—*Act. Eccl. Mediol.,* Pars II, p. 907; Cf. also *IV Con. Mediol.,* c. VI, Mansi, XXXIV, 296.

proved to be unfaithful to his duty in any way, but especially by calumny or falsehood, was to be subjected to a punishment called *talio,* which was of a purely retaliatory character, measuring out like for like or to the same punishment which the real transgressor, whom he had fraudulently concealed and shielded, should have undergone.

§ v. Public witnesses were to be designated during the Calends if for some reason the diocesan synod could not be held.[400]

In order to appreciate this *Decretum* of the Manila Council, the times and the condition of the people must be understood. In the first place there were too many complaints at that time against the friar *curas,* such as their despotic rule practiced over the natives, their greed for gain (extorting all they could get from the natives, although they received large stipends and contributions from the government, and acquiring large estates, besides engaging in a lucrative trade), their negligence in their spiritual work (doing nothing to check the vagrant life of many natives), and certain abuses among them in their treatment of the natives.[401] On the other hand, there were many natives who were apostates from the Holy Faith, idolators, profaners, heretics, usurers, sorcerers, witches, magicians, men addicted to superstition, adultery or concubinage, and transgressors in general of God's and the Church's commandments.[402] The designation of public witnesses and *zelatores* served certainly to discourage both priests and laity from their evil ways; it could also help the proper ecclesiastical authorities to know their priests and the faithful in such a way that admonition, correction, and punishment could be administered whenever necessary. The testi-

[400] Cf. *supra,* p. 238; Bouix, *Tract. de Episc.*, II, 362.

[401] Viana, MS. book, *Cartas y Consultas,* fol. 39V-46, (1767); Pedro de Tavera, *Memorial de Anda y Salazar* (Manila, 1899) (as found in Montero y Vidal, *op. cit.*, II, 66-70, 115-140, 220-382, and *passim*); Blair and Robertson, *op. cit.*, L, 118-190- *passim.*

[402] *Manilanum,* Actio V, Tit. II, Decreta I, II, IV, X, XIII, and XV; *supra,* p. 230; Blair and Robertson, *op. cit.*, L, 227.

mony of the public witnesses and the *zelatores* could furnish the bishops with reliable evidence regarding the conduct of the clergy and the laity, which evidence in turn could serve as proof by means of which to deny or to confirm the accusations leveled against pastors or the laity by the civil authorities before the King of Spain.[403] But, of course, this system was not without its weakness. There was never completely precluded the sinister temptation for the public witnesses or the *zelatores* themselves to yield to the allurement of bribery or to espouse a policy of personal vengeance.

[403] Blair and Robertson, *op. cit.*, L, 136-190.

CONCLUSIONS

1. The bishop's *familia inferior* refers to his lay servants.

2. The Manila Council prohibited the bishops from wearing *monilia aurea et argentea.* The chain of the bishop's pectoral cross and the ring were not included in that prohibition.

3. The *familia superior* of a bishop had to be composed of elderly priests of good reputation, wide experience and solid learning on account of the delicate functions entrusted to them.

4. A bishop in the Philippines at that time, even if he was not legitimately impeded from preaching personally, was not obliged to preach in view of the diversity of the dialects of the people.

5. Five courses of food were still within the frugality of a bishop's table in the Philippine Islands at that time.

6. For seeking out the truly poor, the bishops could employ the help of the civil authority. Therefore the provisions for aid to the poor were combined with police measures.

7. Bishops were specifically to attend to it that no cleric go unaccompanied to institutions for girls. They themselves were warned not to go to the *colegios* and *beaterios* (institutions for girls) without the company of other clerics.

8. The *Catechismus Romanus* mentioned by the Fathers of the Manila Council referred to the abridged Catechism of the Council of Trent.

9. By the Laws of the Indies, bishops in the Philippines were given the right to examine books before their printing or use, and accordingly no catechism was printed or used without first having been examined by them.

10. The use of the expression *vacent orationi* referred not only to vocal prayer but to mental prayer or meditation as well.

11. The term "consultors," as mentioned by the Fathers of the Manila Council, referred to the private consultors of

the bishop. It could not refer to the diocesan consultors, for there was no need of them in the Philippines at that time inasmuch as cathedral chapters were already established. It could not be identified with parish priest consultors for the juridic institution of parish priest consultors dates only from the Pontificate of St. Pius X, when the Sacred Consistorial Congregation issued the decree *Maxima cura* on August 20, 1910.

12. The only reason or cause mentioned by this Council for employing another person for the visitation of the diocese was the geographical expanse of the diocese and the inaccessibility of parochial churches.

13. Although the *Decretum* entitled *De non Gravandis Parochis* indicated concern for lessening the burdens of pastors, nevertheless it also aimed to nullify every attempt that sought to defeat the purpose of the visitation by means of currying episcopal favor through the setting of sumptuous meals for them, through the rendering of personal service from outstanding people of the parish, through the furnishing of entertainment by singers and musicians, and through the bestowal of generous gifts.

14. The provision of the Manila Council regarding the holding of provincial councils, apart from being conditional, was only exhortatory. It could never have had the binding force of a law, even if this council had been approved by the Holy See with an act of due recognition.

15. Unlike the frequency prescribed for the celebrating of provincial councils in the Indies ecclesiastical provinces, the traditionally established frequency for the celebration of diocesan synods was not changed by any indult or privilege.

16. The Manila Council granted the further concession that, if on account of some definite cause (which cause was to be manifested to the bishop) a pastor could not attend the diocesan synod, then the public witnesses were to present a letter informing the bishop what things in the diocese needed reform and also were to attend the synod.

17. As in many parts of the world, the Tridentine law on the annual celebration of diocesan synods was not observed in the Philippine Islands. Some obvious reasons for it were the scarcity of priests and the territorially large size of the dioceses.

18. The Manila Council declared that by a *legitima causa* for non-attendance at the synod was to be understood whatever confined one to bed or necessitated a preoccupation with some important business.

19. The system of employing public witnesses and *zelatores* to report on the conduct and life of the priests and the laity was indeed a vulnerable one for the reason that the public witnesses and *zelatores* could all too readily be induced to yield to bribery or be prompted to evince a personal vengeance.

BIBLIOGRAPHY

Sources

Acta Apostolicae Sedis, Commentarium Officiale, Romae, 1909-

Acta et Decreta Concilii Provincialis Manilani Celebrati Anno MDCCLXXI sub Illustrissimo et Reverendissimo Archiepiscopo Manilano Basilio Sancho a Santa Justa et Rufina (unpublished).

Acta et Decreta Concilii Plenarii Americae Latinae in Urbe Celebrati Anno Domini MDCCCXCIX, Romae, Typis Vaticanis, 1901.

Acta et Decreta Sacrorum Conciliorum Recentiorum, Collectio Lacensis, 7 vols. auctoribus C. Schneemann (Vols. I-VI) et T. Granderath (Vol. VII) Friburgi Brisgoviae, 1870-1892.

Acta et Decreta Concilii Provinciae Remensis Anno MDCCCXLIX Celebrati, Lutetiae Parisiorum, 1850.

Annuario Pontificio, Citta del Vaticano: Tipografia Poliglotta Vaticana, 1956.

Appendix ad Concilium Plenarium Americae Latinae Romae Celebratum Anno Domini MDCCCXCIX, Romae, Typis Polyglottis Vaticanis, 1910.

Bruns, Hermann, *Canones Apostolorum et Conciliorum Saeculorum IV-VII*, 2 vols., Berolini, 1839.

Bullarum Diplomatum et Privilegiorum Sanctorum Romanorum Pontificum Taurinensis Editio, 24 vols. (in 25), 1857-1872.

Catechismus Romanus ex Decreto Concilii Tridentini ad Parochos Pii V Pontificis Maximi Iussu editus, 4. 3rd., Ratisbonae, Romae, Neo Eboraci et Cincinnati, 1907.

Codex Iuris Canonici Pii X Pontificis Maximi Iussu Digestus Benedicti XV Auctoritate Promulgatus Praefatione Fontium Annotatione et Indice Analytico-Alphabetico ab Emo Petro Card. Gasparri Auctus, Reimpressio, Westminster, Maryland: The Newman Press, 1952.

Codicis Iuris Canonici Fontes, cura Emi Petri Cardinalis Gasparri editi, 9 vols., Romae, Typis Polyglottis, Vaticanis, 1923-1939 (Vols. VII-IX ed. cura, et studio Emi Card. Seredi).

Collectanea S. Congregationis de Propaganda Fide, 2 vols., Romae, 1907.

Concilii Plenarii Baltimorensis II in Ecclesia Metropolitana Baltimorensi, a die VII ad diem XXI Octobris A.D. MDCCCLXVI, Acta et Decreta, Baltimorae: John Murphy, 1876.

Concilium Provinciale Mexicanum III, 5 vols. in 1, Mexico, 1770.

Concilio Provinciale Mexicano IV, 5 vols. in 1, Queretaro, 1898.

Corpus Iuris Canonici, editio Lipsiensis secunda post Aemilii, Ludovici Richteri curas... instruxit Aemilius Friedberg, 2 vols., Lipsiae: Tauchnitz, 1879-1881.

Doctrina Christiana, The First Book Printed in the Philippines, Manila, 1593, Philadelphia: Stern & Co., 1947.

Hardouin, J., *Acta Conciliorum et Epistolae Decretales ac Constitutiones Summorum Pontificum*, 12 vols., Parisiis, 1715.

Hernaez, Francisco Javier, *Coleccion de Bulas, Breves, y Otros Documentos Relativos a la Iglesia de America y Filipinas*, 2 vols., Brussels, 1879.

Jaffe, Philippus, *Regesta Pontificum Romanorum ab condita Ecclesia ad annum post Christum Natum MCXCVIII*, ed. correctam et auctam auspicis Gulielmi Wattenbach, curaverunt S. Loewenfel, F. Kaltenbrunner, P. Ewald, 2 vols., Lipsiae, 1885-1888.

Lorenzana, Francisco, *Concilios Provinciales, Primero y Segundo*, Mexico, 1769.

Mansi, Joannes, *Sacrorum Conciliorum Nova et Amplissima Collectio*, 53 vols. in 60, Parisiis, Arnhem, Lipsiae, 1901-1927.

Monumenta Germaniae Historica, Legum Sectio III, Concilia, 2 vols. in 4, ed. F. Maassen, A. Werminghoff, H. Bastgen, Hannoverae et Lipsiae, 1893-1924.

Morelli, Cyriacus, *Fasti Novi Orbis et Ordinationum Apostolicarum*, Venetiis, 1776.

New Testament of Our Lord and Saviour Jesus Christ, The Episcopal Committee of the Confraternity of Christian Doctrine, St. Paul, Minnesota: Catechetical Guild Educational Society, 1953.

Pallottini, S., *Collectio omnium conclusionum et resolutionum quae in causis propositis apud Sacram Congregationem Cardinalium S. Concilii Tridentini interpretum prodierunt ad eius institutione anno MDLXIV ad MDCCCLX, distinctis titulis alphabeticis ordine per materias digesta*, 17 vols., Romae, 1868-1893.

Pontificale Romanum Summorum Pontificum iussu editum, a Benedicto XIV et Leone XIII, Pontificibus Maximis recognitum et castigatum, Mechliniae, 1895.

Ratti, Achilles, *Acta Ecclesiae Mediolanensis ab eius initiis usque ad nostram aetatem*, Vol. II, Mediolanae, 1890.

Recopilacion de Leyes de los Reinos de las Indias, Mandada Imprimir y Publicar por la Mejestad Catolica del Rey Don Carlos II, Nuestro Senor, dividida en 4 tomos, con el Indice General, y al Principio de cada tomo el especial de los titulos que contiene, 5 edicion, Madrid, 1851.

Schroeder, H. J., *Canons and Decrees of the Council of Trent: Original Text with English Translation*, S. Louis: B. Herder Book Co., 1941.

Sancho, Basilio Rufina y Santa Justa, *Documentos Importantes para la Cuestion Pendiente sobre la Provision de Curatos en Filipinas*, Madrid, 1863.

Streit, Carolus, *Atlas Hierarchicus*, Paderbonae in Guestfalia, 1913.

Tejada, Juan Ramiro, *Coleccion de Canones y de todos los Concilios de la Iglesia Española*, 5 vols., Madrid, 1849-1855.

The Great Encyclicals of Leo XIII, Translation from Approved Sources, with Preface by Rev. John J. Wynne, S.J., 3rd edition, New York, Cincinnati, Chicago: (Copyright 1903 by Benziger Brothers).

Turrecremata, J., *Gratiani Decretorum Libri Quinque*, 2 vols., Romae, 1726.

Ugarte, Ruben Vargas, *Concilios Limenses, 1551–1772*, 2 tomos, Mexico, 1952.

REFERENCE WORKS

Abbo, John A.-Hannan, Jerome D., *The Sacred Canons*, 2 vols., St. Louis: Herder, 1952.

Alip, Eufronio, *Political and Cultural History of the Philippines*, 2 vols., Manila, Philippines: Alip & Briones Publication, 1949.

Altamira, Rafael y Crevea, *Historia de Espana y de la Civilizacion Española*, 2 vols., Barcelona, 1909-1911.

Alzona, Encarnacion, *A History of Education in the Philippines 1565–1930*, Manila, 1932.

Augustinus, Antonius, *Iuris Veteris Doctoris et Iuris Pontificii Veteris Epitome*, 3 vols. in 1, Parisiis, 1641.

Bañas, Raymundo, *Brief Historical Sketches of the Philippine Catholic Churches*, Manila, 1936.

Bannon, Jr.-Dunne, P., *Latin America: An Historical Survey*, Milwaukee: The Bruce Publishing Company, 1947.

Barbosa, A., *Collectanea Doctorum in varia Concilii Tridentini Decreta et Canones*, Lugduni, 1672.

———, *De Officio et Potestate Episcopi*, Lugduni, 1656.

Benedictus XIV, *De Synodo Dioecesana*, 2. ed., 2 vols., Parmae, 1764.

Blair, Emma-Robertson, James, *The Philippine Islands*, 55 vols., Ohio, Cleveland, 1903-1909.

Blake, Frank, *A Grammar of the Tagalog Language*, New Haven, 1925.

Bouix, Marie Dominique, *De Concilio Provinciali*, 2. ed., Parisiis, 1862.

———, *Tractatus de Episcopo ubi et de Synodo Dioecesana*, 2 vols. in 1, Parisiis-Insulis, 1873.

———, Tractatus de Judiciis Ecclesiasticis, 3. ed., 2 vols., Parisiis, 1884.

Buzeta-Bravo, *Diccionario Geografico, Estadistico, Historico de las Islas Filipinas*, 2 vols., Manila, 1850.

Campbell, Thomas, *The Jesuits 1534–1921: A History of the Society of Jesus from its Foundation to the Present Time*, 2 vols., New York, 1921.

Catholic Directory of the Philippines, Manila: Catholic Trade School, 1956.

Catholic Dictionary, A, (2). ed., St. Louis, Mo., U.S.A.: B. Herder Book Company, 1951.

Catholic Encyclopedia, The, 15 vols., Index and Supplements, New York: Appleton Co., 1907-1922.

Chapman, Charles E., *A History of Spain Founded; in the "Historia de España y de la Civilizacion Española,"* by Rafael Altamira, New York: The Macmillan Company, 1941.

Chirino, Pedro, *Relacion de las Islas Philipinas*, Roma, 1604.

Concepcion, Juan de la, *Historia General de Philipinas*, 14 vols., Manila, 1788-1792.

Craisson, D., *Manuale Totius Juris Canonici*, 4 vols., 5. ed., Pictavii, 1877.

Cuevas, Mariano, *Historia de la Iglesia en Mexico*, 5 vols., Mexico, 1921-1928.

Cunningham, Charles Henry, *The Audiencia in the Spanish Colonies*, Berkeley, 1919.

Curson, Barbara, *The Jesuits: Their Foundation and History*, 2 vols., New York, Cincinnati and St. Louis, 1879.

Cutts, Edward L., *Parish Priests in the Middle Ages in England*, London, 1898.

De Meester, A., *Juris Canonici et Juris Canonico-Civilis Compendium*, 3 vols. in 4, Brugis, 1921-1928.

Desrochers, L'Abbe Bruno, *Le Premier Concile Plenier de Quebec et Le Code de Droit Canonique*, The Catholic University of America Canon Law Studies, n. 152, Washington, D.C.: The Catholic University of America Press, 1942.

Donnelly, Francis Bernard, *The Dioecesan Synod*, The Catholic University of America Canon Law Studies, n. 74, Washington, D.C., 1932.

Enciclopedia de la Religion Cristiana, (incomplete vols.), Barcelona: Dalmau y Juer, 1950-1954.

Espasa, *Enciclopedia Universal Illustrada Europea-Americana*, 70 vols., Barcelona, 1907-1930.

Fagnanus Prosper, *Commentaria in Quinque Decretalium Libros*, 5 vols. in 4, Venetiis, 1709.

Ferraris, Lucius, *Bibliotheca Canonica, Juridica, Moralis, Theologica, necnon Ascetica, Polemica, Rubricistica, Historica*, ed. novissima, 9 vols., Romae, 1885-1899.

Foreman, John, *The Philippine Islands*, 2. ed., London, 1899.

Frasso, Petrus, *De Regio Patronatu Indiarum*, 2 tomos, Madrid, 1775.

Girardey, F., *Commentary on the Catechism of Rev. Faerber*, 16. ed., St. Louis, Mo.-London, W. C.: B. Herder Book Co., 1939.

Gomez, Rafael Hoyos, *Leyes de Indias y el Derecho Eclesiastico en la*

America Española e Islas Filipinas, Medellin, Colombia: Ediciones Universidad Catolica Boliviana, 1945.

Harney, Martin, *The Jesuits in History—The Society of Jesus Through Four Centuries,* New York: The America Press, 1941.

Hefele, Charles-Clark, William, *A History of the Christian Councils,* 5 vols., Edinburg, 1876-1896.

Hostiensis, Cardinalis (Henricus de Segusio), *Commentaria in Quinque Decretalium Libros,* 6 vols. in 4, Venetiis, 1581.

Lee, Muna, *A History of Spain from the Beginning to the Present Day* by Rafael Altamira, 1. ed., Toronto, New York, London: D. Van Nostrand Company Inc., 1949.

Levillier, Roberto, *Organizacion de la Iglesia y Ordines Religiosas en el Vireinato de Peru en el Sigle XVI,* 2 Partes in 1, Madrid, 1919.

Malcolm, George, *The Commonwealth of the Philippines,* New York-London: D. Appleton-Century Company, 1939.

Mandieta, Geronimo de, *Historia Ecclesiastica Indiano,* Mexico, 1870.

Marin y Morales, Valentin, *Ensayo de Una Sintesis de eos Trabajos Realizados por las Corporaciones Religiosas Espanolas,* 2 vols., Manila, 1901.

Martinez, Bernardo, *Apuntos Historicos de la Provincia Agustiniana,* Madrid, 1909.

Medina, Toribio, J., *La Imprenta en Manila,* Santiago de Chile, 1904.

Menendez, Marcelino y Pelagio, *Historia de los Heterodomos Españoles,* 3 tomos, Madrid, 1880-1881.

Migne, J. S., *S. Bernardi Opera Omnia,* editio nova, 6 vols. in 4, Lutetiae Parisiorum, 1854-1855.

Montero y Vidal, Jose, *Historia General de Filipinas,* 2 vols., Madrid, 1887-1894.

Murphy, Francis Joseph, *Legislative Powers of the Provincial Council,* The Catholic University of America Canon Law Studies, n. 257, Washington, D.C.: The Catholic University of America Press, 1947.

Parker, Donald, *The Church and State in the Philippines 1898–1906,* Chicago, 1936.

Peers, Edgar Allison, *Spain, the Church and the Orders,* London: Burns, Oates & Washbourne, Ltd., 1045.

Perez, Laureano Nier, *Iglesia y Estado Nuevo, Los Concordatos ante el Moderno Derecho Publico,* Madrid: Ediciones Fax, 1940.

Petra, Vincentius, *Commentaria ad Constitutiones Apostolicas seu Bullas Singulas Summorum Pontificum in Bullario Romano Contentas Secundum Collectionem Cherubim,* 5 vols., Romae, 1705-1726.

Quaranta, Stephanus, *Summa Bullarii earumve Summorum Pontificum Constitutionum,* Venetiis, 1672.

Reiffenstuel, A., *Jus Canonicum Universum*, 5 vols. in 7, Parisiis, 1864-1870.

Retaña, Wenceslao E., *Origines de la Imprenta Filipina*, Madrid, 1901.

Reyes-Santamaria-Beyer-Veyra, *Pictorial History of the Philippines*, Manila: Capitol Publishing House, Inc., 1953.

Sadaba, Francisco, *Catalogo de los Religiosos Agustinos de la Provincia de San Nicolas de Tolentino de Filipinas*, Madrid, 1906.

Santa Ana, Alonso de, *Explicacion de la Doctrina Christiana en Lengua Tagala*, Manila, 1672.

Santa Ines, Francisco de, *Cronica de la Provincia de San Gregorio Magno de Religiosos Descalzos de N. P. San Francisco en las Islas Philipinas, China, Japon, etc.* Escrita en 1676, Manila, 1892.

Schmalzgrueber, F., *Ius Ecclesiasticum Universum*, 5 vols. in 12, Romae, 1843-1845.

Schroeder, H. J., *Disciplinary Decrees of the General Councils*, St. Louis: B. Herder Book Co., 1937.

Selvagio, Julius Laurentius, *Institutionum Canonicorum Libri Tres ad Usum Seminarii Neapolitani*, 3 vols., Neapoli, 1839.

Slafkosy, Andrew Leonard, *The Canonical Visitation of the Diocese*, The Catholic University of America Canon Law Studies, n. 142, Washington, D.C.: The Catholic University of America Press, 1941.

Solorzano, Pereira J., *De Indiarum Iure*, 2 vols., Lugduni, 1672.

Tamayo, Serapio, *Sobre una Reseña Historica de Filipinas*, Manila, 1906.

Tavera, Trinidad Pardo de, *Biblioteca Filipina*, Washington, 1903.

———, *Reseña Historica de Filipinas desde su Descubrimiento hasta 1903*, Manila, 1906.

Thomassinus, Ludovicus, *Vetus et Nova Ecclesiae Disciplina circa Beneficia et Beneficiarios*, ed. postrema, 3 Partes in 10 vols., cum Parisiensi accuratissime collata, Magontiaci, 1787.

Thornton, Mary Crescentia, *The Church and Freemasonry in Brazil 1872–1875, A Study in Regalism*, The Catholic University of America, Washington, D.C.: The Catholic University of America Press, 1948.

Van Hove, *Commentarium Lovaniense in Codicem Iuris Canonici*, 1 vol. in 5 tomes, Tom. I, *Prolegomena*, 2. ed., Mechliniae-Romae: H. Dessain, 1945.

Vera, Fortino Hipolito, *Aputamientos Historicos de los Concilios Provinciales Mejicanos en dos Partes*, Mejico, 1893.

Wernz, Franciscus Xav., *Ius Decretalium*, 6 vols., 2. ed., vols. I-IV, 1905-1912, Romae; vols. V-VI, 1914 & 1913 resp., Prati.

———, Vidal, P., *Ius Canonicum*, 7 vols. in 8, Romae: Apud Aedes Universitatis Gregorianae, 1925-1938; Vol. II, 3. ed., 1943.

Worcester, Dean, *The Philippines, Past and Present*, 2 vols. in 1, New York, 1921.
Yabes, Leopoldo, *A Brief Survey of Iloko Literature*, Manila, 1936.
Zaide, Gregorio, *Catholicism in the Philippines*, Manila: Sto. Tomas University Press, 1937.
———, *Philippine Political and Cultural History*, 2 vols., Manila: Philippine Education Company, 1949.
Zamora, Eladio, *Las Corporaciones Religiosas en Filipinas*, Vallodolid, 1901.
Zamora, Matias Gomez, *Regio Patronato Español e Indiano*, Madrid, 1897.

Articles

Costa, Horacio de la, "The Development of the Native Clergy in the Philippines," *Theological Studies*, VIII (1947), 219-250.
Cunningham, Charles Henry, "The Institutional Background of Spanish American History," *The Hispanic American Historical Review*, I (1918) 24-39.
Williams, Schafer, "The First Provincial Council of Manila of 1771," *Seminar* (annual extraordinary number of the *Jurist*, Vol. XIII (1955-1956), 33-47.

Abbreviations

AAS—Acta Apostolicae Sedis.
Act. Eccl. Mediol.—Acta Ecclesiae Mediolanensis.
Bull. Rom.—Bullarium Romanum, editio Taurinensis.
CE—Catholic Encyclopedia.
Coll. Lac.—Collectio Lacensis.
Con. Pl. Balt. II—Concilium Plenarium Baltimorense II.
Dic. Geog. Est. Hist. Fil.—Diccionario, Geografico, Estadistico, Historico de Filipinas.
Disciplinary Decrees—Schroeder, Disciplinary Decrees of the General Councils.
Eccl.—Ecclesiasticus.
Fagnanus—Commentaria in Quinque Decretalium Libros.
Ferraris—Prompta Bibliotheca Canonica, Iuridica, Moralis, Theologica, nec non Ascetica, Polemica, Rubristica, Historia.
Fontes—Codicis Iuris Canonici Fontes cura . . . Gasparri editi.
Hardouin—Acta Conciliorum et Epistolae Decretales ac Constitutiones Summorum Pontificum.
Hist. Edu. in Phil.—History of Education in the Philippines.
Hist. Gen. Phil.—Historia General de Philipinas.
Hostiensis—Commentaria in Quinque Decretalium Libros.

Levillier—Organizacion de la Iglesia y Ordenes Religiosas en el Vireinato del Peru en el siglo XVI.

I y II Mexico—Concilios Provinciales, Primero y Segundo de Mexico.

III Mexicanum—Concilium Mexicanum Provinciale III.

IV Mexicano—Concilio Provincial Mexicano IV.

MGH—Monumenta Germaniae Historica.

MS—Manuscript of the Acts and Decrees of the Manila Provincial Council of Manila of 1771.

Pallottini—*Collectio Omnium Conclusionum et Resolutionum Quae in Causis Propositis apud Sacram Congregationem Cardinalium S. Concilii Tridentini Interpretum Prodierunt ab eius Institutione Anno MCLXIV ad MDCCLX, Distinctis Titulis Alphabetico Ordine per Materias Digesta.*

Phil. Pol. Cult. Hist.—Philippine Political and Cultural History.

Pol. Cult. Hist. Phil.—Political and Cultural History of the Philippines.

Pont. Rom.—Pontificale Romanum.

Recopilacion—Recopilacion de las Leyes de las Indias.

S. C.—Sacra Congregatio.

S.C.C.—Sacra Congregatio Concilii.

S.C. Ep. et Reg.—Sacra Congregatio Episcoporum et Regularium.

S.C.S. Off.— Sacra Congregatio Sancti Officii.

Tract. de Episc.—Tractatus de Episcopis.

Vet. et Nov. Eccl. Discip.—Vetus et Nova Ecclesiae Disciplina.

BIOGRAPHICAL NOTE

Pedro Natividad Bantigue was born on January 31, 1920, in Hagunoy, Bulacan, Philippine Islands. He received his elementary education in the Hagunoy Elementary School. After finishing the second year of High School at the Hagunoy Institute he attended the Archdiocesan Seminary of Manila in 1936, and was ordained to the priesthood on May 31, 1945, by the late Archbishop Michael J. O'Doherty. While he was a curate in San Jose de Trozo, Manila, he enrolled in the School of Education at the Catholic University of the Philippines in 1946, and received the Bachelor of Science in Education in 1948. After serving two years as curate in San Miguel Pro-Cathedral, Manila, he was appointed Prefect of Discipline at the Manila Cathedral School. He also served as secretary to the Apostolic Visitation of the seminaries in the Philippines, Vicar Econome of San Miguel Pro-Cathedral parish, and instructor of the Filipino Language in the Archdiocesan seminary. From 1949 to 1954 he served as private secretary to the Archbishop of Manila. He enrolled in the School of Canon Law at the Catholic University of America in October, 1954, and received the degree of Bachelor of Canon Law in June, 1955, and the degree of Licentiate of Canon Law in June, 1956.

ALPHABETICAL INDEX

CANON LAW STUDIES*

375. Kelleher, Rev. Francis T., A.B., J.C.L., Judicial expenses.
376. Bantigue, Rev. Pedro N., J.C.L., The Provincial Council of Manila of 1771. (Its text followed by a commentary on *Actio* II, *De Episcopis*)
377. Burns, Rev. Dennis J., J.C.L., Matrimonial indissolubility: contrary conditions.
378. Deutsch, Rev. Bernard F., J.C.L., Jurisdiction of pastors in the external forum.
379. Dunnivan, Rev. John P., A.B., J.C.L., Prejudicial attempts in pending litigation.
380. Ernst, Rev. Albert C., A.B., J.C.L., Free admission to church for sacred rites.
381. Frattin, Mr. Peter Louis, J.C.L., The matrimonial impediment of impotence: occlusion of the spermatic ducts and vaginismus.
382. Henry, Rev. Charles W., O.S.B., A.B., S.T.L., J.C.L., Canonical relations between bishops and abbots at the beginning of the tenth century.
383. Hoffman, Rev. Lawrence J., A.B., S.T.B., J.C.L., Clergy conferences: Canon 131.
384. Markham, Rev. James, A.B., S.T.L., J.C.L., The Sacred Congregation of Seminaries and Universities of Studies.
385. McGrath, Rev. John J., A.B., LL.B., J.C.L., A comparative study of crime and its imputability in ecclesiastical criminal law and in American criminal law.
386. McGuire, Rev. James D., O.R.S.A., J.C.L., The postulancy.
387. Munday, Rev. James E., J.C.L., Ecclesiastical Property in Australia and New Zealand.
388. Murphy, Rev. Joseph P., A.B., J.C.L., The laws of the State of New York affecting church property.
389. Pickard, Rev. William M., J.C.L., Judicial experts: a source of evidence in ecclesiastical trials.
390. Ruddy, Rev. James, J.C.L., The Apostolic Constitution *Christus Dominus*: text, translation and commentary, with short annotations on the Motu Proprio *Sacram Communionem.*
391. Vanyo, Rev. Leo. V., A.B., J.C.L., Requisites of intention in the reception of the sacraments.

* For a complete list of the available numbers of this series apply to the Catholic University of America Press, 620 Michigan Avenue, N.E., Washington (17), D.C., for a general catalogue.

www.ingramcontent.com/pod-product-compliance
Lightning Source LLC
LaVergne TN
LVHW050253080826
844660LV00012B/633